At the Heart of Freedom

*

At the Heart of Freedom

FEMINISM, SEX, AND EQUALITY

*

DRUCILLA CORNELL

PRINCETON UNIVERSITY PRESS

PRINCETON, NEW JERSEY

Library of Congress Cataloging-in-Publication Data
Cornell, Drucilla.
At the heart of freedom : feminism, sex, and equality /
Drucilla Cornell.
p.   cm.
Includes bibliographical references and index.
ISBN 0-691-02897-4 (cl : alk. paper). —
ISBN 0-691-02896-6 (pb : alk. paper)
1. Feminism.   2. Women's rights.   I. Title.
HQ1101.C64   1998
305.42—dc21   98-3548

This book has been composed in Sabon

FOR ELOISE SEGAL

*

✳ *Contents* ✳

* Preface *

THE IMAGINARY DOMAIN

No more ten that toil so one reposes
But a sharing of life's glories
Give us bread and give us roses;

The rising of the women
Means the rising of the race.
(from the Union song "Bread and Roses")

THE RIGHT to the imaginary domain takes us beyond hierarchical definitions of self, whether given by class, caste, race, or gender. The freedom to create ourselves as sexed beings, as feeling and reasoning persons, lies at the heart of the ideal that is the imaginary domain. Without it, we will not be able to share life's glories. To say that the imaginary domain is a right is to say that the freedom to be ourselves and the participation in the richness of life is not an arbitrary wish, but an essential right of personality. The imaginary domain can also help us address the pressing political and ethical issues of prostitution, gay and lesbian marriage, adoption, reproductive rights and new technology, and the fathers' rights movement. Moreover, it provides us with a new way of including women's issues in the international human rights agenda.

Feminism's demand for formal equality has certainly opened the doors of many professions previously slammed in our faces, and this impressive accomplishment should be recognized. But many women remain dissatisfied with the need to show we are really like men even though we are without the support systems many men have. Professional equality has, for many women, meant sacrificing love and family life. Some formal-equality feminists have ignored the reality that "hearts" continue to starve, no matter the new opportunities available to women.

The simple answer for this would seem to be more social services for women so that they might avail themselves of equal work opportunities without sacrificing either their emotional lives or their health. But, as socialist societies have shown us, simply providing social services does not allow women the chance to share in life's glories. Child care can relieve women of the bone-crushing weariness of having to work as well as assume full responsibility for their husbands and children, and most of the socialist states provided women with crucial social services. And for those of us for whom child care is a daily problem, such state-supported day care at a reasonable cost would be an important gain. But these benefits were provided because women were necessary both as reproducers and as workers. Indeed, the benefits and social services shifted in accordance with the needs of the state bureaucracy because they were given not to enhance women's freedom, but to support the state. Thus, for example, in socialist countries, when the state needed more children, women lost the right to abortion, but when the state wanted to cut population growth, women were again given the right to have abortions.

Something is missing in both the limited formal equality for women found in the United States and in the social equality provided women in the socialist states. Clearly, neither system has delivered on the promises that women would share in life's glories and that by freeing women, men would be freed as well.

What has been missing is the protection of each person's imaginary domain, that psychic and moral space in which we, as sexed creatures who care deeply about matters of the heart, are allowed to evaluate and represent who we are. That love and sex are personal should be obvious. But what is less obvious is that most societies impose upon their citizens a conception of good, or normal, sexuality as a mandated way of life, thus refusing them the freedom to personalize who they are sexually. This stifles our choices of how we want to live out our sexuality and express our love. This need is in us all, men, women, straight, and gay. And the freedom to be ourselves must be understood as a right that cannot be displaced whenever it is economically convenient to do so. I refer to this right as the right of each person to represent his or her sexuality, or what I call sexuate being.

One popular view of feminism is summarized by the T-shirt slogan "His glass has more than mine, and I'm going to get it," suggesting that feminists want to take what men have and make it their own. But that is not the feminism I want to defend in this book. Rather, feminism should demand sexual freedom for all of us in at least two ways. Yes, feminists do insist that the engendering of sex be confronted. But social, historical, and cultural examination of gender inequality does not necessarily mean we must conclude only that women should finally get "theirs." Rather, our response should be that we all be freed from state-imposed sexual choices that limit all of us in varied aspects of our lives. Legal reinforcement of rigid gender identity can be incredibly cruel, since many of us are different from imposed gender forms. Our emancipation from state-imposed sexual choices and from their reinforcement by the basic institutions of society demands much greater social equality than we have now. Some social services tailored to the freedom they are to serve would be provided to us. When all persons have this right to the imaginary domain, states can no longer force women to play the role of the primary caretaker in families, either directly by law or indirectly by the manipulation of social institutions. Some women who continue to do so would be freely expressing themselves in an intimate life that is their own.

Socialist states were notorious for the repression of sexual freedom; in most, gay and lesbian relationships were explicitly outlawed, and those who refused to give in to the dictates of the state endured brutal treatment. Further, women's sexuality was tightly controlled because women were primarily to serve as the "people's" reproducers. The psychic space people need if they are to shape their own sex and intimate lives was often condemned as bourgeois decadence. The very idea that people be allowed to maintain an imaginary domain so as to draw boundaries between themselves and the state would have controverted the pretense that the state represented what was good, even in the bedroom. Indeed, totalitarian societies as they have been imagined in literature and actualized in political life erect themselves against the individual's imaginary domain.

The Western democracies have not been much better than the socialist societies in recognizing the right of women, let alone gays and lesbians, to represent their own sexuality. Sexual privacy has been almost exclusively limited within the parameters of "normal" heterosexuality, so significant social equality is often deemed unnecessary because heterosexual women can always turn to their husbands for support. Of course this argument won't hold water given the current reality of family lives in the United States.

We do not want sexual freedom to replace social equality; we want social equality redefined so as to serve freedom. In the working class and socialist movements of the last century, issues of women's participation in those movements as well as issues of sexual freedom for all have come to the fore again and again. One of the most profound lessons I learned as a union organizer is that it is a form of class elitism to think that yearnings of the heart are available only to the middle class and the wealthy. Nor are matters of sexual freedom separable from economic justice. It is indeed an economic issue if the stigmatization of a person's sexuality leads her to face discrimination in everything from housing and job opportunities, to custody and access to financial support for her children.

The feminism I defend sets the reconciliation of sexual freedom with social equality at the heart of its political program. But we need to rethink the fundamental premises of our feminism if we are to achieve that reconciliation. This book is devoted to showing how the reconciliation between freedom and equality can be made possible.

* *Acknowledgments* *

EACH AND EVERY ONE of the chapters in this book has been improved enormously by my engagement with colleagues in innumerable colloquiums, seminars, and lecture halls. I particularly owe a debt of gratitude to my graduate students at the University of Warwick, where I was a Visiting Distinguished Professor in the Philosophy Department in May 1997. My students were relentless in exploring all aspects of my ideal of the imaginary domain. Their criticisms went right to the heart of the difficult issues with which I was struggling, and I learned greatly from them.

My participation in Herbert Dreyfus and David Hoy's National Endowment of the Humanities Institute "Background Practices" gave me another forum to further work through someof the central ideas of feminism and philosophy with which I grapple in this book. The "Roundtable on the Limits of Gender" at the Pembroke Center of Brown University put me in touch with some of the most important feminist thinkers and allowed me an invaluable exchange at a crucial moment in the writing of this book. Wendy Brown taught chapter 4 in several different versions, and I am grateful for the criticism she and her students gave me. Sara Ruddick also gave me crucial comments on chapter 4. Roger Berkowitz brought all of his insight into Kantian philosophy to his helpful remarks on the text. Judith Butler has been both a constant source of friendship and an intellectual critic, always willing to engage with the work that I am writing. bell hooks read the entire manuscript and graciously spent an evening with me discussing the book. I benefited greatly from our conversation. Thomas Nagel's extremely helpful remarks on chapter 3 led me to reframe the central arguments in that chapter. Our discussion of chapter 7 helped me clarify my own thinking on utopianism. Ronald Dworkin has been a source of support and criticism. The questions he posed on key concepts in the manuscript were invaluable to me. His intellectual engagement with me over the years has helped me clarify the general direction of my own understanding of the relationship between feminism and liberalism.

Colleagues at the Rutgers Law School—William Bratton, Gary Francione, Dorothy Roberts, and Sherry Colb—all gave helpful criticism and comments that I tried to take into account in rewriting the book. Their intellectual support has been extremely important to me. My colleagues Linda Zerilli, Cynthia Daniels, and Sue Carroll in the Women and Politics Program of the political science department at Rutgers University have also provided me with a constant source of both criticism and sustenance. Their questions on the central ideas that I presented at a seminar in the political science department helped give the book its initial form.

The Study for Law, Philosophy, and Social Theory at the New York University School of Law and the veterans of that seminar have played a larger role than they may know by providing me with an intellectual engagement on the deepest level.

Isabelle Barker has been an assistant only the gods could send. She has participated in every aspect of the production of this book, including research on notes, endless critical commentary, and editorial assistance so that my sentences would not go on for paragraphs. She has been a source of intellectual inspiration for me as well as a reminder of why relationships between older and younger feminists prevent feminism from growing stale and possibly dying out. It is no exaggeration that this book would not have been written without her, or if it had been written, it would have been with considerably more strain and a good deal less happiness. If Isabelle ever got tired of hearing my ideas, she never let on. Sheila Kinney helped me run my office so that I could dedicate as much time as possible to the writing of this book. Her efficiency made it certain that none of my other academic responsibilities fell by the wayside while I was writing. Deborah Milgate worked untiringly on the notes and devoted herself to making sure that the manuscript took on its final form. She brought her excellent legal analysis to bear on how we should integrate case law when we chose to do so.

Lee Smolin, friend over a lifetime, spent a number of critical sessions with me helping me to rework key chapters. Sara Murphy and Laurie Gaughran have not only read the entire manuscript, they have read all eighteen versions of the entire manuscript. Their criticisms were always on point and their suggestions for corrections were extremely helpful. Their presence in my life as constant intellectual interlocutors keeps me on my toes in the best sense. My exchanges with Nancy Lublin over her own book *Pandora's Box* led me to rethink my own interpretation of the crucial issue of surrogacy and high-tech babies more generally.

My daughter Sarita is a hint from the future, a constant reminder of what it might be to grow up with the expectation that a female can be free. I marvel at the gap between us as she realizes in her day-to-day life the freedom that I try to project for her but cannot imagine as my own. This book is in a profound sense an effort to keep up with where my daughter has already demanded that I be. My lifetime partner, Gregory DeFreitas, has struggled to keep this book in touch with what he saw as the important political issues so that it would address as wide an audience as possible. His continual questioning of everything I write makes me endlessly need to return to the economic realities that underlie so much of women's suffering. His own book *Inequality at Work* deeply influenced the sixth chapter of this book. I of course owe him the time off to write because of the diligent and loving care he gives to Sarita. During the writing of this book, my mother-in-law, Carol DeFreitas, has made the house run and done all the small things that made it possible to keep my head screwed on straight and still be a mother and a professor. She is certainly a reminder of how important intergenerational friendship is in a feminist household that can run without any one person bearing the full burden of the tasks demanded by day-to-day life. Irena Moletoris, a deeply loved member of our extended family, has been indispensable both in the love she gives to my daughter and in the time she spends organizing our house. Irena along with Sarita's Uncle Larry made it possible for me to travel so that I could take this book on the road to get the feedback that was needed. Maritza Maestra has helped me out with the care of my daughter and made sure that she remains bilingual. She has gone beyond the duties of her role as my daughter's Spanish teacher, always caring about both her and the rest of the family. My editor, Malcolm Lichtfield, was a hands-on editor in the best sense. His editorial criticism went right to where there were difficulties that needed to be corrected. His diligence and concern that the book be as accessible as possible have certainly helped to make it so.

But there is one person who played a role that Novalis eloquently described: "It is certain any conviction gains infinitely the moment another soul will believe in it." Eloise Segal embraced the ideal of the imaginary domain from the moment I told her about it. A poet and a novelist herself, she brought her own talents to bear on this manuscript, poring over the writing so that my ideas would be given the best possible expression. I cannot thank her enough both for her belief in this book and the effort she put into it. It is at best a small token of what she actually gave that I dedicate it to her.

At the Heart of Freedom

*

* CHAPTER ONE *

Introduction: Feminism, Justice, and Sexual Freedom

> Each person possesses an inviolability founded on justice
> that even the welfare of society as a whole cannot override.
> For this reason justice denies that the loss of freedom for
> some is made right by a greater good shared by others.
> (*John Rawls*)

THE FAILED IDEAL OF GENDER EQUALITY

WHERE does women's freedom begin? It should begin with the demand that we free ourselves from the use of gender comparison as the ideal of equality. I know that this statement runs against mainstream feminist legal analysts, who have fought so valiantly for our formal equal treatment to men. Indeed, some feminist litigators and legislators have explicitly fought against more expansive legal definitions of sex or of sexual equality.[1] Were they right to do so? The most obvious conservative implication of the legal interpretation of sex as gender is that it continues the exclusion of gays and lesbians from the reach of discrimination law. Lesbians are of course women. But by current discrimination law they are excluded from making a claim for sexual equality and sexual freedom because, as lesbians, they do not fit onto the scale of gender comparison. If they are to legally press their claims, they must proceed as straight women even though the injustices thrust upon them are often completely different from those endured by heterosexual women.[2]

Gay men cannot claim legal rights either because they are purportedly being treated differently because of their "sexual orientation," not their gender. Ironically, straight men can pursue discrimination claims if they can show they are being treated

3

differentially from similarly situated women, just because this treatment can be conceived of as gender discrimination. As with lesbians, so for gay men—because of the legal interpretation of sex to be gender, their differential treatment is an inequality not reached by the current form of discrimination law.

If the feminist answer to the question "equality of what?"[3] is *only* formal equal opportunity between men and women, another very difficult problem arises: how to "average out" what that would mean in our public and social lives, how to normatively justify what that "average" should be. How difficult it would be to assess what overall equality between men and women would mean for life opportunities and prospects, since these differ sharply among men themselves. I have already given the example of gay men, some of whom may seemingly "pass" into the mainstream,[4] but men's life chances are also shaped by race and class, and national and linguistic identity. Obviously, an egalitarian theory cannot limit formal equal opportunity to men and women of the same race and nationality without implicit or, worse yet, explicit endorsement of hierarchies based on race and nationality—"what is good for the gander is good for the goose." Put this way, the idea should be particularly shocking for feminists, since some women's aspirations could be viewed as still legitimately thwarted, even though they have purportedly reached equality with "their" men.

To worry about the racism of a feminism that commits itself only to formal equal opportunity is not to deny that gender affects life chances. Whether one is raised as a man or a woman affects almost every aspect of life in our world today. The horrifying statistics gathered by committed human rights activists show how women in alarming numbers are subjected on a day-to-day basis to premature mortality through starvation, lack of medical attention, rape, domestic violence, forcible prevention of access to education, and denial of the right to work or own land.[5]

Amartya Sen has used population ratios—the average ratio of men to women in North America and Europe is 1.05—to demonstrate that in spite of women's longer life expectancy, there are many more men than women in the world. Sen estimates that even if we took the sub-Saharan African ratio of men to women rather than the average in North America and Europe, there would be *100,000 million* "missing women" worldwide.[6] Confronted with such staggering and sobering statistics, it would be perverse to argue against the proposition that because their society degrades them as the lesser sex, women continue to endure life-shattering mayhem. The struggle against this inequality is obviously a matter of life and death for many women. But formal equality, because of its inherent exclusions, and because it is too limited in its demands upon the basic institutions of society, cannot bring justice to the millions of women around the world who demand it.[7] In the United States, women of color have taken the ideal of formal equality to task, charging that the theory effectively silences their claim for just treatment by limiting what can be considered injustice. Even abortion and reproductive rights, issues that seem to be in the interest of all women as women, have at best been uneasily addressed under formal equality.

What do we do when we are not like men in a way that seemingly implies an ontological difference—that is, that we get pregnant and they don't? Further, how do we measure ourselves against men and then make up for other inequalities that occur in marriage, in the workplace, and vis-à-vis sexual relations? To endorse a "white-knuckling" feminism that insists that since we asked for equality, we must live with its consequences seems a cruel response when, in this world of ours, many women, from the poorest to the most wealthy, are impoverished by divorce because they cared for their families instead of pursuing careers. Some feminists have come to reject equality altogether because they identify it with the formal equality that, to them, has merely become one more way of blaming women for their own suffering.[8] But then what standards would a postegalitarian feminism employ to address the injustices they take so seriously?[9] Could we not replace formal equality with substantive equality and so take into account the inequality found in family life? Maybe, but we would still be taking an idealized representation of men as our measure of comparison. Clearly, the gender comparisons inherent in formal equality confine us to traditions inseparable from the view that women are unequal to men, while excluding innumerable forms of sexual difference from the reach of justice.[10] Implicit in our insistence upon freedom from gender comparison is the demand for the space to reimagine our sexual difference beyond the confines of imposed notions of what it means to be a man or a woman.

Of course, the demand to be freed from this measure of gender comparison is made in the name of freedom, not in the name of neutered selves. Indeed, because sexual freedom demands that we be able to recognize the hold that gender forms have upon us, both as confinement and as exclusion, the question of who we are as sexed creatures must be asked at the beginning of every theory of justice. Further, a concept of right that recognizes this freedom must be tailored to provide space for imagining sexual difference.

Sex, Gender, and Sexuate Being

Throughout this book I will use *sex, gender,* and *sexuate being* in the following way. By gender I mean the "commonsense" view of sexual difference, that human beings come in two "kinds," men and women. The sex/gender distinction was used by the feminist theorists of my generation to make the distinction between the socially constructed and culturally imposed meaning of sexual difference, and the natural biological underpinnings of the body. Along with many other feminist theorists, I reject this understanding of the difference between sex and gender because it fails to see how the sexed body is symbolically constructed by a "space of interlocution"[11] and an imago—a primordial image of how we hang together that each one of us lives out.[12]

I use the word *sex* to indicate our unconscious identifications as beings who have been sexed, who have been formed, and who can see themselves only through a sexual imago. We cannot know ourselves outside of these identifications that formed us into beings sexed in a particular way and, as a result, turned us toward particular objects of desire. I also use the word *sex* when I seek to highlight how straight women, gays, and lesbians are treated as things rather than persons because of the meaning society gives to attributes of their bodily difference (in the case of women) or because of society's fantasies about their sexuality (in the case of gays, lesbians, bisexuals, and transgendered persons).

I use the phrase *sexuate being* to represent the sexed body of our human being when engaged with a framework by which we orient ourselves; because we are sexuate beings we have to orient ourselves sexually. And, because the categories of race and class have historically been deployed to define sexuality, and vice versa, they are inextricably linked to the framework by which we develop our sexual identity. Inevitably, we code ourselves, and are coded, along the lines of race and class—all of us, including straight white men. After all, being a straight white man is itself a sexual orientation, although, as Simone de Beauvoir reminds us, it is an orientation that mistakes itself as the state of true human being because it has historically been identified as such.[13] Of course, we can never reach all the way back and simply uncover the framework of our sexuate being because knowing ourselves as "sexed" means we have already assumed a persona that at least partially dictates the way we think of ourselves as having sex and having a sex. Still, the ideal of the free person must be reconciled with the recognition that we must orient ourselves as sexuate beings.

Both sex and gender have become loaded with assumptions that there will be some specific form either to our body or to our desire. This has most obviously been the case for women when, for example, it is assumed that our sexuate being will be almost entirely shaped by our reproductive capacity. I make these dis-

tinctions so as to make clear that although we are sexuate beings, we are not fated to be sexed in any particular form. Sexuate being is meant to be a concept abstract enough to be consistent with the ideal of the free person. I use the expression to
imply that although we are all sexual creatures, there are as
many different possible forms to our sexuate being as there are
people. Once this basic insight into our sexuate being is grasped,
our claim to our person has to include our right to be legally and
politically recognized as the legitimate source of meaning and
representation of our existence as corporal, sexuate beings.

The freedom to orient ourselves to our sexuate being is inspired by Immanuel Kant's definition of freedom before the law,
although we have learned much about "sex" since his time. Certainly, there is widespread agreement that sex is not just a simple
fact of our natural being. Since sex, gender, and sexuality are
not just given to us, we need the space to let our imaginations
run wild if each of us is to have the chance to find the sexual
orientation that can bring us happiness. To even aspire to the
self-representation of our sexuate being we need freedom to explore without fear the representations that surround us. This
place of free exploration of sexual representations, and personas, is the imaginary domain.

FEMINISM AND THE DEMAND FOR "SPACE"

The imaginary domain is the space of the "as if" in which we
imagine who we might be if we made ourselves our own end
and claimed ourselves as our own person. bell hooks has eloquently described the contest with imposed personas as necessarily implicated in imaginatively recollecting herself.[14] She
imagined a place where she could take on different personas:

> I was just reading a quotation from Monique Wittig's *Les Guer-*
> *illeres:* "There was a time when you were not a slave," which
> evokes the idea of *remembering who you were.* I was thinking
> about being in that emotionally abusive, bittersweet relationship,

and was trying to remember when I was *not* in the matrix like that. But coming from a family where I had been routinely tortured and emotionally persecuted, it was hard for me to even imagine a space where I wasn't involved with people who seduce and betray—who make you feel loved one minute, and then pull the rug out from under you the next—so you're always spinning, uncertain how to respond. The point is: performance art, in the ritual of inventing a character who could not only speak through me but also for me, was an important *location of recovery* for me.[15]

The "location of recovery," what I call the imaginary domain, demanded that bell hooks not only re-represent herself but that she create an ideal representative for herself, the imaginary healer, the therapist who could hear and see herself differently. This ideal representative was imagined as from the other space and thus could come to embody the self not ensnared in the matrix of abuse.

Let me give another example to help us understand the relationship between the imaginary domain and the struggle with assumed personas. As a young girl, hooks needed the other space to be represented so she could show where she imagined herself to be. Art class gave her the tools to paint the space that she claimed as her imaginary domain:

> The picture I am painting is of the wilderness my spirit roams in. I told him [her art teacher] I left the cave and went into the wilderness. He tells me to let the color show what the wilderness is like. All around are fading colors that contain bits and pieces of their earlier brightness. I call this painting *Autumn in the Wilderness*.[16]

Spatial metaphors abound in feminist literature. For now, I want to use Virginia Woolf's demand for every woman to have a room of her own as an example. Woolf's demand has often been literalized. But the demand for room is inseparable from Woolf's own battle to claim herself as a writer, and thus to free herself from the "angel in the house" that constantly overcame her. The "angel in the house" is the Woolf who manifests herself as the one beholden to others and who must serve them well. The claim for the room to write is inseparable from the need for the woman writer to represent herself as just that, a writer, rather than, in Woolf's case, her father's ever-so-good daughter.[17]

The demand that each of us have our imaginary domain protected as a matter of moral and legal right does not turn on an appeal to our likeness to other women. Even to imagine femininity as confinement and exclusion, as Woolf does, is not at all to write that women experience these prohibitions in the same ways. For example, white and African American women obviously do not live with or engage in the same imposed and internalized identifications. For an African American woman there is the brutal legacy of slavery, which is inseparable from how she imaginatively recollects herself as an African American woman, that no white woman can know. Patricia J. Williams has eloquently described how her own recognition of the importance of legal—and, I would add, moral—right is inseparable from the history through which she has to engage to recollect herself.[18] That history which inevitably marks her includes the remembrance of her grandmother as a slave. For Williams, the white law professor whose critique of rights she is answering fails to see the importance of her claim to right because he has never not had it. The imaginary domain gives to the individual person, and to her only, the right to claim who she is through her own representation of her sexuate being. Such a right necessarily makes her the morally and legally recognized source of narration and resymbolization of what the meaning of her sexual difference is for her. As Williams has noted, this right is part of what it means to escape from the status of being the degraded other: "where one's experience is rooted not just in a sense of illegitimacy but in *being* illegitimate, in being raped, and in the fear of being murdered, then the black adherence to a scheme of both positive and negative rights—to the self, to the *sanctity of one's own personal boundaries*—makes sense."[19]

Certainly elite men have long been given the right of self-representation—even if expressed as a right to passage to a higher good—as essential to the recognition of who they are, in some cultures as an individual, in others as a member of a religious, national, or racial group. The bourgeois revolutions of the West gave the right to vote to men only because they were supposed to have a capacity for self-representation.[20] Women, on the other hand, have for too long been judged capable only of passive imagination and the ability to mimic the persona deemed proper for women.[21]

FEMINISM AND KANTIAN POLITICAL PHILOSOPHY

What would a concept of right that would allow us to be recognized as the source of our own evaluations and representations of our sexual difference look like and how can we justify it? First and foremost, we must demand that before law and within the basic institutions of society, women be evaluated as free and equal *persons,* whose inviolability cannot be easily overridden in the name of some greater good. Following Kant, we should privilege the freedom of every member of society simply as a human being. For women, it is this freedom that has historically been denied. Second, we should demand the equivalent evaluation of our sexual difference, a demand clearly mandated by any *fair* theory of distributive justice. In the first instance, equivalent evaluation is a demand for women's inclusion in the moral community of persons as an initial matter. On the second level, which follows because we have gained recognition as free and equal persons, it is a demand for fair, and thus, equitable treatment whenever and wherever our sexual difference needs to be taken into account.[22] This fairness would ensure our equal ability to make use of the basic liberties guaranteed to all citizens and would require fair access to opportunities, goods, resources, or capabilities.

11

The crucial question is: What moral methodology is needed to defend both forms of equivalent evaluation? The answer seems to me to be found in Kant, since Kantian political philosophy defends a concept of right that postulates each one of us as a free and equal person:

> The civil state, regarded purely as a lawful state, is based on the following *a priori* principles:
>
> 1. The *freedom* of every member of society as a *human being*.
> 2. The *equality* of each with all the others as a *subject*.
> 3. The *independence* of each member of a commonwealth as a *citizen*.[23]

In *A Theory of Justice* and *Political Liberalism*, John Rawls has developed a theory of justice deeply inspired by Kant, although Rawls justifies the a priori conditions politically, not metaphysically.[24] In Kant, the concept of right foregrounds the general law of freedom as the organizing principle of a civil state.[25] Rawls's central focus, however, has been on fair terms of agreement on the principles of justice for society's basic structure that could be accepted even by those holding strongly divergent views—particularly when these are tied into deeply held religious convictions.[26]

Still following Kant, Rawls postulates a purely hypothetical original position of equality as the test for the rightfulness of law or, in his case, principles of justice. Within the original position, ideal representatives are shielded from knowledge as to their class position, race, gender, nationality, and abilities and assets. This original position, in which a veil of ignorance is set in place, represents the moral space demanded by the recognition that we are free and equal persons, so that agreement on principles of justice is fair. If the principles of justice are agreed to in an initial situation that is fair, "it will then be true that whenever social institutions satisfy these principles those engaged in them can say to one another that they are co-operating on terms to which they would agree if they were free and equal persons whose relations with respect to one another were fair."[27] Rawls further assumes that the original position does determine principles of justice. These are: (1) equal maximum basic liberty and (2) *fair* equal opportunity that yields to social and economic inequalities only when they are to the greatest benefit of the least advantaged.[28] In that the conditions of the original position are fair, those accepting them can be understood to be acting autonomously, in Kant's sense, solely in accordance with their own rationality.[29]

Rawls's second principle of justice turned Kant's interpretation of the condition of "the equality of each with all the others as subjects" on its head. The uniform equality of human beings as subjects of a state is, for Kant, perfectly consistent "with the utmost inequality of the mass in the degree of its possessions, whether these take the form of physical or mental superiority over others, or of fortuitous external property and of particular rights (of which there may be many) with respect to others."[30] Rawls, to the contrary, argues that it would not be rational for representatives behind the veil of ignorance to agree to these kinds of gross inequalities precisely because they would not know their own gender, race, or class position or their natural abilities. Therefore, the only kind of inequalities that would be rationally accepted behind the veil of ignorance are those that better the worse off because no one can know that she might not end up in just that position. The sweeping egalitarianism of Rawls's theory would seemingly appeal to feminists, and I have argued strongly that we should find an ally in Rawls.[31] Yet feminists have been critical, and indeed at times perplexed, as to how feminine sexual difference, and sexual difference more generally, could be addressed by his theory.[32]

While in *A Theory of Justice* Rawls unabashedly focused on class, in *Political Liberalism*, his latest work, he has focused almost exclusively on the second two conditions Kant stipulated as the basis for a just constitutional order. This emphasis is consistent with his focus on class hierarchy and his determination to defend a reasonable conception of justice rising out of our public culture alone so that citizens can find agreement about principles of justice despite any heated disagreement over important life values they might have. For Rawls, the free person of a freestanding concept of political liberalism is the citizen. Therefore, the political concept of the free person is tailored to these conditions of reciprocity that must exist between citizens if they are to reasonably justify their stances on constitutional essentials to one another.[33] But in Rawls's theory, citizens are already included in the moral community of persons, and thus have to be granted equal maximum liberty. Indeed, this inclusion, granting each person equal citizenship, is crucial to Rawls's elaboration of the symmetry of the original position.[34]

THE FEMINIST CHALLENGE: THE IMAGINARY DOMAIN AND FREEDOM

Theories of justice, or of an ethics of social arrangements, deal with the scope of claims on resources and goods and with the manner in which conflicting claims are to be resolved. All moral theories, including Rawls's, seek to develop a legitimate procedure for balancing conflicting interests. As we have seen within Kantian political philosophy, an initial requirement of universalizability must be met if the procedure is to be legitimate. To do this, any procedure must postulate all idealized participants, or representatives, as symmetrical entities, in this case human beings who have a claim on and to their person so as to be representatives of other persons.[35]

What it means for human beings to make this claim as "sexed" and, thus, seemingly ontologically dissimilar is the question feminism demands that we ask. This problem must be addressed if the requirement of legitimate universalizability is to be achieved; it demands that we explicitly recognize the moral space necessary for equivalent evaluation of our sexual difference as free and equal persons, a demand that must be met at a crucial moment in the evolution of a theory of justice before we move on to the broader egalitarian theory. It is this moral space that I have named "the imaginary domain." The imaginary domain is a heuristic device that can help us see that questions of what it means for sexed beings to be included in the moral community of persons as an initial matter must be explicitly addressed before principles of distributive justice can be defended by the moral procedure. If not addressed, the moral procedure will be unfair, and the public culture will lack a legitimate overlapping consensus.

The Place of the "Should Be"

The failure to "see" that there is a prior moral space of evaluation of the entities to be placed in the procedure in order for us to determine the crucial scope issues of distributive justice has hindered the ability of Kantian political philosophy to grapple with sexual difference on many crucial issues, including abortion and fetal protection laws.[36] Some feminists have sought to find a place in reality, even in far distant history, where women were fully equal with men, but their searches have faltered. In spite of their careful work, feminist anthropologists have undertaken to dismantle any simplistic understanding of the edifice of gender hierarchy, and indeed of the meaning of gender; no known society has been shown to be completely free from the symbolic traces of an ideological masculinity and a correspondingly degraded feminine other.[37] Alternatively, the imaginary domain must be recognized if a proceduralist conception of justice is to realize its claims to fairness. Put somewhat differently, it is the place of prior equivalent evaluation that must be imagined no matter what historical and anthropological researchers tell us is "true" about women's nature. Pessimism about whether or not any culture or society can ever recognize women's freedom as human beings is not at issue at this point because Kantian political philosophy demands that we focus on what *ought* to be, not on what *is*. The moral demand lies at the heart of the hypothetical situation of the imagination, and it is

15

out of this hypothetical situation that a fair proceduralist conception of justice can be developed. This demand for what ought to be does not, however, turn us directly to the real world for its justification.

As we will see throughout this book, many analytic difficulties of feminism, and issues of feminine sexual difference that feminism demands we address, become easier to resolve once we recognize the prior space of the imaginary domain. Once recognized, we can deploy the imaginary domain to interpret what it means for a sexed being to be included in the moral community of persons as an initial matter. This inclusion demands that our sexual difference be equivalently evaluated so that no one's sex can be dispositive of the denial of personhood. Of course, this insistence that we stop and reflect on the conditions of women as free persons in no way denies the need to articulate a relationship between all three Kantian conditions or the importance of embracing Rawls's egalitarianism as crucial to feminism in any theory of justice.

The fierce feminist critique of all forms of liberalism can in part be traced to the disappearance of this prior space.[38] At the heart of that critique is the argument that if the paradigmatic person entered into the scales to resolve competing interests, and if the scope of the claims persons can make on society is conceptualized as sex neutral, she (or he) is unconsciously identified as white, straight, and masculine.[39] As a result, so the charge goes, in the balancing that current Kantian moral methodologies offers, the scales are already tilted in favor of the paradigmatic person. For example, in Rawls's *A Theory of Justice* the idealized representatives of free and equal persons are heads of households.[40] In the explicitly patriarchal political philosophy of an earlier century, the head of household was the one who represented not only himself but his family.[41] In Rawls's own phrase, the male head of household was the one who was truly recognized as the "self-authenticating source of valid claims."[42] This right of self-representation was interpreted to be foundational to what it meant to be an equal citizen but was explicitly granted only to men.[43] Crucial to this concept of the citizen was the recognition that these persons possessed non-tradable interests, and freedom guaranteed that these interests could be represented by the person as self-authenticating. That the feminine other was politically defined as a member, but not as a representative, of a household meant she could not represent herself or her interests. The definition of those interests formed a constellation defined by family position and her duties within it. These clearly were not the interests of a free person who was recognized as the self-authenticating source of valid claims.[44]

Freedom for Its Own Sake

In a profound sense, feminism starts with our demand for freedom because only freedom will let us take up our rightful positions as free and equal citizens in the conditions of public reciprocity that make agreement on constitutional essentials a legitimate overlapping consensus. The kind of freedom feminism demands does ultimately run deeper than Rawls's description: "how citizens think of themselves in a democratic society when questions of political justice arise."[45] True, this freedom is absolutely basic to women's inclusion into the moral community as an initial matter; yet it is irreducible to Rawls's conception of the free person because freedom, particularly sexual freedom, is not simply a value to ourselves as citizens. Thus, the second feminist intervention into Kantian proceduralist conceptions of justice takes us back to Kant's insistence that freedom must be foregrounded in a concept of right because there is nothing more fundamental for a human being. For Kant,

> man's *freedom* as a human being, as a principle for the constitution of a commonwealth, can be expressed in the following formula: no-one can compel me to be happy in accordance with his conception of the welfare of others, for each may seek his happiness in whatever way he sees fit, so long as he does not infringe upon the freedom of others to pursue a similar end which can be

17

reconciled with the freedom of everyone else within a workable general law—i.e. he must accord to others the same right he enjoys himself.[46]

As feminists and gay and lesbian activists have shown again and again, we have been compelled to be "happy" in ways that we have not wanted to be. Do I need to say here—and given the fierceness of the debate, I know I do—that to deny a woman the right to an abortion in the name of someone else's good, a good she has made clear she does not want to pursue, overrides her freedom in exactly this sense? When we ask gays and lesbians to closet their sexuality in the name of the welfare of others who are disturbed by a sexuality not their own, we are compelling people to confine and restrain their freedom in the name of the good of others. The central argument in this book is that a person's freedom to pursue her own happiness in her own way is crucial for any person's ability to share in life's glories.

Kant's Concept of Right and the Free Person

Although sexual discrimination in all its varieties impedes people's chances to pursue their own happiness, there is still little agreement that, as sexual creatures, all of us actually should have this right. For Kant, a concept of right provides each person with the authority to coerce others to use their freedom in a way that harmonizes with her freedom.[47] Of course, it would be preferable to reach an overlapping consensus on an equivalent evaluation of women as free and equal persons. But when this fails, their inclusion in the moral community of persons means that they too are to be given this authority and this power to coerce so as to claim their freedom as long as it harmonizes with that of others. To quote Kant: "Thus the *birthright* of each individual in such a state (i.e. before he has performed any acts which can be judged in relation to right) is absolutely *equal* as regards his authority to coerce others to use their freedom in a way which harmonizes with his freedom."[48] For women to have this kind of authority and power of coercion as well as full inclusion in the moral community of persons has been scary to a good many people. To further extend these rights to gays and lesbians may be even scarier for some. But scary or not, it is what a politically liberal society in which all of us are included as free human beings in the moral community of persons demands.

What I mean by sexual freedom does not hinge on the concept of free will or of pure autonomy. As sexed creatures we are not free in any pure metaphysical sense. Still, because sex and intimate life are so important to us, we need to be recognized as the source of our own evaluations and representations of how we are to live out our sexuality. In this way the imaginary domain is consistent with the priority that political liberalism gives to liberty.

The Idea of Our Equal Intrinsic Value

In my interpretation, the idea of intrinsic value derives from the political concept of the free person. Each of us is a unique person who has one life to live and whose integrity and freedom must be recognized by the law and other basic institutions. We all have equal intrinsic value and should be recognized as capable of generating our own evaluations of our life plans. Equal intrinsic value is not a metaphysical proposition, but an aspect of the politically conceived free person.[49] There are clearly differences among liberal political philosophers as to whether or not one needs a detailed justification of an objective viewpoint to support the claim of equal intrinsic worth. I rest the political claim of our equal value as persons on an interpretive, historical appeal to the struggle in the bourgeois revolutions against naturalized, stratified differentiations.[50] In feudal society, for example, lords, just because they were lords, were thought to matter more than serfs. The normative and political significance of the struggle against social and political hierarchy can be interpreted, and certainly has been interpreted, as entailing an individual's moral and legal claim to the right to her person in that

19

none of us should be legally reduced to our place in a social hierarchy;[51] if so reduced, we are not politically recognized as free.

Maximum Equal Liberty

Feminism has at its heart the demand that women be treated as free human beings. We claim the right to be included in the moral community of persons as an initial matter. Inevitably, persons are involved in integrating, struggling with or against, re-imagining or accepting their "nature" as they draw themselves together to represent who they are. Coming to terms with the meaning of our "sex" is part of this undertaking. Further, the equivalent evaluation of our sexual difference cannot be used to deny us political and legal recognition, which provide a source of meaning as to how we wish to live out our lives. Negative constructions that preclude this recognition stamp us unequal and must be disallowed at this level of abstraction.

I am not arguing that we should cease to address issues of gender discrimination as matters of social inequality. I *am* arguing that if we are not equivalently evaluated as free persons as an initial matter, we will be unable to *fairly* correct that definitional inequality; our life chances and prospects will be limited by the very definition of our inequality. For example, if women are defined as disadvantaged, then a legal reform program will focus on making up for this disadvantage. This is a very different proposition than that women, recognized as free persons, be given the chance to live out their lives to the fullest and be provided with the full scope of rights, resources, capabilities, or primary goods that a theory of distributive justice defends. Further, and consistent with my foregrounding of freedom, *any definition* of what a woman is makes the imposed definition, not the woman, the source of the meaning of her sexual difference. If the subject of the theory of justice is the basic "structure" of society, the subject of feminism, for purposes of right and legal reform, is first and foremost the free person.

A person who is recognized as politically free in the way I have described is by definition individuated enough to represent herself as the source of evaluation of her life plans and to make her claim upon society without appealing to her social position or her duties to society. A just society would then further recognize that as a matter of liberty of conscience, the boundaries of individuation become the person's to "draw." The "space" in which those boundaries are personalized and represented is the sanctuary of the imaginary domain. Our bodies and our sex should be ours to claim—certainly, if women's bodies become dispositive of the denial of personhood, then we are effectively banished to the realm of the phenomenal.[52]

I use the phrase "banished to the realm of the phenomenal" to mean our exclusion from the moral community of persons as an initial matter. To be banished to the realm of the phenomenal is to be rendered socially dead.[53] In *The Doll's House,* the nineteenth-century playwright Henrik Ibsen succinctly illustrated the social death imposed upon a woman whose legal life was defined by her duties as a wife. When Nora left the doll's house and a stifling marriage, she lost her social existence, including her legal status as a mother.[54] On the other hand, the demand for our full inclusion in the moral community of persons necessarily mandates that we no longer be defined as beings whose social existence can be taken away from us simply because we do not live up to imposed definitions of what a good woman should be.

Let me put this point as strongly as possible: our right to our person should *not* turn on the resolution of theoretical disputes about the nature of the female body and its relationship to culturally imposed norms of femininity. There is an important feminist reason for separating our claim to be a person from disagreement over the concept of "woman." The reason we should not justify our claim to our person through such an appeal has been argued by women of color.[55] A theoretical appeal to our *likenesses* as women denies the full significance of race and other differences in the constitution of sexual difference. In other words, the category of woman as it has been developed and used by some straight, white women is a description of an internalized habitus that mirrors the externalized limits of femininity as they are imposed on them. Yet individual women experience their sexual difference in the innumerable ways shaped by race, sexuality, ethnicity, disability, and so forth.

The Conflict between Patriarchy and the Sanctuary of the Imaginary Domain

By patriarchy I mean first and foremost the state-enforced and culturally supported norm of heterosexual monogamy as the only appropriate organization of family life. This norm, as traditionally defined, has placed the father as the head of his line. A crucial aspect of this is that women continue to be defined mainly by their reproductive capacity and place in the family, and so are denied the right to the self-representation of their sexuate being.

Gays and lesbians as well, since they have no place in this kinship system, continue to be denied their right to the self-representation of their sexuate being. They cannot assume the status given to the father of a heterosexual marriage as head of his line; they do not even have the kind of protection that binds women to their roles in households.[56] Under a patriarchal system, heterosexual women, gays, lesbians, and transgendered persons are in different ways degraded in that their "sex" or way of having "sex" is used to deny them full standing as persons.

Obviously, the legal coherence of patriarchy has been disrupted by feminists and by the struggles of gays, lesbians, and the transgendered for their rights to their persons. At least in their public life, women have in the last hundred years been given their right to represent themselves.[57] But as feminist family-law lawyers have vigilantly fought to reveal, patriarchy continues to have a hold on almost every aspect of the legal governance of kinship relationships.[58] Thus, the granting to women of their basic rights as citizens has not been coincident with a recognition that they must be granted the right to the self-representation of their sexuate being. We see this only too evidently in the debates over abortion, surrogacy, and the growing number of regulations, accepted as a matter of law, that are being imposed upon women. Thus patriarchy, although disrupted, is hardly a phenomenon of the past and, as I have defined it, is inconsistent with equal protection of the sanctuary of the imaginary domain. As such, it can no longer be legally imposed on free and equal persons as a state-conceived norm for the regulation of family life.

Is There a Conflict between Equality and Sexual Freedom?

Regulations of kinship and sexuality must be tailored to protect the sanctuary of the imaginary domain and must therefore be consistent with each person's equal right to self-representation of her sexuate being. Feminist legal reform must also be consistent with recognition of the sanctuary of the imaginary domain.[59] The feminism I advocate, which justifies the equal protection of the imaginary domain, necessarily demands equality for women as *free* persons, but does not seek to make law the main vehicle for restructuring the current meaning of our sexual difference. Indeed, such a law would fall afoul of the equal protection of the imaginary domain, since it would make the state and not the individual the source of the representation of her sexuate being. We can then use the ideal of the sanctuary of the imaginary domain to answer a frequently heard objection made by liberal analytic philosophers, that feminist substantive theories of gender inequality undermine liberty. This objection has taken two forms: the first, that these theories of equality deny freedom of expression by attempting censorship; and the second, related to the first, that full substantive equality for women would violate our privacy and moral autonomy.[60]

The first objection is answered by making a new distinction.

Law can emancipate us from the legal constraints imposed upon us by patriarchy and can recognize us all as free and equal persons. It can give us the right to represent our sexuate being, and can protect the imaginary domain as the space we need to contest, imagine, and engage with the meanings given to gender, sex, and sexuality. But it cannot give us a substantive definition of what constitutes actual freedom for any individual person, because to do so would violate her right to self-representation of her sexuate being.

There is a necessary aesthetic dimension to a feminist practice of freedom. Feminism is inevitably a symbolic project. We have to struggle to find the words to make sense of what it means to be rendered "the second sex."[61] The "second" wave of feminism has successfully named experiences that prior to this naming could not be signified to others. A woman who is sexually assaulted on a date can now condemn what happened to her as date rape. A woman who has had to endure sexual advances on the part of her boss can now externalize it as sexual harassment, as a wrong.

We have named the wrongs we have had to endure. But that is only the first step. The effort to challenge, engage with, and imagine who we are sexually demands that we have the courage to look into the crevices in ourselves to see things frightening indeed. We need to sink ourselves into our dreams. We need to play with metaphor to undercut the rigidity of engendered meanings that embed themselves in the images and symbols by which we can represent ourselves. The question of who we are as sexed beings takes us into the deepest recesses of what lies buried under civilization. At the same time, the struggle to make our sex our own pushes us forward to try to embody ways of being sexual that are not molded by the objectification of feminine sexual difference. New representations of our sexuate being are difficult to hold on to, let alone live out. They slip away from us like a mirage because they often belie our current forms of sexual representation as masculine and feminine. We have to demand the widest possible space for expression, precisely because without it, we legitimate foreclosures on what can be said, written, or imagined, and thus undermine and reshelve the project of each of us representing her sexuate being in all its fluidity and incessant opening to new possibilities.

Ultimately, we seek nothing less than to displace static representations so that we may dream on and unhinge the unconscious connections we make between race, sex, and desire, connections that ensnare us in hierarchies. When Sula, in Toni Morrison's novel of the same name, evokes the time and place when there will be a "little room for a woman with glory in her heart," this place is imagined only as the sense of our world turned on its head:

"Oh, they'll love me all right. It will take time, but they'll love me." The sound of her voice was soft and distant as the look in her eyes. "After all the old women have lain with the teenagers; when all the young girls have slept with their old drunken uncles; after all the black men fuck all the white ones; when all white women kiss all the black ones; when the guards have raped all the jailbirds and after all the whores make love to the grannies; after all the faggots get their mothers' trim, when Lindbergh sleeps with Bessie Smith and Norma Shearer makes it with Step'n Fetchit; after all the dogs have fucked all the cats and every weathervane on every barn flies off the roof to mount the hogs . . . then there'll be a little love left over for me. And I know just what it will feel like."[62]

It should be clear that censorship would interfere with the symbolic practices that are inseparable from our imaginings of freedom.

The second objection to feminist substantive theories of inequality, in its most sophisticated form, worries that full substantive equality, for example in reproduction and the care and raising of children, will involve the state in every aspect of our intimate lives.[63] This worry has informed critics of Susan Mol-

25

ler Okin's attempt to defend the application of justice to the family.[64] I offer a full critique of Okin and an account of the difference between my position and hers in chapter 3. To anticipate, my argument against Okin is that she advocates perfectionist measures that would violate the imaginary domain. The equal protection of the imaginary domain does not demand that every aspect of life be controlled in the name of substantive equality. As should be evident by now, the opposite is the case. That protection seeks to get the state out of the business of giving "form" to our intimate lives. And since equal protection proceeds in the name of our right to claim our persons and to represent our sexuate beings, it would not protect violence or abuse against women in the home in the name of privacy. This objection to feminism is best understood as a concern that the scope of egalitarian claims could undermine sexual freedom and freedom of association. But the demand for women to be recognized as persons with the right to self-representation does not substantively define what a normal family should look like. On the contrary, it says that we cannot have any state-imposed definition of the "ideal" family.

The problem with most theories of justice, from a feminist perspective, is that they have not adequately addressed conditions of inclusion because they have failed to address the relationship between the ideal of the free person and the project all human beings have of orienting themselves as to their sexuate being. An equivalent law of persons would clearly demand that the scope of distributive justice be sufficient to ensure the right to the self-representation of each person's sexuate being. Take, for example, the issue of reproduction. Inclusion, as I have argued, demands that women be given the right to bodily integrity as part of their moral right to make themselves their own ends. Some issues of reproduction that inevitably implicate bodily integrity and a woman's representation of her body would be resolved by an appeal to what it means to be included in the moral community as an initial matter. But obviously issues of reproduction go beyond issues of conception, pregnancy, and the right of the woman to change her mind about a surrogacy contract.

If a woman is designated by a legal or cultural definition of her sex to be responsible for reproduction and child rearing, her right to represent herself is undermined. Why shouldn't a woman be able to follow her own path and be a parent, too? Straight men do it all the time. To argue that one has to give up mothering, as many of our own symbolic mothers in the feminist movement have urged us to do, as the only way to make ourselves an end in ourselves, is an enforced sexual choice.[65] Part of our struggle is to explode the barriers of such enforced sexual choices. Mothering has meant enslavement to many women, but that is because women have been forced to take on a particular persona only because they are mothers.

Thus, if we are to include women as true members of the moral community as an initial matter, we will have to design some more equitable arrangement for the care of children. Given the moral demands inherent in an equivalent law of persons, such arrangements could not assume the heterosexual family to be a given. Consider Swedish family law reform, which has attempted to excise imposed definitions of gender and heterosexuality from the definition of the right to parenting leave and to a family allowance. I am not attempting to defend the Swedish family law system. I offer the example only to emphasize that treatment of women as free and equal persons demands some form of equitable distribution of these responsibilities, but does not mandate any one particular scheme.[66] But it does guide us in judging different conceptions of an equitable social arrangement for the sustenance of children. Since under my definition of an equivalent law of persons we would no longer have patriarchy as we now know it, the scope of a more equitable system would also involve the expansion of the number of possible parents. I will return to a full discussion of family law reform in chapter 4. For now, I want to argue only that how the scope of rights is tailored would have to be consistent with the equal protection of the imaginary domain together with its right to the self-representation of the meaning of one's sexuate being. Thus, it would have to be consistent with our emancipation from any state definition of what a normal family should look like. The imaginary domain can function as the avatar of both sexual freedom and the protection of freedom of intimate association.

THE CHAPTERS

The terms defined in this introduction will help us think beyond some of the seemingly insurmountable dilemmas presented by feminist theory, most particularly in programs offered as legal reform. In chapter 2 I will defend in fuller detail the imaginary domain as both politically and ethically necessary for the protection of freedom of personality. I will argue that the imaginary domain, rather than privacy, offers a better way to understand what is at stake in the protection of sexual freedom. Thus, I will more fully develop what is demanded by the right to the self-representation of our sexuate being by looking at different meanings of representation. To contrast the imaginary domain with privacy as that concept has been used in legal doctrine, I will examine the jurisprudence of Justice Harry Blackmun, since he has struggled to articulate our constitutionally protected liberty interest in the self-determination of our sexuality and our intimate relationships.

I will then defend the sanctuary of the imaginary domain by an ethical appeal to our need for the moral and psychic space in which to orient ourselves sexually. By ethical, I mean the practice of trying to figure out our vision of the good life. The claim for the imaginary domain is that it gives each of us the chance to become a unique person. I make an ethical defense of the imaginary domain by an appeal to two ancestral principles that Ronald Dworkin argues are the "ground" of liberalism: that we are all of equal worth as persons and that we are all uniquely responsible for our own lives. The second principle is particularly important to feminists, who often obscure the question of responsibility for our lives. This is not surprising, because if we are not regarded as free, how can we be responsible? My only disagreement with Dworkin is that the Western understanding of the individual need not be used as the basis on which we demand the equivalent evaluation of our personhood, at least not when we consider the thorniness of imperialist legacies in the context of international law.

In chapter 3, I will address the question of whether or not feminism, because it purportedly deals with a natural originary difference, is in some way outside the scope of justice. As I have argued, the equivalent evaluation of sexual differences must be made prior to the beginning of the operation of a proceduralist theory of justice. If the theory is to meet the requirement of legitimate universalizability, it must evaluate our sexual differences equivalently, as part of what it means for women and gays and lesbians to be included in the moral community of persons. Moreover, I will answer Thomas Nagel's argument that if women's sexual difference is understood to be "caused" by nature, even if only partially, it *may* (Nagel is unsure) not be appropriately addressed by justice. Here I will return to my argument that questions of sexual difference demand equivalent evaluation on two levels. First, women must be included in the moral community of free persons as an initial matter. Equivalent evaluation of our sexual difference as it is relevant to a fair theory of equal opportunity must always be consistent with this inclusion. Since women cannot be banished to the realm of the phenomenal because they are free persons, this demand for equivalent evaluation must be pressed in the name of justice. Hence, my central disagreement with Nagel is that no theory of natural causation can exclude women from the reach of justice. If women are not included in the moral community as an initial matter, then a fair theory of equal opportunity will falter, because the deontological procedure has already undermined its own claims to fairness. Second, fair equal opportunity would then have to be tailored to sustain our equal maximum liberty.

In her pathbreaking book *Justice, Gender and the Family,* Susan Okin also attempts to elaborate on what justice, as fairness, would demand for women. I agree with her that families must be just, but disagree that Rawls's two principles of justice tailored to other social institutions should simply be applied to the family. Because of my insistence on freedom, I disagree with some of Okin's proposals as to how families could be made. Her attempt to end gender by state-imposed meaning implies perfectionism and, as such, violates the sanctuary of the imaginary domain.

In chapter 4 I will use adoption to give a concrete example of how patriarchy continues to dominate our legal conceptions of kinship. I will critique feminists, such as Martha Fineman, who argue that we should take a postequality position in order to defend women against the devastation imposed by divorce and custody battles. Fineman wants to end the sexual family and put in its place the mother/child dyad as the legally privileged unit, excluding lovers and husbands from this legal entity. The men to be viewed as the woman's family would be her male line—her father and grandfather. My argument against Fineman is that we should not legally privilege *any* family as the good one.

Luce Irigaray, another eloquent spokeswoman—from a very different tradition—for a reciprocal right of women and children, still naturalizes sexual difference in her advocacy of sexuate rights.[67] The naturalization of sexual difference in sexuate rights would once again impose a limit on the horizon in which our sexuate being could be expressed. Furthermore, it would privilege sexual difference as an originary split into two sexes so as to seemingly privilege it over the differences of race, nationality, and nonheterosexual representations of sexual difference. Adoption demands that we look not only at sexual difference but at class, race, and national privilege as well. In order to protect the imaginary domain of adopted children and birth mothers, we need to outline what the legitimate interests of the state would be in the regulation of kinship. I conclude chapter 4 with such an outline.

In chapter 5 I continue my discussion of the limits of state intervention in enforcing an ideal of gender and, with it, one of the family by focusing on straight, mainly white men. Here I argue that the purported fathers' movement and the legal reforms it advocates cannot be morally defended because they banish men to the realm of the phenomenal. Thus, I strongly disagree with the fathers' movement, which assumes men can be legitimately conscripted into the family, because to do so denies them their claim to their person. Chapters 3 and 5 both argue that "nature" cannot be used to deny our equivalent status as persons.

Chapter 6 anticipates the charge that the advocacy of an equivalent law of persons and the protection of the imaginary domain, if it is in any way universalized as a conception of right, is necessarily imperialistic. The charge would be that it is imperialistic because it imposes the Western philosophical imaginary on postcolonial peoples. Here we will look more closely at exactly what is being demanded by a feminist human rights agenda—an agenda that has gained considerable international support. In this chapter, I will engage the issues of genital mutilation and polygamy because the charge of immoral or illiberal universalization has been used against those in the human rights movement who would outlaw these practices as a matter of right. I will conclude that something like the imaginary domain is necessary for a human rights agenda that addresses sex and that it need not rest on the Kantian justification I have used to defend it in this book.

In chapter 7 I will address the question of whether or not feminism is utopian. First, I will examine whether or not the basic claim in this book—that we each must have the sanctuary of the imaginary domain and the right to the self-representation of our sexuate being—is utopian. To do so I will explore different meanings of utopianism. Any Kantian political conception of right is utopian in one basic sense: it cannot concede any claims, made in the name of reality, that some of us are graded down as less than free and equal persons. This utopianism is basic to ethical and political liberalism, and we must insist upon it against those who seek to justify social hierarchies and inequalities because "nature" makes them inevitable. Feminism that insists on the imaginary domain guides itself by recollective imagination that keeps us from losing our dream that there might be a society in which all share in life's glories.

* CHAPTER TWO *

Freed Up: Privacy, Sexual Freedom, and Liberty of Conscience

Besides defending the idea that our sexuate being and the way we choose to represent ourselves sexually is basic and personality-defining, and must therefore be protected by any meaningful concept of liberty of conscience, I will show how the concept of the imaginary domain works normatively to define the limits of the regulation of any person's sexuality. Furthermore, I will point out how the imaginary domain can help us move past the "which side are you on" rhetoric that has accompanied debates among feminists over the controversial issue of the moral stature of prostitutes and porn workers. Feminists who think of prostitutes and porn workers as "sexual slaves" will disagree sharply on what should be done about sex work with those who consider sex workers to be persons with the right to represent their sexuate being. Last, I want to separate the demand for the moral and psychic space needed for orienting ourselves as sexuate beings from the concept of individualism.[1] Even so, the demand for moral and psychic space can be reconciled with what Ronald Dworkin has named the "ancestral" principles that protect freedom of personality in a politically liberal society—principles that for Dworkin cohere into ethical individualism—thus providing an ethical, and not simply a political, justification for the imaginary domain. The two principles that Dworkin advances are that each of us has equal intrinsic value and that each of us is uniquely responsible for his or her own life.[2]

33

Bodily Integrity and the Sexual Imago

Human creatures are sexual beings. From the moment we project an image of ourselves as a self, a creature whose body is recollected as hers, sex is in the picture. The pulling together of the body into an image of wholeness is crucial to the delicate process by which the infant individuates herself from others as both subject and object. Sigmund Freud considered the development of an ego to be first and foremost bodily.[3] Infants are conglomerates of fleeting experiences; they are bombarded by sensations, including those coming from their own body. The child develops a bodily ego in part by finding her own body parts a libidinal source of pleasure. This primordial sense that libidinal pleasure comes from her body gives the infant her first stabilized sense of herself as a coherent being: Bodily integrity is not just a given, but demands that we view ourselves as an integral whole, as a self. Freud's concept of the bodily ego was deeply influenced by the neurophysiology of his time, and in particular by the discovery of the sixth sense. The twentieth-century neurologist Oliver Sacks describes how without the effective operation of this sixth sense there is no sense of self:

> Our other senses—the five senses—are open and obvious; but this—our hidden sense—had to be discovered, as it was, by Sherrington, in the 1890's. He named it "proprioception," to distinguish it from "exteroception" and "interoception," and, additionally, because of its indispensability for our sense of *ourselves;* for it is only by courtesy of proprioception, so to speak, that we feel our bodies proper to us, as our "property," as our own.
>
> What is more important for us, at an elemental level, than the control, the owning and operation, of our own physical selves? And yet it is so automatic, so familiar, we never give it a thought.[4]

The sixth sense is what allows us to perceive ourselves as physically coherent beings—as selves. The bodily ego is what gives us the ability to organize our perceptions of ourselves as

our own.[5] More developed representations of ourselves as cor-
poreal beings rest on this sixth sense and on our bodily ego.
Through the bodily ego, the body becomes meaningful as our
self, not only as a functional source of delight or a means to an
end. Our investment in our bodies is in this sense inseparable
from our most basic sense of self. The psychical map of the
body's libidinal delights is both internalized and projected out as
the body image through which the self is "grounded." I put
grounded in quotation marks only to indicate the paradox and
fragility of grounding oneself in an image.

Jacques Lacan's addition to Freud's understanding of how we
become a self only through the process of developing a bodily
ego is twofold.[6] First, he emphasizes that the infant's psychical
mapping of her body involves more than a simple tracing of her
own sources of delight, or remembrance of them as her own
because certain of these body parts of hers repeatedly and pre-
dictably give pleasure. Lacan sees us as depending on others for
the experience of projecting ourselves as whole; he records how
human beings differ from chimpanzees when confronted with
their self-images in the mirror. This "stage" of jubilation at seeing oneself as a whole, as a being that coheres as its own object
and subject, begins between the ages of six and eighteen
months. Relatively helpless at this stage of life, the infant is only
beginning to have some limited control over her body. But because the infant's perceptual apparatus is more advanced than
her other physical capacities, when she sees herself mirrored she
can perceive a wholeness that she does not experience physically. A human infant's mirroring does not only take place in
front of a mirror: the primary caretaker both represents an individuated being to the child and serves as a mirror. The primary
caretaker appears as whole to the baby, who invests in the primary caretaker because there she sees bodily coherence she can
count on to meet her needs. By identifying with the primary
caretaker's own projected wholeness, the child finds another
means of achieving a sense of continuity for her own fragile
bodily ego.

Lacan's second contribution to Freud's basic insight stresses the temporal dimension in the development of coherent egos. The stabilization of the bodily ego and, with it, a primordial sense of self must have not only continuity in confirmation of it in order to lay the basis for the baby's internalization of its body image, but also must have a projected future in which this process of "pulling oneself together" is experienced as a sense of self-identity over time.

The significance of Lacan's insight can be understood by the example of the post-traumatic stress syndrome experienced by victims of rape and other violent experiences, symptoms that result not just from reliving the brutal moment of assault.[7] Because an attack on the integrity of the body is an attack on the ego itself, the ability of the self to pull itself together is wounded. Thus, the symptoms of post-traumatic stress syndrome include a sense of collapse, paralysis, and an inability to collect oneself and go on. Part of this feeling that one cannot go on comes from the loss of a sense of a secure future for the self to project its continuing self-identity into. Because the shattering of the bodily ego disrupts the semiautomatic process by which most adults pull themselves together as a self, recovery demands that one go back and actively and imaginatively recollect oneself before projecting oneself once more into the future.[8] This projection into the future of an embodied self that can collect herself, and thus give meaning to herself, is crucial, and is truly the basis for the experience of selfhood.[9] Although this process of pulling oneself together through recollective imagination becomes obvious in victims of crime, it is necessary to all of us even if it has become so automatic that we are hardly aware of it.

The right to bodily integrity has to be an essential component of our being recognized as persons: bodily integration is composed of a body image and a sexual imago.[10] In our culture the "sex" we are designated to be at birth certainly matters a great deal. Indeed, to be viewed as of one gender or another, either male or female, affects the way we are confirmed as selves by the adults who mirror us and give us our ability to experience ourselves.[11] Since we project ourselves only through an ego that psychically maps its libidinal intensities, this mapping inescapably implicates sex. Not only is this so because of primordial pleasure, but also through the meanings communicated to us by both the mirroring of ourselves by adults and their tactile engagement with us. The result of these experiences is that our egos are not neutrally developed, but are "sexed" so that we cannot see ourselves from the outside as men or women, gay or straight. Instead, we see ourselves so deeply from the "inside" as "sexed" that we cannot easily, if at all, re-envision our sexuate being. This inner "sexed" sense is the sexual imago that is the basis of the unconscious assumed persona through which we represent ourselves.

Sexual orientation cannot be called a choice since it implicates a sexual imago that is inseparable from the bodily ego. To deny a person the space to live out her sexuate being as it is presented and represented in her persona is potentially to undermine her most basic sense of self. Bodily integration and sexual representation go hand in hand. To have a sexual identity thrust upon one by state-imposed meanings of normal sexuality when it does not suit one's sexual imago or reimagined representation of one's sexuate being is inconsistent with the politically liberal ideal of freedom of personality. If the state forces any one of us into the closet because of our sexuate being, it denies us our standing as persons because we are no longer recognized as having the right to define ourselves and to set forth our own vision of what a good life for us would be. Freedom of conscience, the hallmark of a politically liberal society, denies the legitimacy of such enforced closeting.

CONSCIENCE AND SELF-REPRESENTATION OF SEXUATE BEING

I am using *conscience* in the sense of the freedom given a person in a politically liberal society to claim herself as the "self-authenticating source" of what the good life is for her. Conscience is the "sanctuary" of personality, in that who we are as unique beings is inseparable from how we mark out a life with its commitments, fundamental values, and responsibilities as *ours*. By this definition, conscience is not simply an inherent moral faculty that enjoins one to conform to a moral law, although it does involve the development of an "inward monitor" of how we should guide our lives. This "inward monitor" is what we turn to when we look to ourselves for the right answer for us to the big life-determining questions we inevitably have to confront as we attempt to design a life in a world as beset by moral complexity as our own. I put "inward monitor" in quotation marks because it is a metaphor for the constant and complex process of internalization through which we embrace and identify ourselves with a set of moral convictions and political commitments we personalize as part of ourselves and then appeal to as standards by which to judge how our life is going.

None of us starts from scratch—each of us wrestles with the ideas of the good life that are culturally available to us. Formed as we are by the world into which we are thrown and which engages us because we are set in the midst of it, the process of mining and shifting our values as we make them our own is a lifelong project. We can never draw a clear line between the values "out there" and the ones we have internalized and embraced as personality defining. We cannot actually be the fully original source of our own values, or even know the extent to which we have absorbed conventional morality, unconsciously sanctifying it rather than rebelling against or critically appropriating it. Although we cannot be the fully authenticating source of our own values, in reality we should nonetheless be politically recognized as if we were. The abstract ideal person is normatively recognized as the node of choice and source of value. *Abstraction—defining the person only through a normative outline—is the only way we can preserve freedom of personality.* If the person were given "substance" by state-imposed meanings, say, of "normal" sexuality, then her freedom would be denied. That is to say, freedom of personality as a political ideal need not be rooted in a truth about the human condition, or in a metaphysical justification for autonomy.[12] I return to this point later on in this chapter when discussing why the ideal of the imaginary domain does not entail an individualist anthropology.[13]

For now, I want to return to why I have named this sanctuary of personality the imaginary domain, and why, as the moral space to orient ourselves sexually, the imaginary domain differs from privacy, the constitutional doctrine used most frequently and yet inconsistently to defend freedom to define one's sexuality.[14] The inconsistency stems from the Supreme Court's using two bases for the justification of the line of cases beginning with *Griswold*.[15] *Griswold* protected married people's right to use contraception.[16] But because of its subject matter, *Griswold* also represented the tension in the Court's reasoning. On the one hand the Court offered an interpretation of the Due Process Clause of the Fourteenth Amendment, arguing that any meaningful concept of "ordered liberty" would have to include a married couple's right to make crucial decisions about when to begin their family. That is, the state was not to climb into the marital bed and impose the view that sex for the purpose of reproduction is the only morally acceptable sex. But at the same time, the Court appealed to the state's interest in promoting and protecting the monogamous heterosexual family. Since *Griswold,* the state's interest in promoting the integrity of the institution of monogamous heterosexual marriage has continued to figure prominently in privacy cases. Indeed, in *Bowers v. Hardwick,* the state's interest in promoting the integrity of marriage was appealed to as an argument against the rights of two gay men to express themselves sexually in the privacy of their own home.[17]

The argument throughout this book is that the promotion of the integrity of heterosexual monogamous marriage in a politically liberal society is illegitimate because it violates the sanctuary of personality, the imaginary domain. Some libertarians have tried to use privacy to argue either implicitly or explicitly against the state interest in promoting the sanctity of the monogamous heterosexual family.[18] In their interpretation, privacy means that the state must leave us alone in our fundamental value decisions, and certainly in the places of retreat we choose for ourselves. Feminists have attacked this relentless interpretation of privacy as the demand to be left alone by the state, certainly in one's home and in one's bed, as a cover that hides rampant sexual abuse and domestic violence.[19] The imaginary domain allows us to separate what is of value in the doctrine of privacy from its illegitimate promotion of the heterosexual nuclear family as the good family, and does so without reducing the value of privacy to the right to be left alone. Simply demanding that the state leave us alone inadequately protects what is at stake in the right to self-represent one's sexuate being.

First and foremost, the right to self-represent one's own sexuate being cannot meaningfully separate speech from action, expression from actualization.[20] Self-representation of one's sexuate being involves not only representing oneself in and through sexual personae[21] but setting forth a life that expresses one's moral and affective orientation in matters of sex and family. The demand to exercise one's sexuate being through bonds and associations with others is structurally analogous to the protection of the right not only to appeal to conscience alone in religious matters but to be allowed space for the practice of one's faith.[22] Historically, the political ideal of the protection of the space for conscience was inseparable from the demand for religious freedom.[23] This freedom was interpreted to mean that the person had to make her own decisions and follow her deepest convictions in the pursuit of her faith. But faith in most religions is expressed not just privately. Meaningful religious freedom would not be protected if a person were allowed to pray only in solitude, nor would it be protected as long as others who did not like the particular practices of members of a certain religion were allowed to refuse to have them "in their face." Freedom of religion demands the full reach of the right to self-representation.

In like manner, the right to the self-representation of one's sexuate being demands a full reach. The freedom to announce that one is gay or a lesbian, or even to hang a sign from the Empire State Building to that effect, does not meet the right to the self-representation of one's sexuate being. For example, life for a gay man obviously includes the right to live out his sexuality, live openly and at peace with his lover or lovers, and take on the commitment of parenting if he so chooses. When we think of orienting ourselves as sexuate beings, we think not only of with whom we will have sex and what kinds of relationships we will have with lovers, questions that are basic and personality-defining, but about whether to marry or not, a question whose answer is fundamental to a person's life. Just as these questions have expressive, moral, and political dimensions in the straight community, so they do in the queer community in the struggle for the right of gays and lesbians to marry. The debate has in part been over the meaning of *queer* as a political identification.[24] But for feminists too, certainly those in their midforties, the question of whether to marry or not has been inseparable from how women represented themselves as feminists and as persons. Indeed, some feminists argue that heterosexual marriage is a patriarchal institution inconsistent with the recognition of women as persons.

Setting forth a life as a sexuate being certainly, when it is explicitly political, fosters the right to seek out political associations and to represent one's politics in the public realm. But even if the person wants to avoid politics, the expression of sexuate being demands that one be allowed to associate with any others, *a choice that can involve political stances*. This right involves not only sexual relationships with other adults, but decisions whether to parent or to find other forms for intergenerational friendships.[25] If gays and lesbians are denied the right to parent or are forced to face prohibitive hurdles against creating families, then the state clearly is taking a space that should be left to the person. The *Bowers v. Hardwick* decision shows just how far we are from allowing gays and lesbians the right to self-represent their sexuate being; the threat that the law will close down what little space has been gained for gays and lesbians to live openly as lovers and as families is still unallayed. Only very recently, indeed within the last three decades, have white heterosexual women felt free enough of the cultural stigmatization imposed on the single mother to raise children born "out of wedlock."[26] The recent welfare reforms aimed at making it economically prohibitive for single women to have more than two children show how fragile the acceptance of single motherhood is in our society.[27] And only in the last fifteen years have single, heterosexual women been allowed to adopt children in the United States.[28] Whether and how one represents oneself as a mother is clearly a personality-defining decision that is as fundamental to the way we orient ourselves as sexuate beings as are decisions about with whom we have sex.

Throughout most of Europe in the nineteenth century, a woman who left her marriage automatically lost her children. There are still many structures in our family law that effectively prohibit women who choose to live freely sexually from maintaining custody of their children.[29] Self-representation of oneself as a sexuate being carries with it one's demand for freedom to bond and create unions with others, a demand that does not sit easily with one particular interpretation of privacy. In his dissent in *Bowers v. Hardwick*, Justice Blackmun eloquently argued that a community of ordered liberty must recognize a right to intimate association if there is to be any real meaning to personal freedom in matters of the heart.[30] For Blackmun, such matters exemplified the kind of deep-seated, personality-defining decisions that, in a politically liberal society, must be left to the individual.[31]

Morris Kaplan has correctly argued that the right to intimate association transcends the concept of privacy as understood to be the right to be left alone:

The freedom of intimate association requires not only a negative right to be left alone, but also a positive capacity to create intimate spaces and social support for personal choices that establish and maintain personal relationships and identities. These intimate spaces are often referred to as "home." Domesticity is the metaphorical and actual space of intimacy: the privacy cases demonstrate the dependence of such a sphere on its recognition by legal and social authorities.[32]

These spaces in which we reimagine the meanings of "kin," "love," "sex," and "intergenerational friendship" are not places we have necessarily been or know and so they demand imaginative creation. We are dreaming them up as we constitute our families, even as we struggle with what it means to be a family member. And the imaginary domain is crucial for these dreams. First, it allows the sexual imago in and through which we come to represent ourselves in the first place. Second, it is the psychic space in which we are allowed to freely imagine ourselves as sexuate beings, representing ourselves as persons who define our own moral perspectives in matters of sex, love, and intergenerational friendship. Third, it allows for imagined modes of relationships that help us give body to the ways we wish to set up our intimate relationships.

Of course, these imagined settings need to be translated into real space if they are to be actualized and effectively represented. We don't want simply to dream about intimate relationships; we want to have them. Housing laws that refuse a gay couple real space prevent these lovers from living out their commitment to each other.[33] Because they are so precious and fragile, relationships can falter before much less explicit forms of discrimination. Freedom to live out one's love involves all the small and big gestures, from holding hands in public to being affirmed as the beloved at a lover's deathbed.

Some of us may think we are only copying the families we grew up in, but copying involves some degree of creativity because it can never be exact. Others of us who think of ourselves as making psychic maps for outer space surprise ourselves by patterning relationships in ways we thought we had rejected.

Ironically, all the hoopla about family values highlights the extent to which families can no longer be assumed to be part of what someone inherits and passes on to the next generation in the course of life. New kinds of families are being made that do not necessarily follow biology, evidence that they are being made and are not just "expressing nature."

Clearly, there is a perceived crisis in families in the United States.[34] That many families are not even close to the idealized family picture of the 1950s is only too evident.[35] The image of the traditional nuclear heterosexual family was based on the premise of a lifetime marriage and a male breadwinner. Although most families in the United States never matched the image,[36] many Americans have been held captive by the image as an ideal to which they should aspire. Indeed, just such a family in a privately owned home surrounded by a white picket fence has been the quintessential representation of the American Dream.

But an image is just that—an image, a representation. Certainly, those who accept that ideal have the right to bond with others and set forth on a life together that they believe matches or comes close to matching that ideal picture. This innate right is of course protected by their imaginary domain. Feminists have often been accused of trying to impose their view of the family on everyone else.[37] But a feminism that demands equal protection for every person's own imaginary domain does the opposite. True, the public contest over family values demonstrates how differently people picture what a good family is, and how fiercely people hold on to their ideals. But it is at just such moments of heated contest that we can see how tightly we each hold on to our vision of our intimate relationships' needs. People cannot claim that their love is better than any other, or that their way of love should be imposed upon anyone else. Our political commitment to freedom of conscience has been severely tested by this precisely because we are all so wrapped up in our particular intimate relationships and their meaning for us. An equivalent law of persons demands the recognition that we all have the right to the self-representation of our sexuate being: nothing less and nothing more.

Complete deregulation also does not adequately protect the right to intimate association if implicit or explicit discrimination is allowed against gay couples. As I have already pointed out, self-representation of one's sexuate being cannot be reduced to literal privacy of an individual to be left alone in his or her bedroom. Of course, in post-*Bowers* America, gays and lesbians do not even have that right—which would be an improvement for gay couples, but is not adequate to the right to self-represent one's sexuate being.

If a gay couple is forced to "hide" their love in order to even get a roof over their heads, then they are being denied the right to self-representation of their sexuate beings. President Clinton's suggested solution for the military, "don't ask, don't tell,"[38] also violates the imaginary domain of gays and lesbians. If a lesbian couple is denied the right to legally establish themselves as a family, then the state is thrusting a way of life upon them that violates how, if free, they would set forth their intimate relationships with one another and with their children. As I have argued, the right to self-representation must protect a person's ability to design a life. What designing a life means varies according to circumstances. It can mean being a proud lesbian sergeant. It can mean choosing not to be a mother by having an abortion, or it can mean setting forth a relationship with a same-sex partner and then deciding to parent openly and lovingly together. The latter instance will involve the state-protected right of the lover who does not bear her child to adopt him or her, a right that cannot be protected by the right to be left alone.

THE CASE OF PROSTITUTION

The argument for the equal protection of the sanctuary of the imaginary domain and the corresponding right to self-represen-

45

tation of our sexuate being can help us to develop politically principled guidelines for the areas of sexual relationships and family life. These guidelines must of course be made accordant with the protection of the freedom of personality from which they find their justification. The question of how to involve the state in the area of intimate relations is particularly tricky because regulation can so easily trample on the person's right to self-representation. Some feminists have tried to develop a theory of male sexual domination to be used to morally and legally judge our sexual relationships. Their theory would then be used to determine what are necessarily degrading representations of our sexuate being and, thus, should be legally prohibited. The state, so the argument goes, should be put to use to end male sexual domination, particularly in its most obvious and brutal forms, no matter what the women involved say about their freedom. Male domination purportedly creates its own "willing" victims. The state must save women who participate in its perpetuation from their own false consciousness. Prostitutes and pornography workers exemplify women who have been "had" in the most tragic sense. By ending porn work and prostitution, the state saves them from themselves.

Without denying the harsh economic or psychic history that led them into prostitution or pornography, some prostitutes and porn workers have loudly protested that they do not want or need to be saved. They argue that they no more need saving than do the white, middle-class feminists who are out to save them from themselves. Although both prostitutes and porn workers have formed union-type organizations, the question that continues to be posed for feminists is whether or not to support them since such organizations inevitably begin with a demand for the decriminalization of sex work and legal recognition for sex workers. The fierce debate over the regulation of pornography is inseparable from the legal status of prostitution, since porn workers have sex in exchange for money. The two industries also intersect because many porn workers also do "outwork." The debates over the regulation of pornography demand an answer to the question of the legal status of porn workers and prostitutes, although the connection between the two has not always been recognized, nor consistently applied, in feminist programs for regulation. What kind of regulation, if any, is appropriate when a woman insists she is involved in the self-representation of her sexuate being by becoming a porn worker and/or a prostitute? What does it mean for a feminist to advocate that the state should save a woman from herself?

Are Prostitutes Persons?

Currently, the most sophisticated feminist argument for the legal prohibition and, thus, criminalization of prostitution is that prostitution involves indentured servitude or, worse yet, sexual slavery. That is, a woman does not have the right to cancel herself out as a source of rights, as a person, by selling her "sex." This argument takes the form of that made against slavery: slavery must be prohibited even if a woman "chooses" to sell herself, because the institution violates her standing as a source of right and this violation, even if self-imposed, is inconsistent with recognition of her as a free and equal person. If a woman represents herself in a manner that is inconsistent with her personhood, should we not protect her from doing so in the name of the personhood she has forsaken?

Within what has now come to be called the second wave of feminism, the sides have been drawn: one is either for or against the continuation of legal prohibition of prostitution. But there are actually more than two "sides" among feminist activists. For many feminists, even those who disagree with the continuing criminalization of prostitution, the ambivalent social acceptance of prostitution as necessary for men functions to support the wrong kind of legislation for the protection of prostitutes. The historical legacy of the haphazard enforcement against the prostitutes and not the johns, and only against prostitutes when there is some other purpose served by rounding them up, exposes the hypocritical underside of patriarchy. The picture of the patriarch has two sides: flip over the picture of the good family man and you find a john eagerly pursuing a streetwalker.

Historians have shown how the regulations of "illegitimate sexualities" in nineteenth-century Great Britain and France functioned as attempts to control disorder. Even though the prostitute was a manifestation of illegitimate sexuality, both countries tolerated prostitution within the parameters of highly regulated systems enforced by laws and by the medical establishment. The prostitute was viewed as a depository for the excesses that could not be contained within the parameters of the Victorian family; according to one French physician, she was a "seminal drain."[39] Her existence, although dangerous, was therefore necessary. Because specialists on the subject contended that unregulated prostitution would lead to the spread of disease and immorality, the state put into place a system of laws and medical procedures aimed at regulating the prostitutes' activities.

In 1836 the French social scientist Alexandre Parent-Duchâtelet wrote that

> prostitutes are as inevitable, in an agglomeration of men, as sewers, garbage-heaps, and refuse-dumps; the conduct of the authorities ought to be the same with regard to one as to the other; the duty is to watch over, to diminish by all possible means the inconveniences inherent in them, and, certainly, to hide them, to relegate them to the darkest corners, to make their presence as unnoticed as possible.[40]

The French government adopted Parent-Duchâtelet's suggestions and established a complex system of tolerance of illegitimate sexuality. The government enlisted *maîtresses de maison,* women who managed *maisons de tolérance,* or brothels, and made their workers available to the state for regular inspection. Individual prostitutes were required to register with a brothel, and police were granted the authority to arrest any woman they suspected to be a prostitute not registered with a state-authorized brothel.

Great Britain took France's lead and enacted the Contagious
Diseases Acts of 1864, 1866, and 1869. The acts designated
women, and not their male clients, as the source of disease.[41]
Police were required by the acts to identify individual women
whom they suspected to be prostitutes and subject them to bi-
weekly gynecological exams; if a woman was diagnosed with
gonorrhea or syphilis, she could be hospitalized for several
weeks or months.

In both France and Great Britain, feminists mounted cam-
paigns against these state regulations, charging that the regulations, in the words of Great Britain's Ladies National Association (LNA), "punished the sex who are the victims of vice and
leave unpunished the sex who are the main causes both of the
vice and its dreaded consequences."[42] Organized feminist re-
sponses to state tolerance of prostitution grew out of the "rescue work" many middle-class feminists took part in throughout
the nineteenth century. Charity work engaged middle-class
women's "maternal, angelic nature" as they sought to convey
standards of bourgeois family life to members, usually women
and children, of the working classes. Charity work expanded to
include the task of rescuing "fallen women" from the "instrumental rape" of the regulations enacted in France and Great
Britain. Feminists argued that the tolerance system in France
and the Contagious Diseases Acts in Great Britain served to legitimate and perpetuate male vice at the expense of young
women. The LNA depicted prostitutes "as women who had
been invaded by men's bodies, men's laws and by that 'steel
penis,' the speculum."[43]

Throughout the nineteenth century, the task of rescuing the
prostitute from state regulations provided feminists an occasion
to further define women's inherent difference from men. In various registers, feminists couched their demands for social and
political equality in terms of women's difference. In 1848 the
feminist newspaper *La voix des femmes,* declared that "the
morality of the nation depends especially on the morality of
women."[44] Women, feminists argued, deserved equal rights

because then the state could benefit from women's unique qualities. Since the rescue of the prostitute became a way for feminists to further proclaim women's virtue, they could conceive of
the prostitute only as the victim of men's inherent licentiousness. They could not imagine her as having chosen the profession voluntarily. Although feminists did suggest that if granted
greater opportunities, women would be unlikely to turn to prostitution for their survival, this economics-based argument was
more often than not obscured by the "obsession" with male
vice.[45]

In Great Britain, the Contagious Diseases Acts were repealed
in 1883, and in France, the last state-regulated brothel closed its
doors in 1946. Yet the moral tenor of the feminist repeal campaign had taken hold of policy makers and enabled the passage
of laws that, in effect, placed more restrictions on women than
had the system of tolerance or the Contagious Diseases Acts.

This legacy haunts contemporary feminist appeals for state
regulation of sex work. This being said, some activists argue for
deregulation and decriminalization based on everyone's right to
express her sexuality as she sees fit, even if it involves danger to
herself and others, as long as it stops with nonconsensual violence.[46] This argument continues to be a powerful response to
those who have favored either criminalization of prostitution or
decriminalization with regulation. Many feminists contend that
such activists ignore the reported suffering of prostitutes and the
conditions of prostitution, and have felt justified in denouncing
these advocates as merely perpetuating the patriarchal abuse of
women.[47] The feminists see deregulation as a license for rampant male sexual abuse against terribly vulnerable women.[48]
Yet, given that women in many of the world's countries in the
1990s are formally recognized as equal persons before the law,
the question of the personhood of prostitutes is unavoidable. In
the nineteenth century, the question was how feminist organizations should represent prostitutes. In the twentieth century, the
question is whether prostitutes can or should represent themselves. The question of whether prostitutes have sacrificed their

standing as persons and thus their right to represent themselves is therefore on the table.

Alternative Programs of Reform in Our Time

In 1974 there was a feminist meeting in New York to air the differences among feminists over the issue of the legal prohibition against prostitution. A number of prostitutes' organizations attended, as did advocates for the legal prohibition of prostitution, as well as organizations offering medical attention, food, and shelter to prostitutes on the streets. The prostitutes, arguing against any kind of criminalization and regulation that would deny them their status as persons, were completely opposed to forced registration, imposed hospitalization, or forced medical treatment, which had all been regulations of the tolerance system a century before. More broadly, the prostitutes' organizations opposed any regulation made in the name of moral decency, and feminists advocating prohibition were accused of wanting the state to impose their own sexual morality.

The bitterness of the fights at that conference reflected the divisions of race and class that seem to create such gulfs between women. Many of the prostitutes were African American or Latina. White prostitutes involved with the prostitutes' organizations were mostly of working-class origin. The women who advocated prohibition and criminalization, many of them lawyers, seemed to many of the prostitutes to be from a world of racial and class privilege. Indeed, prohibition and criminalization were virulently attacked because these reforms would throw women out of the best jobs many of them could get. There was deep resentment against the women who wanted to put prostitutes out of business; they were seen as out of touch with the suffering that their support for more rigorous enforcement of the criminal law—for prostitution was illegal in New York state—would mean for women who might end up with jail sentences. There was great cynicism that effective law enforcement against johns, let alone pimps, would ever become a reality. Prostitutes also militantly refused to accept the view that they were victims.

The feminists who favored prohibition and the abolition of prostitution through vigorous criminal enforcement argued that the prostitutes were participating in their own oppression, and accused them of false consciousness. The prostitutes' organizations counterattacked. Using the feminist terminology of the time, they argued that if all women's sexuality was caught up in patriarchal limitations imposed upon them, then there could be only a continuum. No woman could claim that her sexual life was pure or that she had never sold herself for a date or in marriage. Prostitutes argued that feminist self-righteousness, demanding the backing of the state, would be only another barrier against women's sexual freedom.

I attended the conference with my consciousness-raising group, all Latina and African American except for me. Our program called for decriminalization and self-organization into a union-type organization. One of the women in our consciousness-raising group also called for the women who were sincerely interested in the suffering of street prostitutes to set up organizations to take on the dangerous business of helping defend individual prostitutes against the violence of pimps. The call for a unionlike organization was supported by most of the prostitutes' organizations, and then, naturally, decriminalization was seen to be the first step toward unionization. The debate was not about whether everything was "A-OK" in the lives of prostitutes, although there was clear recognition that there were hierarchies among prostitutes, and that those who worked the streets (often to support a serious drug habit) were in the most need of organized assistance. Rather, the question was whether or not prostitutes could form their own organizations and represent themselves, all the while welcoming support from feminists to back their efforts at self-organization. Clearly, our group believed they could. The conference did not resolve the dispute, in part because of the terms of the debate. The fierce disagreement about prostitution was displaced by the discord between feminists over the regulation of pornography. The disagreement over the standing of prostitutes and porn workers rages on today, the terms of the debate as yet unchanged.

Let me now put the debate into the terminology developed in this book. The question to be addressed is the one presented earlier: by selling their sex, have prostitutes excluded themselves from the moral community of persons? Let me begin by reasserting that my insistence on abstraction is inseparable from the political recognition of the person as the node of choice in all crucial personality-defining decisions. Therefore, such an abstract ideal of the person, with its insistence on the space to orient oneself as a sexuate being, would have a presumption against state-enforced sexual morality, including state regulation of prostitutes. Yet if the state is called on to give equal protection to bodily integrity as instant in the imaginary domain and as a minimum condition of individuation, can't we make the argument that someone who has violated her own bodily integrity no longer has a self to represent? To put it somewhat differently, hasn't she shown that her imaginary domain has been completely shattered, that she has not been able to become a self, a subject of a life, and thus cannot represent herself because she has reduced herself to an object, her sex? If we answer yes, then it follows that there is nothing left except a thing to be filled in by the desires of others. Following this argument, it would seem that the state should prohibit this kind of self-objectification in the name of the minimum conditions of individuation that I have defended elsewhere.[49] By prohibiting prostitution, the state is protecting prostitutes' chances to become the persons they now are not, since they have reduced themselves to pieces of property.

Prostitutes' organizations have argued forcefully against this kind of comparison with sexual slavery. First, they argue that they have sold themselves not for all time, but only a *part* of themselves for a *period* of time. Second, unlike slaves, they are paid for specific acts. Last, they argue that, unlike slavery, prostitution is an extremely lucrative "profession," indeed one of the most lucrative ways for a woman to make a living. Some prostitutes' organizations agree that in an ideal society, prostitution should not exist, but ours is far from an ideal society. Thus, self-representation and self-organization are the best solutions for the often poor working conditions some prostitutes, particularly streetwalkers, have to endure.

I want to return to the argument that my own defense of state protection of bodily integrity as a minimum condition of individuation could lead to the continuing legal prohibition of prostitution. First, as I argued earlier, we need to protect bodily integrity not because we have pregiven integral bodies, but because we *do not* have such bodies. Bodily integrity is understood to be instant in the imaginary domain because it is not a reality but a representation of ourselves. How we represent our bodily integrity is inseparable from how we represent our sexuate being. The body is invested in as part of the self through a highly individualized process of psychic mapping. Thus, it would be possible to admit that the development of the primordial sense of self has been disrupted in many women who sell their "sex," and yet still argue that it is not for the state but for them to find out what the meaning of prostitution is for themselves. For example, Ona Zee Wiggers, who tried to create a union for porn workers in the 1990s, pointed out that many prostitutes and porn workers have endured sexual traumas at an early age that disrupt the development of an integrated sense of self, leading them to experience a kind of splitting off from the body instead:

> I think that most of the women in the business had something go kaflooey, for lack of a better word. I don't think little girls just wake up one day and decide that they are going to have sex for a living. I don't believe it happens that way. I believe something happens to your psyche. Whether their Mom was a prostitute, or their Daddy treated them badly. In my case my step-grandfather molested me repeatedly. Whatever it was that happened, something happened that made them decide. And I am not saying that

this is a bad thing. For me, it has been the best thing in the world.[50]

Yet Wiggers also recognized that having "sex" for money demanded that she split herself off from what she was doing:

> O. Z.: I think that the truth is when you have sex for a living you split yourself off. And what I have learned in my therapy is that I learned to split myself off from the moment that, probably even before, I was even conscious because of what was going on in my home. When my grandfather was incesting me I had to split off or I would not have been able to tolerate it. So when I got into the sex business, splitting off was something I already knew how to do really, really well. When you get the exchange of money, the money is what is really gratifying. I guess that is part of what you were saying . . .
>
> D. C.: Yes, it's literally a payback in a sense.
>
> O. Z.: But there does come a time when you stop splitting off. That's what happened to me.[51]

For Ona Zee, part of the end to her splitting off came when she started organizing the union. But Wiggers still insisted that her life as a prostitute was a representation of her sexuate being, a persona that she had to live out.

Again, to quote Wiggers speaking of her own "journey" to express and come to terms with her sexuality, including her life as a prostitute:

> It's such an incredible process. I wish every woman in the world could have a night with someone for money because it's such an eye opener. It is beyond belief. You come to grips with your power in a magnificent way. You can either make it a magnificent journey or the worst thing that happened to you in the world. I've swung back and forth on that pendulum. Overall though it has been a privilege to work in the industry and make a contribution to these men because they needed it so badly. And I've worked privately. I've worked in some of the biggest prostitution

rings in the world. I wanted to try that. I wanted to see what it was like. I did that as a choice. I made a conscious choice.[52]

What does it mean for a feminist to argue that Ona Zee should not have been allowed to go through this journey, when she recognizes it may have been necessary for her, to make up for her grandfather's abuse? We might regret that she had no other means to do this; we most certainly should regret and indeed despair over the horrific violation that is an incestuous childhood. We have to fight back on every political level we can dream of to end the sexual abuse of children. For Ona Zee, the abuse necessitated her taking on the persona of the prostitute. She does not pretend she would have done so if she had not been abused. How could we accuse her of false consciousness, of not understanding the connection between porn work and child-hood incest, when she so clearly articulates the connection? As difficult as it is to face, in a world of abuse some women will take on the life of a prostitute in order to work through their incestuous and violent pasts.

Of course, choosing to become a prostitute may be reactive; Ona Zee says her decision was. But how many of us can say that our own representations of our own sexuate being are not reactive? How can any of us know for sure? Thus, given the level of abstraction at which the ideal of the person must remain if it is to protect freedom of personality, I would strongly argue against dismissing Ona Zee and other prostitutes from the moral community of persons. Besides, if prostitutes and porn workers are not recognized as persons, they are stripped of their civil rights. Andrea Dworkin and Catherine MacKinnon's pornography ordinance in Minneapolis sought to give porn workers the right to sue their production companies for violation of their person.[53] Yet, ironically, the ordinance can make no sense unless porn workers and prostitutes are recognized as persons.

Thus, a prostitute should be given the right to the self-representation of her sexuate being, as well as the right to form representative organizations for prostitutes and porn workers. As Rosalind Pollack Petchesky has eloquently argued, the process of claiming title to oneself is a political and ethical process and turns on a view of what it means to own oneself that differs from the static idea of ownership presented in feminist critiques of prostitutes' self-organization.[54]

As feminists, we clearly want to be on the side of both recognizing and supporting the collective effort of prostitutes to claim themselves. For many who became active in the prostitutes' organizations movement, part of this struggle for bodily integrity is to join in a movement in which the personhood of the prostitute is proclaimed as essential to a program of reform of the conditions of prostitution. If we separate bodily integrity from collective representation, the chance to claim oneself as a prostitute and as a person is taken away.

State prohibition of prostitution and the move for vigilant criminal enforcement rob women who are porn workers and prostitutes of the most effective weapon against the abuses that have been graphically described—unionization. As I wrote earlier, if porn work and prostitution are criminalized, then these women cannot form legitimate unions. Do I think that prostitution would exist in a just or ethical world? Certainly it would not exist as it does now for the poorer streetwalkers, whose need for protection is supposedly provided by pimps who are too frequently themselves abusers. Even when they are not outright abusers, the pimps take a good portion of what the woman makes. Prostitutes who are not streetwalkers do not have to cope with being in that precarious position; there are hierarchies among prostitutes, as there are in almost every walk of life in the United States.

The pornography industry has hierarchies as well, so that some directors of sexually explicit videos, such as feminists, gays, and almost all lesbians, are excluded from the industry association, which has a distribution network and holds awards ceremonies. Conditions of work on the sets run by these outsiders are often completely different. For example, some lesbian production companies are run collectively. Do I think there would be sexually explicit videos in a just world? Indeed, I do, both for education and for pleasure. Candida Royalle and her seminars and videos would be missed, as would Annie Sprinkle's performance art.

Certainly any "ideal" world worth the name would be completely free from the high rate of incest and child abuse that we have come to know exists in this society. Since any ethical theory for social and political arrangement would have to include a theory of the scope of rights that inclusion in the moral community demands, women would not be driven into prostitution by poverty and drug addiction. But how do we move closer to a just or even ethically acceptable social and political arrangement if as feminists we join with conservative movements that would turn women over to the hands of the state rather than to their own organizations? State-enforced moralism hinders what we as feminists should seek: the psychic, political, and ethical space for women to represent themselves.

The Political and Ethical Justification for the Imaginary Domain

Let me begin with the political justification. I have already explained why the imaginary domain should be protected under any meaningful political conception of the freedom of conscience. Because it gives the person the right to represent her sexuate being, the imaginary domain is basic to the freedom of personality; there is nothing more personal to a human being than how she chooses to organize her sexual and familial relationships. The intensity with which ideals of personal life are defended is not surprising. So be it. There will always be competing and often opposing views as to what kind of sexual and familial life is the good one. Precisely because it so personal, we must allow each person to pursue her vision of what love, sex, and family mean for her. The deeply personal nature of these decisions leads me to defend an interpretive justification of what Ronald Dworkin has named the "discontinuity thesis." In our morally complex world we sometimes need to insist on discontinuity between what we think is good for ourselves and the people close to us and what we would allow the state to impose as the general evaluation of the good. When it comes to sexual relationships and family life, we most definitely should privilege the right over the good.[55]

I defend this interpretation of the discontinuity thesis because we can no more expect agreement on sex and family than we can on religion. Indeed, if we successfully grant each of us the right to represent our own sexuate being, there are sure to be more contests over what counts as the good life because many more sexualities will be freed from the closet. As Rawls continually reminds us, a proliferation of visions of the good life is inseparable from the *freedom* to pursue one's own. Because sexual and family decisions are so deeply personal, they must be left to each one of us to make.

To deny someone the right to the self-representation of her sexuate being would effectively mean excluding her from the moral community of persons. This would involve thrusting someone else's conception of the good or natural family upon a person who has chosen to organize her sexuality in a manner that is not in accord with that view. The sole justification for the violation of a person's imaginary domain can be only that the way in which she represents her sexuate being is so bad for her, or for others; the state then can warrant prohibiting it outright, or at least can try to discourage it. But I have argued that we should not do this even in the case of prostitution; history shows the dangers of allowing the state to be the source of meaning of acceptable "sex."

If the state were to favor only one form of representation of sexuate being, it would violate the basic mandate of a politically liberal society that all of us are to be given equal concern as persons. This equal concern follows from the equal intrinsic value of each one of us as a person. Dworkin has forcefully argued that what is demanded by the recognition of our equal intrinsic value is *treatment of each of us as an equal* and not just equal treatment.[56] To prohibit, discourage, or encourage one form of representation of sexuate being over another clearly favors some persons over others. The demand, then, is not only for toleration of "different" forms of family. Whose standards of the good could we use to judge what is "different," let alone what is deviant? The demand is for freedom and equality, for the recognition of each one of us as the node of representation for our own sexuality and therefore of our own equivalent value, despite the forms with which we choose to represent our sexual difference. The state must show us equal concern by recognizing our equivalent value as persons who inevitably express their sexuate being. Sexual difference has all too often been used to effectively banish people to the realm of the phenomenal, and to use their "sex" as dispositive of the denial of full personhood.

There are only two limitations on the right of each one of us as a person to the self-representation of her sexuate being. The first is the obvious prohibition that no one can use force or violence against another person in representing her sexuate being. The second is the "degradation prohibition,"[57] which prohibits any one of us from being graded down because of her form of representation of her sexuate being. By graded down I mean to denote when our sexuate being is used to create gradations that would have some of us judged as not truly persons in that abstract sense I have defended in the introduction and in this chapter. If a lesbian couple is not allowed to live openly with their children, then they are not being allowed to set forth their life together as they have chosen to represent it. The degradation prohibition is not to be justified as a moralistic defense of state intervention against offensive behavior.[58] The opposite is the case: the prohibition would prevent the state from degrading anyone in the sense of excluding her from the normative community of persons, which is exactly what happens to people who are denied their lives as sexuate beings because their way of life offends someone else.

What are we to do when there is an open and public clash between our different representations of our sexuate being, particularly as these are necessarily involved with our other basic identifications—race and national and linguistic identity? A classic example in recent years was the demand made by organizers of the St. Patrick's Day Parade that gays and lesbians not be allowed to organize an "Irish and Proud" contingent.[59] Here was an open clash between the ways competing groups interpret the meaning of Irish-ness. Of course, there are some in the Irish community who think that it is a contradiction in terms to be Irish and gay. There are some who feel equally as intensely that, for example, part of their identity as Irishwomen is open rebellion against all oppressive norms. I am one of them. A homophobic Irishman may be deeply offended by having to march in a parade with gays and lesbians. But he is not degraded. He is allowed to be openly straight and Irish. What is the solution? The answer offered in this book is that there cannot be any state-ordered solution because such an intervention inevitably involves the state in deciding whose representation of Irishness is "better," more worthy of participation in rather than exclusion from the march. The conflict should be left in the street, not taken to court.

The justification of the imaginary domain is ethical as well as political. Dworkin gives us two "ancestral" principles that justify liberal institutions. His goal is to develop a comprehensive interpretive theory of the values of what makes up a successful life, to justify a continuity between what he calls ethical individualism and the institutions we associate with political liberalism. My own goal is different.[60] I have argued only that freedom of personality for a sexuate being demands the equal protection of the imaginary domain for all persons. But the argument for the imaginary domain is ethical as well as political—ethical in the sense that freedom of personality is valued not only because it is what allows us to represent *ourselves* as citizens. (I am using *ethical* broadly to encompass questions of what constitutes the good life, or what Dworkin calls a "successful" life.) Freedom of personality and, in the case of sexuality, the imaginary domain is valuable because it is what lets us make a life we embrace as our own. Thus, I accept Dworkin's second ancestral principle, that each one of us has a unique and special relationship to her own life despite the recognition that her life has no greater inherent value than anyone else's.[61]

The right to the self-representation of one's sexuate being is essential to an environment in which unique responsibility for one's life can be exercised. How can a person take responsibility for her life, design it as she imagines it should be, if the most intimate decisions about sexual and familial life are thrust upon her by the state? How can she personally embrace her life if she cannot even—as she cannot in many states—openly and proudly live out her role as a lesbian mother because she is forbidden to adopt the child that was planned for and raised by both mothers, but that her lover bore? A person not allowed the right to self-representation cannot take responsibility for her own life, and the denial of this right contradicts Dworkin's second ancestral principle.

Given that the right to represent one's sexuate being demands space for setting forth sexual as well as kin relationships, it does not embrace an individualistic ethic more broadly. First and foremost, my argument does not embrace an individualistic anthropology; indeed, it is our inevitable immersion in a world out of which we individuate ourselves that makes the sanctuary of the imaginary domain so precious. Surely, the very choice of the word *individuation* recognizes that what we think of as the individual is a lifelong process of engagement with the constitutive relationships upon which we base our identities. The person is, at least in part, constituted by recognition that she is a person with rights.[62] Precisely because our individuation and differentiation cannot be taken for granted, we must demand the protection of the imaginary domain as a matter of right.

It should be noted here that Dworkin's own ethical individualism is complex. He too realizes how important participation in our communities and families is for what he calls a successful life, and indeed that we need political recognition of the freedom of personality in order to have the chance to make our lives our own. Still, the very word *individualism* carries within it connotations of the possessive or solitary individual.[63] In spite of that connotation, Dworkin clearly wants to break with that meaning. He also wants to avoid endorsing a metaphysical notion of autonomy in his understanding of the second principle of ethical individualism.

> We must take considerable care not to misunderstand that assignment. It assumes and demands a kind of freedom but this is not metaphysical freedom—it is not, that is, people's power, by an act of a free will, to alter the chain of events predetermined by physical or mental causation. The second principle is not offended or undermined in any way by a commitment to determinism, because it neither demands nor presupposes anything to the contrary. The principle presupposes what we might call *relational* freedom: it insists that, so far as your life is guided by convictions, assumptions or instincts about ethical value, these must be *your* convictions, assumptions or instincts. You, rather than anyone else, have the right and the responsibility to choose the ethical values that you will try to embody in your life.[64]

I share with Dworkin the aspiration to separate freedom from its grounding in a metaphysical concept of autonomy. Not only do we not need such a concept; it is actually out of touch with the material and cultural reality in and through which a human being is shaped and which then provides her with the possibility for designing a life. On the other hand, there are clearly echoes of the Kantian notion of dignity in both Dworkin's and my own strong defense of our equal intrinsic value. Freed from its metaphysical underpinnings, dignity points us to the potentiality of human beings to lead a life that is their own.[65]

By potentiality I mean to specifically indicate the chance we all have to design our own life. But it is just that, a chance. Both Dworkin and I endorse the view that, of course, a human being cannot separate herself all at once outside all of the history and culture that make her who she is, leaving only the core of the free self or the pure free will behind. We are creatures in time, not just in circumstance. We project our futures, which include different possibilities of making something new of the self we have been made into by our own struggles and our engagement with the language and culture inseparable from how we have any sense of ourselves to begin with.

Dworkin, however, does not address the vulnerability of individuation, and it is precisely this recognition of vulnerability that I think we need to add to his ethical individualism. Given that we are creatures thrown into a world not of our making and yet which inevitably shapes us, we can be crushed in our efforts to become our own persons. We need to explicitly articulate and recognize that individuation is a project, and one that needs legal, political, ethical, and moral recognition if it is to be effectively maintained.[66] The demand for the imaginary domain is made in the name of the recognition of our own vulnerability as well as our own dignity.

Ironically, some of the more conservative communitarians who advocate community standards of sexual morality force individuals who do not meet those standards into social isolation. The pain of closeting, as Morris Kaplan has eloquently argued, is inseparable from being cut off from associative and intimate ties that one would otherwise seek because those with whom we would associate are also forced to hide.[67] For Kaplan, "coming out" involves the freedom to come into associative and intimate ties. Communitarians who would deny some people the right to form families are not protecting communities against rampant individualism, but are denying to others what they proclaim they value most, and on the premise that their way of forming communities and families is the only proper way and, thus, the only way allowable. This cannot be accepted by a politically liberal state because such a premise violates our intrinsic equal worth as persons. As sexuate beings we need our sanctuaries so as to form and live out intimate relationships. The protection of the imaginary domain is a demand upon the state that simply because we are persons, we should have the right to set forth a life as a sexuate being that is truly ours. Our story, including our story of sex, love, and family life, begins in the space left open by the limits imposed upon the state as a matter of right.

Nature, Gender, and Equivalent Evaluation of Sexual Difference

Congress dramatically declared discrimination against pregnancy to be illegal sex discrimination by overturning the Supreme Court opinion *Geduldig v. Aiello*.[1] Writing for the court in *Geduldig*, Justice William Rehnquist held it not to be per se discrimination when insurance companies covering male-related disorders refused coverage for pregnancy.[2] Insurance companies had argued that their refusal disadvantaged pregnant women only.[3]

Despite Congress's legislative efforts, deeply entrenched views of women and their reproductive capacity have changed little, and discrimination against women continues,[4] particularly against pregnant women in the workplace.[5] Thus, there has been widespread support for recent fetal protection regulations from both women and men, although they can adversely affect women's employment opportunities.[6] Even such invasive and coercive measures as forced hospitalization and incarceration of drug-addicted pregnant women have been publicly supported and even imposed.[7] Women's reproductive capacity is still widely viewed as that real difference from men that explains or justifies women's inequality in employment. At the same time, in the name of the greater good of future life, reproductive capacity and actual pregnancy have continued to be used as reasons for overriding a woman's choice of whether or not to become or remain pregnant. That a pregnant woman is a *person* remains an incongruous if not a preposterous idea in the public imagination: how can anyone claim pregnant women to be the same as men when they are so obviously different?

My argument is that feminists must defend my position that

pregnancy does not and cannot take away a woman's standing as a person. To insist on this in no way underestimates pregnancy's significance for many women. Rather, the demand is that our reproductive capacity not be allowed to deny our claim to be persons. Although pregnant, we, like men and women who are not pregnant, remain the only legitimate moral source of our life's direction.

Thomas Nagel has recently queried whether a deontological approach to justice should address sexual difference and, if so, in what way. The demand for women's inclusion and the recognition of women as free persons is a deontological principle in Nagel's sense: it limits the means by which a society may pursue its other aims. But whatever the cause of our sexual difference, it cannot be used to exclude us from the moral community of persons; therefore the answer to the question should sexual difference be addressed as a matter of justice? has to be yes. Nagel fails to see this because he does not grasp that women's inclusion in the moral community of persons has to be constructed if there is to be "*pure* procedural justice."[8] My own approach is twofold: first, we must demand inclusion in the moral community of persons as a matter of right and demand that, as persons, we be given equal and maximum liberty to determine our sexual lives, including what meaning to give to our reproductive capacity; second, as recognized persons we must demand a scope of rights, resources, and capabilities consistent with our treatment as equals.

To further define my own position, I compare it with Susan Moller Okin's feminist interpretation of deontological theories of justice, more specifically the theory defended by John Rawls. My central difference with Okin is that whereas my program of legal reform emphasizes our equal standing as free persons, her program emphasizes reforms that would make women more equal to men within heterosexual marriage. To do so, she takes Rawls's principles of justice for other basic structures of society and applies them to the family. I agree with Okin that the state must provide a just form to the family. But what this means has to be carefully specified so that any proposed legislation is consistent with our recognition as free persons with the right to represent our sexuate being and to have free, intimate associations consistent with our sexual orientation. Given that women have not been treated as free persons and that many of us have lived traditional lives in the family, we no doubt need transitional programs to ensure that women can come out of broken marriages on an equal footing with men. But on the level of the ideal, we should not retreat from the position that insists on our freedom.

An Uneasy Match: Formal Equality and Pregnancy

The dilemma of how to address women's reproductive capacity within a theory of equality is not new. The weight of history bears down on us. For the last two hundred years, Western feminists have had to battle against the idea that women were unequal by nature. Women's reproductive capacity, so the argument has gone, creates an unsurpassable impediment to our equality because the reforms needed to make us equal to men would be either unnatural and unbearably expensive or would severely limit sexual freedom.[9] Nature, not society, is depicted as the true enemy of women.[10] For over two centuries, feminists have been represented as the new Don Quixotes, tilting at windmills, fighting an enemy within themselves that they cannot defeat.[11]

Those of us lumped together as members of the "second wave of feminism" have militantly refused to accept that "anatomy is destiny."[12] We have insisted that an egalitarian solution be found so that women's biological difference does not perpetuate our inequality. However, there has been intense disagreement among us over how sexual difference is to be addressed under a theory of equality.[13]

68

Feminists who have advocated formal equality for women have found it difficult to reconcile the reality of women's biological difference with their claim that, for purposes of the law, women are "like" men. In the case of pregnancy, the demands of formal equality led feminists to justify pregnancy leave by pointing to a comparable disability in men so that an equality argument could be made for maternity leave.[14] Pregnancy came to be compared to a host of male disabilities, from hernias to prostate cancer. The unfortunate result for women is that, although after the Pregnancy Discrimination Act more insurance programs now cover pregnancy, disability pay does not come close to adequately compensating new mothers until they can return to work.

Troubled by this seemingly irresolvable dilemma in egalitarian theory, and by the suffering imposed upon actual women in the name of equality, other feminists (frequently referred to as "difference," or cultural, feminists) rejected these theories as masculinist in the very structure of their argument—as too abstract.[15] They have critiqued egalitarianism for viewing sexual difference as a phenomenal reality that necessarily falls beyond the reach of theories that consider people as mere disembodied sites of reason.[16] (I argue, to the contrary, that feminist egalitarian theory has not been abstract enough.)

Cultural feminists have argued that feminine sexual difference is erased when reduced to a set of characteristics that can be compared with those of men and thus can be adequately interpreted by formal theories of equality, that is, like should be treated alike.[17] For these feminists, if there is a "causal" link between women's reproductive capacity and a predisposition to care for children and other dependents, it should be valued, not trivialized.[18] Cultural feminists have vehemently rejected the "white knuckling" imposed by inadequate maternity leave programs: to have a baby on Tuesday and be back in the office on Wednesday, all the while acting as if nothing has happened, hardly seems a victory for women.

In the last thirty years a massive literature in anthropology and sociology has effectively challenged the idea that women's reproductive capacity necessarily *causes* the traditional division of labor in the family.[19] Thus, reproduction's effects are shown to be intertwined with the role of families, kinship, and the establishment of social rank in the political and cultural organization of societies.[20] The division of labor in the family itself is deeply influenced by class and rank, leaving some women almost entirely free from responsibility for children they have borne, as well as from confinement to the domestic realm.[21] Whether societies are matrilineal or patrilineal, whether heterosexuality is enforced as the norm of sexual life or not, the way hierarchies are built and legitimated, together with the shape given to representations of religious authority, all interact to form the meaning of sexual difference. Furthermore, these factors determine how rigidly enforced the division of labor within the family will be.

The anthropological literature presents us with a complex analysis that problematizes any easy generalizations about gender, let alone about the causal role of women's reproductive capacity in the formation of family hierarchies. Within our own culture, Judith Butler's pathbreaking book *Gender Trouble* challenged the theoretical adequacy of a feminist analysis of gender that focused almost exclusively on women's reproductive capacity and the division of labor in the monogamous heterosexual family.[22] For Butler, gender identity, and its assumption by an individual through a sexual imago with underpinnings in fantasy, is inseparable from the complex web of meaning produced and reinforced by a whole series of norms and prohibitions of heterosexuality, the cans and cannots through which one comes to recognize himself or herself as primarily identified with either the masculine or the feminine.[23] Rooted in fantasy and given meaning by prohibition, rigid gender identities are always imperfectly assumed because what it really means to be a man or a woman cannot be pinned down with exactitude, since anyone's gendered life is presented only through a *representation* of those terms. Gender trouble is the good news that Butler brings to feminist theory, breaking open the space for freedom, since gender identity cannot determine us. But paths broken are not necessarily followed, at least in part because there has been a lack of clarity, and even serious disagreement, about what "gender trouble" means for feminist political philosophy, and particularly for feminist programs of legal reform.[24]

It is not surprising, then, that the questions of whether and how women's reproductive capacity should be taken into account by the law, and how a program for family law reform should be tailored, have continued to trouble feminist theory. In this chapter I concentrate on the first question, and in chapter 4 I will focus on family law reform. I have separated the two because I see no immediate and necessary causal connection between pregnancy and the traditional division of labor in the heterosexual monogamous family. Still, pregnancy and early postpartum care of both the mother and the infant, including breastfeeding, are clear examples of biological differences between men and women. My purpose then is to show why the equivalent evaluation of biological difference—in this case women's reproductive capacity—is mandated by the inclusion of women in the moral community of persons as an initial matter. Once the full normative significance of this is grasped, certain kinds of legislation, particularly fetal protection laws, would obviously be invalid.

THE CASE OF JOHNSON CONTROLS

A review of the case of *Johnson Controls* shows how the emphasis on inclusion of women in the moral community of persons as an initial matter can provide an analytic framework for justifying reproductive rights when confronting particularly difficult issues raised by our reproductive capacity, such as pregnancy and addiction. The 1980s saw the emergence of fetal "rights."[25] Fetal "rights" (I put *rights* in quotation marks because, as I have argued elsewhere, fetuses are not persons and therefore do not have rights)[26] were tailored and then defended in the legislation of the 1980s in a peculiar fashion. Fetal rights laws were designed to protect the fetus against a mother who took a harmful or potentially harmful action with regard to the fetus. In the case of *Johnson Controls,* the employer asked for state support when their fetal protection policy was challenged, putting themselves on the side of fetuses, fighting against "irresponsible" mothers willing to put their unborn babies at risk.

Johnson Controls, like many other major manufacturers in the United States, hired no women in its battery-production facility before the passage of the 1964 Civil Rights Act.[27] Even then, women were hired only for clerical or administrative positions, and only government pressure made Johnson Controls finally hire women for production jobs (p. 63), much desired because they paid considerably more than clerical positions.

In the United States many on-floor jobs in the production of batteries involve exposure to high levels of lead. Study after study has found lead to be dangerous to the health of children and of adult men and women, causing, among other illnesses, heart disease, high blood pressure, and premature strokes (p. 65). Reproductive toxicity is only one of the dangers lead poisoning presents. There is no doubt, however, that exposure to lead at certain levels can lead to serious birth defects in fetuses, defects transmitted by both men and women, if in different ways. Lead, not surprisingly, was one of the first substances to be regulated by the U.S. government because of its reproductive toxicity (p. 71).

At first, Johnson Controls' fetal protection policy was voluntary. The 1977 regulations warned women of the dangerous effects lead would have on their fetuses if they were to become pregnant; furthermore, the company encouraged women of childbearing age—which was interpreted very broadly as all women not yet in menopause—not to choose jobs in the production facility.

In 1982 the company made the policy mandatory, stating that

"women who are pregnant or who are capable of bearing children will not be placed into jobs involving lead exposure or which could expose them to lead through the exercise of job bidding, bumping, transfer, or promotion rights."[28] Johnson Controls argued that it had to move to a mandatory program because eight women who had become pregnant under the voluntary program had not quit their jobs. Since the company could not control who was to become pregnant, its solution was to control all women of childbearing age—fertile women would no longer be employed in the production facility.

But what of the as yet fertile woman who was already employed in the production facility? She was to be offered a simple choice: be sterilized or lose the job in the production facility. No exceptions. One woman whose husband had had a vasectomy assumed she would be exempted. She was wrong.

> I thought I would be exempt from the policy because my husband had had a vasectomy. However, the plant manager told me that even though my husband had been sterilized, I could still "screw around." I was informed by a personnel representative that I could definitely keep my job in the high lead area if I would agree to being sterilized. . . . I refused . . . and within a few days, I was laid off. I eventually took a job at a fast-food restaurant at a substantial cut in pay.[29]

Johnson Controls defined fertile women as at risk of pregnancy despite seeming "facts" to the contrary, and gave all women the staggering either/or of job loss or sterilization.[30] Some women agreed to be sterilized because high-salaried jobs with equal benefits were so difficult for women to come by (p. 88).

Another effect of the company's policy was that women's reproductive status became public knowledge. Those who remained at their jobs after they became sterilized found themselves the butt of jokes made by male workers:

> The men in the plant knew about the policy and they knew I was sterilized. Some of them harassed me, making jokes and cruel

comments. . . . Someone put a can in my locker with the message, "you didn't have to have it done in a hospital, you could have done it in the maintenance shop." Some of the men referred to me as "one of the guys." (p. 88)

The United Auto Workers (UAW) brought suit against the Johnson Controls Company on behalf of six women and one man who had been affected by the policy. The man had been denied a transfer when he sought to lower his blood levels because he was trying to conceive a child with his wife. The UAW presented evidence that men's reproductive capacity could be harmed by lead, rendering them temporarily infertile. Thus, those men who wanted to fulfill their desire to impregnate their partners would have to transfer to another job. The UAW not only emphasized the evidence that showed impairment of men's fertility; they presented studies that showed a possible link between mutagenic damage to sperm and miscarriage rates and birth defects, including some level of brain damage. These studies were recent, and the link admittedly uncertain. Until then, studies had primarily focused on women. The UAW was hard-pressed to find the "same" kind of documented risk for men as for pregnant women. The UAW argued that this called for more studies on men, not a dismissal of the growing evidence, including that from other occupations, that showed that reproductively toxic substances could be transmitted directly through the seminal fluid. For example, studies referenced by the UAW traced the higher miscarriage rate in the wives of dentists to their husbands' exposure to anesthetic gases (p. 77).

In other words, the UAW insisted that there was comparability of risk to both women and men and their genetic fetuses. To further bolster their argument they quoted the Occupational Safety and Health Administration's standard on lead:

Because of the demonstrated adverse effects of lead on reproductive function in both male and female as well as the risk of genetic damage of lead on both the ovum and the sperm, OSHA recommends a 30μg/100g maximum permissible blood level in both males and females who wish to bear children.[31]

The union put animal studies into evidence as well, studies that draw a link between male-mediated mutagenic effects and birth defects. In a traditional Title VII case, which proceeds under the rubric of formal equality, such a showing of comparability of risk is necessary for making the comparison between men and women in order to show "sex" discrimination. As I argue throughout this book, the necessity for this kind of comparison is an insurmountable obstacle to finding an ethically or politically viable solution to the equality/difference debate that has haunted feminist litigation and legislative proposals on the issue of pregnancy. The analytic problem with the framework is clear: a man does not have the same obvious and direct relationship to the fetus as a pregnant woman does, so the risk of harm to the fetus cannot be the same (in the sense of identical) from both, although it can be extensive and, in terms of the individual or the couple's experience of it, devastating. Faced with this analytic difficulty, the UAW actually downplayed the harm to women and to their fetuses in order to make it more the "same."

Thus, it was not surprising that Johnson Controls harped on the "hard-heartedness" of the union's trivialization of the risks to fetuses when there was so much evidence of the danger. Johnson Controls in turn trivialized the effect of lead on men, disparaging the evidence that the "tangential" relationship of men to the fetus could actually cause birth defects. Of course, this was only *the company's* characterization of the evidence. It did not disparage or deny the damage to men's fertility but insisted that it was not "permanent" and could be "reversible at some point." This "impermanence" was not of much comfort to Donald Penney, who had wanted to try to impregnate his partner at the time he asked for the transfer.

As Cynthia Daniels convincingly argues, Johnson Controls was defending itself by appealing to a cultural narration that has become widespread in our country (p. 76). This story suggests that if a woman does not cede her own interests to her role as mother, she and the fetus become two separate beings in conflict with one another. In their brief, Johnson Controls positioned itself as the responsible employer trying to protect innocent fetuses against selfish women who put their own interests above their duty to care for their "young." To quote Daniels's analysis of the rhetoric of the Johnson Control brief,

> The risk to fetal health is not traced directly to the toxin, lead, nor is it considered the responsibility of the employer. Rather, the risk is mediated by the pregnant woman, always called the mother, who delivers lead to the dependent fetus and who has, by implication, the power to stop the poisoning. The distancing of fathers from the reproductive process and employers from the productive process distances them as well from the responsibility for the harm of the fetus. The woman remains the primary site of responsibility and blame. Furthermore, the man can remove himself temporarily from the workplace to restore his fertility, but women's fertility is permanently damaged by her association with work. The more vulnerable woman stores the poisonous lead in her body, where it may pose a hidden threat to her future children. The risk is never characterized as a risk to the female body itself; the woman worker is never herself poisoned but acts like a conduit, a "maternal environment," for others. Johnson Controls thus draws a narrow circle of causality and places women at the center of this circle. (p. 75)[32]

The Seventh Circuit Court of Appeals upheld Johnson Controls fetal protection policy as nondiscriminatory because the court agreed that women were at the center of the narrow circle of causality, concluding: "the UAW's animal research does not present the type of solid scientific data necessary for a reasonable fact finder to reach a non-speculative conclusion that a father's exposure to lead presents the same danger to the unborn child as that resulting from a female employee's exposure to lead."[33] In other words, the court judged that mutagenesis, which can affect both men and women, was relatively insignificant in comparison with the damage that could be done to a fetus inside a woman. The damage to both the individual man whose sperm or the woman whose ovum could be damaged by mutagenesis was ignored by the court. *This was a fetal protection act.* The question was the comparable risk to the fetus from men and women exposed to lead, not the comparable damage done to adult male and female fertility.

Once the *comparability* of risks was discounted by the court, their legal conclusion was easily reached under the rubric of formal equality. The selective exclusion of women from production jobs if they did not accept sterilization was held to be non-discriminatory because scientific evidence had shown that "harm to the unborn child is substantially confined to female employees" (p. 78). According to the court, the evidence had successfully shown that women were by nature different from men in terms of the harm they could cause to their fetuses. Thus, to treat women differently than men was legally warranted because they in fact differed from men in their relationship to their fetuses.

But then the Supreme Court reversed the Seventh Circuit. Even the conservative Justice Antonin Scalia recognized that the government had no business overriding a woman's judgment as to how to manage the risks posed to her by choosing to stay in a job with high lead exposure (p. 89). Writing for the Court, Justice Harry Blackmun forcefully rejected the Seventh Circuit's reasoning that the fetal protection policy was not discriminatory:

> Concern for a woman's existing or potential offspring historically has been the excuse for denying women equal opportunity. It is no more appropriate for the courts than it is for the individual employers to decide whether a woman's reproductive role is more important to herself and her family than her economic role. (p. 90)

Justice Blackmun also refused to set aside the suffering of adult men and women arising from damage done to their reproductive capacity; his opinion turned attention back to the adults whose lives mattered beyond simply being the reproducers of the next generation. The breadth of the Johnson Controls policy obviously triggered Blackmun's suspicion that women's reproductive capacity was being used once again—as it had been in the earlier history of protective labor legislation stemming from the *Muller v. Oregon* decision—as an "excuse" to deny women equal opportunity.[34]

The Supreme Court's decision was a victory for women, but that decision still leaves open the possibility that a less sweeping fetal protection policy would be constitutionally permissible because it could circumvent judgment that the policy was a "pretense" for excluding women. More important, what kind of victory is it to be given the "right to work" with levels of lead that are undoubtedly toxic to the reproductive systems of both men and women, as well as seriously damaging to their more general health? Certainly, concern for women's reproductive capacity has been used as a pretext for denying women equal opportunity. But as the complicated history of the debate over the value of protective legislation shows, there are also pressing issues of safety that have led some women's groups, and many unions, to endorse such legislation in spite of their wariness of the representations of women that were used to justify reform.[35] Of course, health and safety issues are inevitably pressing matters because of the devastating and often irreversible effects unsafe workplaces have on the lives of workers. The UAW's brief was written not only to show comparability of risk in order to demonstrate discrimination, but to highlight the dire effects of lead on both men and women.

An uneasiness with the decision is inseparable from the inadequacy of the legal categories in which the case was fought, because formal equal opportunity could not yield a satisfactory analysis of what was at stake for both men and women at Johnson Controls. It is hardly surprising that the "grit your teeth and bear it" brand of equality has been hard to sell to many women, particularly those who work in factories. Paradoxically, the demand for equality, when tailored to formal equal opportunity, can often be defended only by appealing to an ethic of sacrifice. If we want only to be treated as equals, then we must live our lives as if we were equal and accept the dangers that come with equal treatment. No doubt it is easier to advocate this position when you are not the one working with lead.

The analytic framework I advocate changes the terms of the battle over the fetal control policy at Johnson Controls and by so doing resolves the paradox inherent in the demand for formal equal opportunity. As Daniels writes:

> To ignore difference is to risk placing women in a workplace designed by and for men, with all of its hazards and lack of concern for the preservation of health and life. On the other hand, to treat women differently from men in the workplace is to reinforce those assumptions and economic structures which form the foundation of women's inequality.[36]

To thrust upon a woman the "choice" to be sterilized in order to keep a job violates her imaginary domain by preventing her from personalizing her own sense of her bodily integrity. This kind of stark either/or is an enforced choice that takes away her unique responsibility for her own life and denies that she has an intrinsic value equal to all other lives. Justice Blackmun had it exactly right: women must be recognized as the only legitimate legal source for the decision as to whether or not to value their economic contribution over their reproductive capacity. Moreover, they must not be put in the position of having to choose sterilization as the only way to keep a high-paying manufacturing job. The scope of rights must be consistent with the recognition that women are the only legally validated source of what to do with their reproductive capacity.

There are many ways to minimize the danger to women and fetuses that would not force women to have to "choose" the almost inevitable risk to their reproductive capacity and to their fetuses. Although pregnancy cannot always be planned, those who are planning it should be allowed to transfer to another job

79

that lowers the lead in their blood and to remain there until the end of their pregnancies. Johnson Controls provided blood tests for women of all ages in order to find out whether they were pregnant. These tests were mandatory, which, of course, they should not have been. But certainly the company could continue to provide women with these tests if women *requested* them. The company could in fact encourage employees to have the tests by continuing to provide them at the company's expense, and if the tests showed dangerously high levels of lead, then the woman (or the man) should be allowed to transfer to another job during the period of trying to have a baby. Of course, the company could put a reasonable time limit on the transfer. Women who discovered they were pregnant should be granted transfers to other jobs where they would not be exposed to lead at all; they should also be able to return to their jobs after the births of their children.

If the Anti-Discrimination Act is to be worth the paper it is written on, then pregnancy cannot be used as an excuse to lay women off from the high-paying jobs they fought so hard to get. To keep women from getting their jobs back when their pregnancies come to term clearly takes away employment opportunities for no other reason than that the woman became pregnant. Inclusion demands the equivalent evaluation of a woman's person, granting her the freedom to struggle for her own form of self-integration. The scope of rights demanded by inclusion are those which are mandated by the value given a woman by her inclusion in the moral community of persons as an initial matter.

Johnson Controls is a relatively easy case for "measuring what equivalent evaluation" would mean because of the extensive evidence of damage done to *both* men and women. In spite of their different biological relationships to the fetus, both men and women need to be accommodated by the company in ways appropriate to their general health and to the protection of their reproductive capacity. The measures I have just advocated involve evaluating what it means to recognize men's and women's difference and still treat them as persons of equal worth.

Let me be clearer: men will not need to be transferred when they are pregnant because they do not *get* pregnant. But if they were planning pregnancy with their partner, the danger of mutagenesis would demand they be transferred. The demand that an actual reform program be based on the equivalent evaluation of sexual difference, in the sense of measuring what is necessary for men and necessary for women, takes us back to the initial demand for our equivalent evaluation as persons since the scope of rights, or protections for each, must be consistent with the recognition of our personhood.

Heartless Feminism?

Some advocates of more moderate fetal protection laws who yet support the need for coercive measures against addicted pregnant women have argued that feminists, in their insistence on equal opportunity, ignore the suffering of fetuses. Let me show that this is not the case: to include women in the moral community of persons would mean that they could not be forcibly incarcerated in order to protect their unborn fetuses. That is, other means consistent with women's freedom will have to be found, and this freedom could be overridden legitimately *only* after other programs had been tried. Further, we need to examine the fantasy that accompanies the calls for retribution against addicted pregnant women who are charged with not caring about what happens to their fetuses, with valuing a night of fun more than a healthy child.

As studies have shown, one night of fun, even many of them, does not necessarily cause a baby to be born an addict or to be marked by other life-threatening birth defects.[37] But then addiction is not about having one night of fun. There is widespread agreement among psychologists and psychoanalysts that addiction is inseparable from a blocked longing to be a person. The substitute, the object of addiction, stands in for both the imagined other self, the one who is not degraded, and the imposed

persona the addict seeks to shed. The substance becomes intertwined with the fantasy of release from an imprisoning reality.
However, the addiction can only further reinforce the truth that
the addict is imprisoned, so the addict has this psychoanalytic
paradox at her core.

bell hooks analyzes how the consumption of the idealized
other can momentarily give the illusion of freedom from the
persona of a degraded self.

In Toni Morrison's novel *The Bluest Eye,* Pecola, the little black
girl who is full of self-hate, who is the victim of incest rape, counters her sense of personal anguish and shame by eating candy.
Fond of a candy that features a picture of a little white girl who
symbolizes the goodness and happiness that is not available to
her, Pecola's addiction to sugar is fundamentally linked to her
low self-esteem. The candy represents pleasure and escape into
fantasy:

> Each pale yellow wrapper has a picture on it. A picture of
> little Mary Jane for whom the candy is named. Smiling
> white face. Blond hair in gentle disarray, blue eyes looking
> at her out of a world of clean comfort. The eyes are petu-
> lant, mischievous. To Pecola they are simply pretty. She eats
> the candy, and its sweetness is good. To eat the candy is
> somehow to eat the eyes, eat Mary Jane. Love Mary Jane.
> Be Mary Jane.[38]

Legal punishment only reinforces the women's internalized
worthlessness, which in turn feeds the need for the fantasized
other who both escapes and yet repeats the anguish of her degradation. It is a mockery of the complexity of addiction to re-
duce its description to one of a night of pleasure. The figure of
the irresponsible, pleasure-seeking woman should be seen for
what it is—fantasy. Many addicted women do take responsibility for their pregnancies. Some are like Marina Greywind, a
Lakota woman with an addiction to alcohol who is living on the
streets of North Dakota; she sought an abortion after becoming

pregnant from an apparent rape.[39] A militant antiabortion group found out about her and offered her eleven thousand dollars to have the baby. She refused to accept the money and continued to plan to have the abortion. The antiabortion group then took her to court for cruelly endangering a fetus, both because of her alcoholism and her intent to have an abortion. She went ahead and had the abortion and, having pleaded guilty, was sentenced to a nine-month prison term. She had had the abortion after she was charged, and yet the prosecutors insisted that the terms of the original charge be retained because she was a drunk endangering her baby. The catch-22 should be obvious here. Marina Greywind sought the abortion because she was an alcoholic and did not want to harm the fetus.

What else should she have done? Could she have realistically sought rehabilitation? Here again we are brought up short by the hypocritical treatment of women. Jennifer Johnson, the first woman convicted for giving birth to a baby who tested positive for cocaine, sought treatment desperately. She was turned away. Johnson gave birth to her first child on October 3, 1987. The doctor who delivered the baby reported that he seemed healthy. Since Johnson had admitted to using cocaine, a toxicological test was performed on both herself and her newborn son. Both tested positive for benzoylecgonine, a metabolite of cocaine.[40] In 1989, Johnson had her second child, who was also reportedly healthy. As before, she leveled with her obstetrician: she had taken crack cocaine during her pregnancy, and was addicted. She was charged with delivering drugs to a minor, through the umbilical cord to two infants after they had been born but before the cord was cut. She pleaded innocent but was convicted. She was sentenced to fifteen years probation and one year of drug treatment in a residential program. As a condition of probation she was to be subjected to regular drug and alcohol testing, and her children were taken away from her.

Three years later her conviction was struck down by the Florida Supreme Court on the grounds that the law used to support the conviction was never meant to be used against drug-addicted women. As of yet, Johnson has neither regained custody of her children nor recovered from her addiction. The cruel irony is that she had sought the rehabilitation that was imposed upon her. Her conviction granted her what she could not otherwise get, but under conditions that degraded her.

The scope of rights and resources made available to pregnant women must begin with access to rehabilitation specifically tailored to the health needs of pregnant women. Both Marina Greywind and Jennifer Johnson sought to take responsibility for their pregnancies. Of course, some women may be so lost in the netherworld of their addiction that they can no longer retrieve enough of their person to take responsibility, but here again incarceration is not the solution.

Principled interventions that aim to take women off the streets and provide them with rehabilitative support are the sensible alternatives. Community programs, particularly in African American communities, have done this, sometimes against the power over her of her own addiction. But rehabilitation, the returning of the person to herself, is the only long-range hope for the pregnant woman and her future child. bell hooks argues, "Living without the ability to exercise meaningful control over one's life is a situation that invites addiction."[41] Of course, the insistence on freedom cannot guarantee that a woman will be able to re-collect herself into a person, but it is a break in the cycle.

The right to become a person is always a chance that must be offered. Given women's reproductive power, granting women personhood has often been considered a risk that society should not take because the lives of fetuses are so highly valued. The risk purportedly justifies treating women as less than persons. But we cannot know even what that risk truly is, given the fantasies about the irresponsible pregnant woman that have governed so much of the discourse about fetal protection laws and other coercive measures against pregnant women. Only when we treat all women as free and equal persons and, in the case of addicted pregnant women, provide them with the health care they often seek to rehabilitate themselves will we ever be able to assess what the risk of letting addicted pregnant women go free *actually* is. The first step is to render justice to women.

DISAGREEMENTS WITH THOMAS NAGEL

Thomas Nagel has questioned whether or not we actually can render justice to women. He queries whether or not gender inequality should be covered by a deontological approach to justice. For Nagel, a deontological approach would involve the equivalent evaluation of biological differences.[42]

He points out, however, that a political assessment and implementation of equivalent evaluation would be a big task. Of course, if gender inequality is to be covered by a deontological approach, then big or not, it *must* be undertaken. His question as to whether that would be wise has implications broader than those of gender because he wonders more generally about the *scope* of inequalities to be addressed by justice.[43] Connected to this question is another: "What must be the causal responsibility of society for an inequality in order for it to be unjust?" (p. 304).

His argument is that there may be a moral difference between inequalities for which the individual is not responsible because they were caused by nature and those for which they are not responsible because they are imposed by societal discrimination. For example, a distinction could be drawn between limited intellectual skill due to lack of education caused by an imposed class position and limited educational ability due to a genetic defect. The first limit implicates society, while the second may not. Rawls sees these two kinds of inequalities as morally arbitrary, so that the issue of divergent cause is not relevant. But Nagel, by wondering whether the second kind of inequality could be put into the "background," questions Rawls's "refusal to accept either the verdict of nature or the demands of individual responsibility as limits on the scope of justice."[44]

But if some inequalities were put into the background, there would be morally significant distinctions between each of them based on cause. This differential illegitimacy could then be used to limit the social space that the demands of justice would fill, thereby allowing inequalities caused by "nature," as Nagel defines them, to lie beyond the reach of justice.

For Nagel, however, the question of whether or not gender inequality should be redressed as a matter of justice would not be easy to answer, even if one accepted the moral relevance of cause, that is, nature or society. If gender were outside the realm of justice, then one-half of the human race would be outside, and their sheer numbers would make the unequal state of women morally and politically significant. Moreover, Nagel clearly recognizes that gender inequality is to a considerable degree caused by social institutions and cultural expectations. But, in part because of the division of labor within the family, he attributes some responsibility to nature (pp. 317–18).

Even so, Nagel recognizes that the "permission" society gives to the status quo of the division of labor in the heterosexual family may make it wrong to think of nature,[45] rather than class or caste, as the cause. But, again, even if the glaring wrong to women comes easily into view when it is analogized as a caste or class oppression, Nagel is still unsure of how to change their situation, rejecting the "end of gender" as either a "reasonable or realistic hope":

> There will inevitably be some general social expectations, of a rough kind, about the division of domestic labor between the sexes. Even the expectation that there will be no "normal" division of labor whatever would be an expectation that society, through laws and conventions, would have to impose on its members, and it might burden some individuals just as unfairly as an alternative norm. It is a platitude, but the aim of justice in this area should be not to eliminate differences but to devise a system that treats men and women comparably by some measure that takes into account their differences.[46]

The claim that the imposition of "no normal" expectations as to division of labor within the family *might* burden some individuals is rather vague, at best. My main counter to Nagel is that society's expectations have to be consistent with a recognition of women's maximum equal liberty, women being the only legally recognized source of whatever meaning they give to their "sex." Let me put this as strongly as possible: there can be no *reason* in a deontological theory for treating women as less than free persons. Even if one agreed with Nagel that there is probably a natural limit on women's ability to truly represent and thus challenge and change the meaning of their sex, a just society would leave this engagement with her "sex" to the woman.

Nagel remarks that all cultures are in the business of transcending the state of nature; yes, and so are persons, so give us our full standing as free persons, something no society has ever done before, and then let's see what remains of the "natural" limit. Nagel writes that even if we could make the difficult judgment as to which aspects of women's inequality are socially caused and which are naturally produced, "it would be amazing if none were natural" (p. 320). I eagerly wait to be amazed. My demand *now* is that, while I'm waiting, I be recognized as a free person.

At the heart of John Rawls's conception of the original position is the recognition of our inviolability as persons. Nagel begins his essay by putting the original position aside in an attempt to assess fairness in the principles of justice themselves. I question whether this can be done, at least given Rawls's understanding of the relationship between the principles of justice and the original position. To quote Rawls:

> Among other things, respect for persons is shown by treating them in ways that they can see to be justified. But more than this, it is manifest in the content of the principles to which we appeal. Thus to respect persons is to recognize that they possess an inviolability founded on justice that even the welfare of society as a whole cannot override. It is to affirm that the loss of freedom for

some is not made right by greater welfare enjoyed by others. The lexical priorities of justice represent the value of persons that Kant says is beyond all price. The theory of justice provides a rendering of these ideas but we cannot start out from them. There is no way to avoid the complications of the original position, or some similar construction, if our notions of respect and the natural basis of equality are to be systematically presented.[47]

Rawls differentiates between inequalities less because of their cause than because some inequalities can arguably be made consistent with the "value of persons."[48] I bring up this difference in our reading of Rawls because the Kantian demand for legitimate universalizability can be met only by a procedure that begins with the recognition of each one of us as a free and equal person and it is only such persons whose consent to any system of right could be consistent with their freedom.[49]

If women are entered into any theory or proceduralist conception of justice as a degraded form of human being, then the theory cannot possibly achieve its goal of defending a fair scope of distributional justice. Therefore, the issue of our inclusion must be resolved prior to any attempt to work out a fair system of distributional justice or equality. If, for example, we simply jump ahead and try to figure out how pregnancy would be fairly dealt with in a distributional scheme when this difference has already weighed in as a "disadvantage," then the scales are already unfairly tilted. Hence the seemingly unsurpassable dilemma of what to do with women's difference in a theory of justice.

Because he has already weighed women into a deontological approach that finds them unequal to men, Nagel runs into difficulties in terms of ends or solutions that can hardly be adequate from a feminist perspective.

Equivalence of opportunities and life prospects, in evaluative terms, can only be roughly defined, given the importance of the differences, but it is the only reasonable goal, if the deontological standard of justice is to be applied to this case.

This means two things. First, women who do not have children should have exactly the same opportunities as men so that the range of results depend entirely on variation in ability and inclination. Second, women who do have children, even if this inevitably affects the shape of the rest of their lives, should not thereby end up worse off than men. But to even define this condition, let alone to say how it is to be realized, and at what cost, is the real task. Some combination of enhanced opportunities, flexible working conditions, shared or assisted child care, and economic compensation or security are clearly necessary to approximate fair equality of opportunity.[50]

The alternative to his proposal is to recognize women as free persons who, like men, must orient themselves as sexuate beings, as persons legally free to do this in their own way as a matter of right. Some issues, such as the right to abortion and the right of pregnant women to be both freed from levels of lead deadly to their fetuses and allowed to continue at work if they choose, are necessary for our recognition as free persons. But once we are equivalently evaluated as free persons with maximum equal liberty, the question of what scope of rights, opportunities, and social goods would be needed to maintain freedom and equality would, of course, have to be addressed. Thus, we would clearly need a more general theory of distributive justice, such as that offered by Rawls, or by Ronald Dworkin's equality of resources, or by Amartya Sen's equality of well-being and capability.[51]

CRITICISMS OF SUSAN MOLLER OKIN

Freedom, in turn, would put a limit on the kinds of legal reforms that can be state enforced, even in the name of gender equality. The arena of family law shows the strength of a feminism that defends women as *free* persons of equal worth, rather than arguing for our formal equality to men. Should not persons be free to set forth lives in accordance with their own particular visions of what they seek from intimacy? The equality that demands we be free to set forth our intimate associations as we wish does not put families beyond regulation; rather, it insists that the regulation be consistent with the recognition of all as free persons.

Insistence on this freedom raises my central disagreement with Susan Moller Okin's bold attempt to bring justice to families. Okin's corrective political theory, at least as regards Rawls, is that the family be considered a basic institution in which justice has to be rendered. Her argument is that the family is basic to society in two senses: first, most people live in families, and therefore their opportunities in life are inevitably affected by how families are structured; second, families are where equality or inequality between men and women is learned and thus are a training ground of sorts for citizens. Since our opportunities are affected by our places in the family, Okin would seek to equalize those positions by means of such basic reforms as funded child care and family leave. I, too, support these programs, as they would allow more equitably shared responsibility for child rearing.

Okin advocates two kinds of reform: one aims to end gender, while the other aims to protect the vulnerable. The programs for moving away from gender are more in line with the guidelines offered in the next chapter as to the state's legitimate interest in family law regulation than those she advocates to protect the vulnerable. Still, there is a significant difference between the values we base our reforms on. Okin emphasizes equality between the genders. I, on the other hand, foreground equal maximum liberty for all persons and so advocate that extending the right of intimate association to different kinds of families must be at the very heart of a feminist program of family reform.

Okin and I share the critique of egalitarian theory for its exclusion and erasure of women and, with this, the removal of justice from the family. However, I do not agree with her that putting gender, or even women's viewpoints, behind Rawls's veil of ignorance is a way to solve that problem.[52] My argument against putting women or gender behind such a veil is that it is philosophically inconsistent with Rawls's idea of the original position. The original position as a representational device is not about bringing all voices or all viewpoints to the negotiating table. Rather, as we have seen, the original position embodies a hypothetical experiment in the imagination in which symmetrically situated and idealized representatives reflect on principles of justice without the encumbrance of this brutal world of ours that drags agreement out of "exhaustion and circumstance."[53] The original position is a *representational device,* a view from an ideal somewhere, a view from those suitably represented as free and equal persons.

Okin is right: whatever being a woman is, it is not "being" an equal. If there is a woman's viewpoint, it is deeply immersed in this world of inequality. Our engendering as women has no doubt put a limit on our dreams. What does it mean for us to ever "see" equality when it can appear to us only through comparisons with men, themselves unfree? The whole purpose of a hypothetical experiment in the imagination is to reason through the "should be" of what free and equal persons must be able to demand as a matter of justice. Putting women or gender behind the veil of ignorance robs the hypothetical experiment of the imagination of just that standing, returning it to the world of give and take, of actual bargaining, even if there is a concerted attempt to give all voices a hearing.

But the imaginary domain, rather than putting women behind the veil of ignorance, insists that a prior place of inclusion in which women are equivalently evaluated must be constructed before the beginnings of the operation of the proceduralist conception of justice, and so fulfills Okin's goal. At first this may seem a purely philosophical debate of interest to few. But it is more than that. If we begin by recognizing women as free persons who can represent their own sexuate being, then the legislation we propose would begin not with an end to gender inequality, but instead with the *realization* of that freedom.

Two examples of Okin's show the political significance of this

91

difference. Although arguing that women endure more of the same everywhere, her legislation proposals are addressed only to heterosexual women:

> Sexual orientation is another matter; it is far more difficult to refute claims that lesbian women are neglected in much feminist theory. . . . As the evidence and argument that follow will indicate, most women in poor countries would seem to have little or no opportunity to live as lesbians. It is therefore impossible to gauge how many might wish to, or how they would wish to do so, if they could. Traditional, including religious, taboos, added to compulsory or virtually compulsory marriage (often at a very young age) and dependency on men, seems likely to make lesbian existence far more impossible, even unthinkable, for many Third World women than it is for Western women.[54]

But is this lack of opportunity really the case? Surely not, since the rights of gays and lesbians have been foregrounded in postcolonial struggles around the world. In many "third world" countries the rigid enforcement of heterosexuality and monogamous marriage has been more lax than in many Western democracies; second, women who have participated in national liberation movements gain an empowerment that can make it easier for them to assert their sexuality in ways that professional women in the West would not dare. That some Western feminists have paid no attention to the politics of sexuality advocated by women involved in postcolonial struggles is an example of what can go wrong when a "woman's viewpoint" is simply assumed.

Jacqui Alexander, a lesbian from Trinidad and Tobago, has argued that the demand for erotic autonomy lies at the heart of the politics of decolonization,[55] and so argues that family law legislation must begin by granting full erotic autonomy to all adults, so undermining the ideology of primogeniture. Her demand is therefore nothing less than that we challenge the way we conceive of lineage and, of course, with it, property.

Alexander's challenge would also allow alternative possibilities for child care by encouraging women to set up house-holds more diverse than the model of the heterosexual couple, creating more flexible communities for their children's care. Feminists have always worried about turning too-young children over to the state in government-supported crèches; the concern is not simply that these facilities will be underfunded and thus unable to provide a safe space for children. Parents also fear that their children will be taught unacceptable values, those which challenge national, ethnic, and personal dignity. More informal arrangements could give women more power over how their children are cared for.

Ruth Anna Putnam notes that when Okin advocates state-funded child care, she is missing the crucial point that these jobs are poorly paid and so, once again, some women will be freeing themselves by climbing on the backs of others.[56] Of course, there is no reason that such jobs must be so horrendously under-paid. Indeed, the low salaries reflect the devaluation of what is viewed as "women's work," and it is this devaluation of the feminine that I have argued must be redressed by the imaginary domain. Programs of family law reform would have to be based on the evaluation of us as free and equal persons, nothing less and nothing more. Let me be clear, however, that I am not simply advocating another kind of "white-knuckling" feminism in the name of some utopian ideal. Thus, I would accept some of Okin's programs to protect the vulnerable as necessary for alleviating the suffering of women who grew up under imposed gender roles, and I agree with her when she argues,

> both post-divorce households should enjoy the same standard of living. Alimony should end after a few years as the (patronizingly named) "rehabilitative alimony" of today does; it should continue for at least as long as the traditional division of labor in the marriage did and, in the case of short-term marriages that produced children, until the youngest child enters first grade and the custodial parent has a real chance of making his or her own living. After that point, child support should continue at a level that

enables the children to enjoy a standard of living equal to that of the noncustodial parent. There can be no reason consistent with principles of justice that some should suffer economically vastly more than others from the breakup of a relationship whose asymmetric division of labor was mutually agreed on.[57]

These programs to "protect the vulnerable," as important as they are, should be recognized as explicitly transitional; otherwise, they could reinscribe a view of woman as the injured party, a view inconsistent with her being recognized as a free person who can represent her own sexuate being.

For Okin gender is inequality, so what she means by an end to gender is the end of inequality. Yet this concern is framed by her concentration on heterosexual families. Indeed, her theory gives these families a special value because in them, citizens learn about equality between the genders. Okin suggests that the family headed by a mother and a father in equal positions is the optimal "training ground" for citizens and, by so doing, implicitly defines gay and lesbian families as ineffectual training grounds. I also worry about her reliance on the state to "supervise" the division of labor and finances within heterosexual families. Thus, although I respect her egalitarian goals for protecting women from dependence, I disagree with her when she writes that

> there is no need for the division of labor between the sexes to involve the economic dependence, either complete or partial, of one partner on the other. Such dependence can be avoided if both partners have *equal legal entitlement* to all earnings coming into the household. The clearest and simplest way of doing this would be to have employers make out wage checks equally divided between the earner and the partner who provides all or most of his or her unpaid domestic services.[58]

Here the reach of the state in supervising family finances is simply too great. Moreover, because Okin seeks to end gender as she understands it, she would institute a perfect, because genderless, family. Once again, the danger of a perfectionist tendency in Okin's work is that it undermines our freedom.

Okin's laudable goal is to end gender as hierarchy, and any feminist would agree with her that gender defined that way cannot have a place in a politically liberal society. However, those of us already in "gender trouble" have to be given the space to set forth our sexuate being in our own way: we do not want the state to supervise the "content" of our imaginary domain. Of course, once children are introduced in the scene, I would agree with Okin that we tailor legal requirements to facilitate child rearing, a theme that belongs to my next chapter.

Adoption and Its Progeny: Rethinking Family Law, Gender, and Sexual Difference

WHY HAVE FEMINISTS been reluctant participants in the politics of adoption? Today, the law in most states pits the two mothers against one another while the media dramatizes the purportedly hostile relationship between the two. Think of the "heart-tugging" pictures of baby Jessica as she is removed from her adoptive parents to be given back to her birth mother and father. The press in general has never shown much sympathy for birth mothers. Nor has the feminist press, wherein for years members of the various birth mothers' associations have tried without success to publish.[1] These organizations have accused feminists of favoring adopting mothers, either because they are adopting mothers themselves or because, like the public in general, they have disdain for the birth mother who gave up her baby.

This reluctance may not spring from conscious attitudes about birth mothers. There are real difficulties raised by adoption when a custody battle is fought. Such battles challenge one of our culture's deepest fantasies—that there can only be one mother and, therefore, we have to pick the "real" mother. Picking one mother over another is a harsh judgment not easily reconciled with feminist solidarity, which supposedly grows out of the shared experience of our oppression as women, uncovered through consciousness raising that gives new meaning to what we have had to endure under male domination.[2] At first glance, however, the so-called birth mother and the adopting mother do not share a reality of treatment. More often than not the privilege of class separates the two mothers. In the numerous contemporary movies we see the scene of the two warring mothers played out in its most stereotypic form: the responsible, married white woman vying against the young, sexually irresponsible, crack-addicted black woman. The woman who is picked by law as the "real" mother is the one privileged by class and race. The politics of imperialist domination and the struggle of post-colonial nations to constitute themselves as independent nations are inevitably implicated in international adoptions. Hence, it is not surprising that one of the first steps in the constitution of nationhood is an end to international adoptions.[3] Adoption is fraught with issues of race, class, and imperialist domination that have persistently caused divisions in the second wave of feminism.

The language of adoption is the language of war. In most states the "birth mother" surrenders her child to the state, which then transfers the child to the adopting, predominantly white, middle-class, heterosexual parents. A recent change is that single mothers are allowed to adopt. There are almost no states in the United States that allow a gay or lesbian couple to openly adopt a baby as a couple. Single or coupled, gay men are almost entirely excluded from access to legally recognized parenthood. It is still the exception to the rule that a lesbian can adopt a child born into the relationship by one mother but raised by both women and ascend to the status of legally recognized parent.

According to current law, what the "birth mother" surrenders is not just primary custodial responsibility of her child, but her entitlement to any kind of relationship with him or her in the future. She is denied even the most basic kind of information as to the child's well-being. In states where records are closed, adopted children have to "show cause" to get any information about their heredity or the whereabouts of their "birth mother" and/or their biological father. For decades now, birth mothers' organizations have militantly protested against the surrender of their entitlement to the status of mother, even if they chose or were forced by circumstances to forsake primary custodial re-sponsibility of their child. Lorraine Dusky eloquently writes:

They call me "biological mother." I hate those words. They make me sound like a baby machine, a conduit, without emotions. They want me to forget and go out and make a new life. I had a baby and gave her away. But I am a mother.[4]

Adopted children are now in the process of challenging as unconstitutional their unequal treatment at the hands of the legal system. After all, nonadopted children have access to information about themselves and their genealogy. On the one hand, it seems obvious that adopted children are indeed being treated unequally. Could there be a compelling state interest that would legitimate such unequal treatment? A feminist answer to that question has to be that there could be no compelling state interest that could legitimate the relinquishment of the birth mother's entitlement to any kind of access to her child or to the child's access to her. We need to have a deeper analysis of why that relinquishment has historically been enforced and felt by many to be so necessary to the protection of "family values." Without this analysis we will continue to establish victors and vanquished in a war that is usually portrayed as being one between women. The issue of adoption demands that we examine our entire family law system from the ground up. In spite of attempts at feminist reform, our family law remains grounded in enforced heterosexuality with its inscription of rigid gender identities and corresponding familial roles and duties.

This chapter will argue that the state-enforced heterosexual, nuclear, monogamous family cannot be sustained under an equivalent law of persons. Enforced monogamous heterosexuality makes the state and not the person the source of moral meaning of her sexuate being and how it should be lived with "all our kin."[5] It is time that we recognize that governmentally enforced sexual choices, let alone the outright denial of the right to parent to some persons because of their sexual lives, is inconsistent with the equal protection of their imaginary domain. Feminists have a strong political interest in insisting that the right to build families and to foster our own intimate lives be privileged over the state enforcement of any *ideal* of the good family. I will conclude with my own proposed guidelines for family law reform, which would change the very meaning of adoption as it is now legally and culturally understood.

Many birth mothers who have given up their babies for adoption have undergone a trauma. A legal system that makes the cut from her child absolute blocks any hope for the recovery from this trauma, for the mother certainly, and maybe for the child. The best law can do for adopted children and birth mothers who feel compelled to seek out one another is to provide them with the space to work through the traumatic event that has to some extent formed them. Law cannot erase the past. It certainly cannot provide a magical "cure" to the emotional difficulties we all face in our intimate associations. Some adopted children will want to search for their birth parents and some will not. Some birth parents will want to be found; others will not. Law cannot take the passion and complexity out of emotionally fraught situations. Still, the imaginary domain will give to the persons involved in an adoption the moral and psychic space to come to terms with their history, the meaning it has for them, and the possibilities it yields for new ways of imagining themselves.

THE MEANING OF MODERN ADOPTION

Why has adoption come to be understood as requiring the complete relinquishment of all access to or even information about the child? We can see all the contradictions wrought by this demand for absolute surrender in recent lesbian coparent adoptions. In such adoptions, the last thing the "birth" mother wants is to give up all access to her child. She wants to share childrearing responsibilities within the relationship. Long before lesbian adoptions became possible to the limited degree they are now, informal "adoptions" in African American communities kept families together by extending them, rather than by shutting out the birth mother. In these communities there are often two mothers, which avoids the demand to pick one as the "real" mother.[6]

Modern legal adoptions are only one form of adoption and are a recent historical event.[7] We have to ask what legal interests are at stake in these adoptions and why adoption has come to demand total surrender of both the child and of all information about her. Why not identify adoption as only the signing away of primary custody? To understand why we define adoption as we do, we need to look at the intersection between women's legal standing in society as a whole and the residues of patriarchy in family law as they effectuate an unjust limit on women's right to claim their own person.

The Relationship between Women's Civil Standing and Their Role in the Family

The imaginary domain gives to women, as well as to men, the chance to become a person, to interiorize and cohere the identifications that make us who we are into a self. Hegel argued that the modern civil law (and in the case of a common law country like our own, the constitutional law) received its only justification and legitimacy because it was the guardian of man's subjectivity.[8] When Hegel wrote "man" he specifically meant men because it was only they who were accorded status as persons in the civil law.

For Hegel, in the genealogically male family, the woman remains bound by her duties in the family as the servant of man's needs. She has no independent standing in civil society. According to Hegel, ethical life includes family life as well as life in the organizations of civil society—corporations, unions, and the like. But unlike the other organizations, the family is natural. Women can participate in ethical life because of their central role in the family. Their nature makes them duty bound, and indeed, their sense of duty to their family is one reason why women as women could play an important role in the ethical life of society.[9]

Man, on the other hand, is able to find his freedom and exercise his subjectivity as both a citizen and a member of civil society because his "natural" side is cared for in the family. Further, law is the guardian of his subjectivity because it protects the space for man to interiorize his identity as an individuated human being who is irreducible to his social role. For Hegel, the crowning achievement of the modern legal system was the reconciliation of the objective power of the state with the legal freedom of individuals.

But the law could not be the guardian for woman's subjectivity, since woman was defined by her exteriority, by state-imposed duties. The state realized her nature by imposing womanly duties on her. Thus, only by taking up her properly allotted role—that is, as wife and mother—did she warrant protection by the state.

Obviously, as a feminist I strongly disagree with Hegel's conclusions that a woman's true nature is to be duty bound to the family and that the state owes allegiance to her only in her role as wife and mother. But his description of how a woman's legal identity is intertwined with her duties to the family, and not in her entitlement as a person, remains a powerful explanation, in spite of his own intent to justify it, of why it has been so difficult to adequately challenge family law. Obviously things have changed since Hegel's time. Women are public citizens. Women can vote. Women can run for public office. They have some independent standing in civil society when unmarried. Women can own property in their own name and can obtain credit. But these changes have been piecemeal because they have not adequately challenged the basis of the legal problem sweepingly called patriarchy.

Patriarchy and Its Legal Effects

For my purposes, the word *patriarchy* indicates the manner in which a woman's legal identity remains bound up with her du-

ties to the state as wife and mother within the traditional heterosexual family. Our feminist demand must be for the full release
of women from this legal identity that is wholly inconsistent
with the recognition of each one us as a free and equal person.

We cannot demand release from a legal identity that defines
and limits what it means to be a woman through state-imposed
duties without challenging the legal institution of the monogamous heterosexual family. The duties that define woman in her
social identity are inseparable from the conjugal institution of
the heterosexual family. The demand for women's release from
the bonds of duty demands the reform of our family law system
from the ground up. Furthermore, it is inseparable from the demands of gays and lesbians to be free to create their own
persons.

If we understand that women's legal identity in both family
life and civil society remains bound up with an externally imposed set of duties, we can at least make sense of why it is that
the so-called birth mother is deemed as giving up all entitlement
to any kind of relationship with her child when she yields her
duty to be the child's caretaker. Under the patriarchal scheme
that Hegel so accurately describes, a woman is entitled to protection by the state because she takes up her duties as caregiver
to her family. If she forsakes those duties she is denied any of the
protection given to mothers. Since she has no independent
standing in civil society, she has no social life. In Hegel's state,
women are mothers, not persons. Let me put it as clearly as
possible: it is only in the context of a system of duties that remains bound up with women's legal identity in the heterosexual
family that we can even begin to understand the unequal treatment of birth mothers and adopted children.

The relationship between legal identity in civil society, or "social life,"[10] and the system of duties in the heterosexual family
can help us understand the driving anxiety about infertility that
has haunted the history of modern adoptions. If a woman's social worth is inseparable from the fulfillment of her duty as a
mother, then if she cannot live up to that duty, she is confronted

with the loss of her only social status. Of course, the obsession with genetic ties is also tied into unconscious fantasies about the meaning of masculinity and racial superiority.[11] The protagonist of the film *The Official Story* sees herself as worthless because of her inability to meet her duty to biologically reproduce her husband's line. She and her husband adopt a child but the adoption is kept a secret to protect her from public notice of her failure. The symbolic reduction of woman to the maternal function is intimately tied to the sexual shame experienced because of infertility.[12]

This protection from public exposure of the adopting mother's failure to be a woman because she has failed to meet the symbolic meaning of womanhood demands the erasure of the birth mother. It is not entitlement but rather the terror before the loss of identity that explains so much of the secrecy that surrounds adoption and, in the case of *The Official Story,* allows the woman to blind herself to the reality of her daughter's tragic history. She discovers that her daughter is a child of a missing person, probably one of those murdered by the Argentinean government. It is only by slowly freeing herself from the imprisonment of imposed duties in the family that she can see her way to her responsibility as a citizen of Argentina. She sheds her exteriorized feminine identity, and in a profound sense becomes for herself when she dons the identity of a citizen responsible for the fate of her country as well as for the destiny of her adopted daughter. Before, she left the world of politics to men. She dons her identity as citizen by taking her place in a demonstration beside the grandmother of her daughter. Her prior life in the conjugal institution of the heterosexual family does not survive her insistence on her political responsibility as citizen and her ethical responsibility to her daughter's grandmother. What relationship the two women will have to one another is left open, but it is clear that there can be no going back once the grandmother is accepted and embraced. The woman's embrace of the grandmother as someone entitled to a relationship to her daughter left nothing in its place. It ended her life in the traditional family.

The Official Story presents in an extreme form the continuing presence of kidnapping disguised as an economic transaction in an adoption. *The Official Story* also graphically demonstrates the ability of the rich and powerful in many of the world's nations to steal children of the poor or the politically dispossessed. This phenomenon is well documented in heart wrenching stories of the mothers of "the disappeared." The dictatorship in Argentina that allowed babies to be stolen for adoption is not an isolated event. Indeed, the open stealing of a person's children is part of the enactment of psychic as well as physical torture.[13] *The Official Story* is clear: disappeared persons do not *have* children because they are deemed socially dead; their social death is a preliminary obliteration foreshadowing their actual murder.

The scene of adoption is ensnared in imposed roles associated with women's legal identity within the heterosexual family. The first step in untangling oneself from these imposed roles is to don the identity of citizen and to demand a full civil identity as a person. Simply put, as feminists we must demand that we are entitled to rights, not because we are mothers, but because we are persons.

THE IMAGINARY DOMAIN AND THE RIGHT OF BIRTH MOTHERS AND ADOPTED CHILDREN

My argument so far has been that, even now, the way in which women have been symbolically sexed is partly constituted by legal duties that have been imposed upon them, so that the very idea of the equal protection of women's imaginary domain challenges the legitimacy of those state-imposed duties. Our "selves" have been buried under these duties for far too long. As Irigaray has written:

Valorized by society as a mother, nurturer, and housewife (the community needs children to make up the future work force, as defenders of the nation and as reproducers of society, aside from the fact that the family unit is the most profitable one for the State in that much of the work that is done within it goes unpaid, for example), woman is deprived of the possibility of interiorizing her female identity.[14]

As we have seen in chapter 2, the value of privacy is expanded and not curtailed in the ideal of the imaginary domain. First, it challenges the idea that heterosexuality has ever been truly privatized. Obviously it has not, since it has been enforced by the state; thus, violation of heterosexuality has meant criminalization of nonconformist sexuality and, in many cases, enforced exile from a home country. Second, it recognizes that we need not only actual physical space, but also psychic space in which to struggle to become a person. The individual, not the state, should be the normative "master" of this kind of struggle in which we seek to make sense of the identifications that make up who we are.

The Rights of Birth Mothers

Would the equal protection of the imaginary domain give rights to birth mothers and adopted children? First let us take the example of so-called birth mothers. It is only too evident that the struggle of every woman to become who she is demands a confrontation with the connection between femininity and motherhood. For some women, oppressions imposed by race, class, national, and sexual identity have forced absolute separation from their children upon them. Carol Austin, who had to hide her own relationship to her lesbian lover in order for them to successfully complete an international adoption, describes the situation of the "birth mother" of their first adopted child as follows:

> A real joy for us was being able to spend a lot of time with Catherine's birth mother, Violetta, a twenty-two year old Quechua Indian who was also Julie's maid. When Violetta had become pregnant out of wedlock, she had been taken in by some distant

105

members who struggled to care for their own five children. Living in a crowded, dirt floored home in a poverty-ridden neighborhood in Lima, the family was not willing to care for another child. And if Violetta decided to keep her child, she could not work. Violetta's and her child's survival depended upon her giving up this first born baby to adoption.[15]

Violetta did not have the economic option to take custodial responsibility for her child. Austin was only too well aware that Violetta's decision to give up her child was not a choice and Austin knew that no amount of emotional support from her could make up for Violetta's loss and sorrow that she could not keep her baby. Still, to whatever degree it might help Violetta, both Austin and her partner wanted her to get to know them—wanted her to know that her baby would be safe. They showed her pictures of where the baby was to live; they left their address with her so that she could check on her baby's well-being.

Certainly, these measures, as reassuring as they may have been, could not make up for Violetta's terrible either/or, a forced sexual choice in the worst sense. Some adopting mothers have spoken of their feeling that their babies were destined for them. Austin was well aware that if this baby was destined for her and her lover, then Violetta was destined to be deprived of her child by economic circumstances. Measures could be taken to ameliorate Violetta's pain, but the poverty of her life circumstances remained. Austin's sensitivity to Violetta's horrible either/or, and the economic poverty and oppression that imposed it, came in part from her own struggles as an adopting lesbian parent.

Austin describes her pain at having to be disappeared in order to adopt a child for herself and her lover. Again, economics played a major role in the lovers' choice of who was to appear as a mother. Of course, Austin's circumstances were in no way comparable to Violetta's, but she did not have the same kind of professional job as her lover, who was put forward as most suitable for the role of (supposedly) single mother because of her professional and financial standing. But, in spite of her realization that this was the best way for the two of them to adopt a baby, Austin rebelled:

> I soon found myself emotionally stranded between anger and guilt. I felt angry and totally left out by my externally forced, yet self-imposed, invisibility. And right on the heels of my anger came my guilt! It was, after all, Jane who was putting in hours of meeting time, and it was her financial and personal history that was being dissected. I didn't envy her, yet I began to have an all or nothing reaction. . . . Finally immersion at *any* level, without recognition of my existence, became impossible. How naive I had been to assume, only a few months before, that my invisibility would be no problem. The entire adoption situation had forced open some of my raw childhood wounds. (p. 106)

Austin's emotional pain at being forcibly rendered invisible sensitized her both to a birth mother's need to be seen and understood and to the adopted child's need to be in touch with her national heritage.

Could a birth mother who chose or was forced to give up primary custody still know herself at the deepest recesses of her person to be a mother? Birth mothers' testimonies have answered yes to that question. To rob her of her chance to struggle through what meaning being a mother still has for her is to put the state, and not the woman, as the master over the construction of her sense of who she is. Birth mothers have rights, not as birth mothers, but as persons who, like all others, must be allowed the space to come to terms with their own life-defining decisions about sexuality and family.

Lorraine Dusky is only one of many birth mothers who have described their anguish at the enforced separation between them and their children. In her case she knew that there was crucial information that the adopted parents needed to have about her daughter. Dusky had taken birth control pills during the early

stage of her pregnancy, before she realized that she was pregnant. Studies later found that the pills could cause serious gynecological problems in the next generation. She tried to get the
agency that had handled the adoption to pass the crucial information on to the adopting parents; she was desperate to know
that her daughter received the proper medical attention. The
agency told her that her daughter was fine. Tragically, the information was in fact never passed along to her daughter's adopting parents. As it turned out, the adopting parents were trying
to locate Dusky because, although Dusky's daughter did not
suffer from gynecological problems, she had suffered severe sei-
zures, almost drowning twice; the adopting parents urgently
needed to communicate with Dusky about her medical history.
Dusky finally found her daughter through the adoption underground. The adopting mother recognized her as Jane's other
mother, and Dusky has for many years had a relationship with
her daughter.

Dusky's story had a happy ending. But why did Dusky—
white, middle class, and on her way to becoming a successful
journalist—give her baby up in the first place? The story of her
decision is inseparable from the sexual shame imposed upon
women in the 1950s who did not get pregnant in the proper
way: that is, within legal marriage. Abortion was illegal, and,
like many women who hoped against hope that they were not
pregnant, she put off searching for alternative routes to get an
abortion. By the time she found access to an illegal abortion in
Puerto Rico, it was too late. Adoption was her only option, because abortion was illegal, and because the blending of personal
and political morality made it close to impossible at that time
for an unmarried, white, middle-class woman to be a single
mother. Dusky's decision exemplifies what I mean when I say
that enforced sexual choice arises from denying women their
equivalent chance to claim their person and to represent their
own sexuate being.

What should a birth mother relinquish when she relinquishes

primary custody of her child? Only that—primary custody. The equal protection of the birth mother's imaginary domain at least demands that she be allowed access to any information she desires to have about her child, and to have the chance to meet and explore with the child what kind of relationship they can develop.

The child should have the same right to access information about his or her biological mother and father as the biological parents have to their child. Again, once we accept that even a primordial sense of self is not just given to us, but is a complicated lifelong process of imagining and projecting ourselves over time, we can see how important it is to have access to one's family history if one feels the need to have it. If the meaning of that history is inseparable from the struggle of postcolonial nations to achieve meaningful economic and political independence, then that history is political from the outset. Heritage has a genetic component, but not only that. A break with the nation, culture, and language of one's birth which is inevitably imposed by an international adoption; these factors must be made available for symbolization. Under our current law an internationally adopted child is already subjected to second-class citizenship. Certain rights of citizenship, including the right to run for the presidency of the country, are denied.[16] But even if we were to remove the taint of second-class citizenship, the child still needs to make sense of the break, to have the chance to recover herself and the meaning of keeping in touch with the linguistic and cultural traditions of her country of origin through her own imaginary domain.

Children should not have to show cause, let alone show that they are emotionally disturbed because of their adoptive status. The demand to show cause is just one more way in which people who do not fit neatly into the purportedly natural heterosexual family are pathologized. Again, the imagined heterosexual adopting family is privileged as the one deserving of protection of the state, even against the child who is a member of it.

My only serious disagreement with some of the literature written by birth mothers is the idealization of biological ties. There is an old Italian saying that blood seeks blood. But blood also robs, rapes, and murders blood. Moreover, as Dorothy Roberts has eloquently argued, the idealization of genetic ties is intertwined with the most profound racist fantasies, including the desire for racial purity.[17]

To conclude, adopted children and birth mothers should be allowed access to each other as part of the equal protection of their imaginary domain. We should have public records in which all adopted children and birth parents can register. A birth mother who was forced to give up her child obviously did not have her right to represent her own sexuate being protected. She had a decision thrust upon her either by economic circumstances or, as in Dusky's case, because of the sexual hypocrisy that dominated this country in the 1950s. *Her right should be based not on the fact of her biological motherhood, but on her personhood.* If, in spite of circumstances, she still represents herself as a mother who has given up primary custody, but only that, she should be allowed to follow through in her efforts to reach her child. The fear of the hysterical birth mother is just that, a fear. The adoption resolves the issue of primary custody except in the few states where lesbian lovers are allowed joint custody; custody laws should be tailored to meet the needs of lesbian joint custody, all the while protecting the established custody of adopting mothers who are not in lesbian relationships. Dusky did not try to steal her daughter Jane from her adopting parents. She knew she could not undo what she had done. Jane has two mothers, and she has had to come to terms with that. She calls Lorraine by her first name and not "mother," perhaps to recognize the differential relationship between the two mothers. Yet everyone agrees that it is better this way.

What of the woman who, when she gives up primary custody, also wishes to escape entirely from any imposition on her self of the role of mother? Such a woman should be allowed her refusal to register. But the law cannot make it illegal for the child to track down the birth mother. In the end it is between them. This is an example of why I argue that we should not expect law to do more than provide us with the space to work through and personalize our complicated life histories. It cannot heal trauma. It cannot protect a birth mother who is tracked by her child from the pain of confrontation with her child. Such a confrontation with her child could undoubtedly challenge her sense of who she has struggled to become. The protection of the imaginary domain demands that space be open to explore and establish relationships, but cannot provide the moral content of those relationships without delimiting the space that its justification demands be kept open.

THE IMAGINARY DOMAIN AND FAMILY LAW REFORM

My defense of the imaginary domain insists that the law protect it as a right and so breaks even with feminists who agree with me that our family law needs to be reconceptualized from the ground up. Recognition of the suffering that formal equality brings in its wake in hierarchically arranged families has led many in the international human rights movement to return to the idea of the expansion of state duties to women and children as part of an overarching concept of the good, which can provide a solution to the continuing reality of inequality between the sexes. Such expanded, affirmative duties are seen as necessary for the protection of women and children. But there are serious problems with the establishment of these kinds of duties. Legislation in some postcolonial nations has attempted to stabilize heterosexual families against the more informal sexual arrangements that had previously reigned among the people.[18] One aspect of this legislation, which is often articulated in terms of the need to protect the reproduction of the next generation of workers, has seemingly had the progressive aspect of imposing affirmative duties on the state to protect women and children,

111

for example, from abuse within the family. But, as Jacqui Alexander has argued, a severe price has been paid for this legislation. As she effectively demonstrated, the protection from abuse was conditioned on the mandate to marry:

> For most women who stand outside the legal definitions of "party to a marriage," no such claims can be made for relief from the court. Domestic violence as a legal construct—or more accurately, women's experience of physical, sexual and psychic violence together, in a space that has been designated as private— operates as a proxy to ensure the allocation of private property within disruptive hetero-sexual marriage (70% of children in the Bahamas are brought into being outside of hetero-sexual marriage) might both increase the state's anxiety around questions of hetero-sexual respectability as well as threaten the ideology of primogeniture.[19]

Because she is a lesbian, Alexander has been outlawed from her own country on the basis of legislation that mandates a return to the patriarchal family structure in which a woman's legal identity is bound up with her duties within the traditional heterosexual family.[20] Duty to the nation and duty to be heterosexual are conflated: Alexander writes,

> The nation has always been conceived in hetero-sexuality, since biology and reproduction are at the heart of its impulse. The citizenship machinery is also located here, in the sense that the prerequisites of good citizenship and loyalty to the nation are simultaneously sexualized and hierarchized into a class of good, loyal, reproducing, hetero-sexual citizens, and a subordinated marginalized class of new citizens who by virtue of choice and perversion choose not to do so.[21]

Since Alexander failed to live up to the nation's demand to be a good heterosexual woman, she lost her legal identity, her very right to citizenship. She was not just rendered socially dead; she was literally banished. So, the beginning of a program of family reform must begin with the recognition of women as persons whose citizenship and civil standing are not bound by traditional female duties within the family.

LIMITING FREEDOM: PROBLEMATIC FEMINIST REFORM PROGRAMS

Before turning to my own guidelines for family law reform, I need to discuss and critique programs of reform offered by Martha Fineman and Luce Irigaray, since both thinkers argue that our current family law must be radically transformed. Although both offer visionary alternatives to our current family law, my disagreement with both is that their programs controvert women's freedom by limiting their right to represent their own sexuate being.

Martha Fineman argues masterfully that the entitlement of women as mothers demands that we replace the sexual family altogether. To do so she would abolish marriage as a legal category:

> In other words, I suggest that all relationships between adults be non-legal, and therefore, non-privileged—unsubsidized by the state. In this way, "equality" is achieved in regard to all choices of sexual relational affiliations. I suggest we destroy the marital model altogether and collapse all sexual relationships into the same category—private—not sanctioned, privileged or preferred by law.[22]

For Fineman, then, once marriage is no longer legally recognized as the core unit privileged in law, the baseline norm for the family would be the mother/child dyad. To the response "but that's sexist—it excludes men," Fineman reminds us that there are other roles for men besides lovers and sexual reproducers. Describing a typical exchange in class, Fineman constructs her response to that charge as follows:

> "Why," I respond, "do you think that men's major, definitive role in the family is only expressed in terms of their sexual affiliation

113

with women? Don't men also find their places within units as sons, or as a mother's brother, as uncles to her children? What about grandfathers? Why are you disturbed by a paradigm that challenges the way we typically think about intimacy between men and women—a vertical rather than a horizontal tie; a biological rather than sexual affiliation, an intergenerational organization of intimacy?" (p. 5)

Fineman would give fathers rights, but these rights would be based on neither a simple biological connection nor a man's marital relationship to the child's mother. Instead, both married and unmarried fathers would have to show "biology plus" in order to claim a parental right to their child. Moreover, paternal responsibility would no longer be coterminous with economic support. Although fathers could claim parental rights by showing an actual caretaking role, they would not be included in the baseline norm for the family as *fathers*. To be included in that norm, a man would have to show that he was a committed primary caregiver, taking on the features we stereotypically associate with the mother. The mother/child dyad functions as a metaphor, which is why Fineman can argue that men could potentially be "mothers." Indeed, for Fineman, men can fully come into the family only as mothers.

> First, I believe that men can and should be Mothers. In fact, if men are interested in acquiring legal access to children (or other dependents), I argue they *must* be Mothers in the stereotypical nurturing sense of that term—that is, engaged in caretaking. (p. 235)

The dyad is a metaphor for the practice of care for dependents that all societies demand. The "child" does not need to be a literal child, but can be anyone who is dependent in the ways children are dependent on adult care and management. Fineman's dyad would be a core family protected by a redefined doctrine of entity privacy. Aware of its patriarchal roots, Fineman is careful to unhook her own concept of entity privacy from its traditional conceptualization as the protection of the man as the head of his household. Still, the inadequacies of individual privacy are only too evident in the case of single mothers who, because they are dependent on the state, cannot claim "privacy" as autonomous individuals. As Fineman rightfully notes, their dependence has left them prey to state violations of their dignity and the dignity of their families.

According to Fineman, her redefinition would end public persecution of single mothers and would instead recognize them for the valuable and inevitable labor they perform:

> Under my intimacy scheme, however, single mothers and their children and indeed all "extended" families transcending generations would not be "deviant" and forgotten or chastised forms that they are considered to be today because they do not include a male head of household. Family and sexuality would not be confluent; rather, the mother-child formation would be the "natural" or core family unit—it would be the base entity around which social policy and legal rules are fashioned. The intergenerational, nonsexual organization of intimacy is what would be protected and privileged in law and policy. (pp. 5–6)

Fineman has written a brave book that challenges us to redefine the family. My disagreement with her is that there can be *no state-imposed* baseline norm that privileges one kind of intimacy over another. For some people, and not just heterosexuals, horizontal sexual intimacy is how they wish to represent their sexuate being. They should be legally allowed to express their horizontal love whether it is called marriage or some newly created legal name for horizontal love that does not proceed by contract alone. Obviously, to the degree that there is marriage, it should be open to us all—gays and lesbians, as well as straight men and women. I agree with Fineman that intimacy and sexuality should not be forced by the state into confluence through recognition of the heterosexual family as the natural family.

However, it is one thing to argue that there should be no state-enforced confluence between sexuality and intimacy, and another to defend the proposition that the two *must* be separated in a new legally privileged baseline for the family.

It is these state-imposed "must be's" that violate the sanctuary of the imaginary domain. If men must be mothers in order to have parental rights, then the state is inescapably in the business of defining those who meet the required level of care. How much caretaking does it take for a man, or for that matter, a woman, to become a mother? What about women who do not meet the standard of the stereotypical caretaker? What of, for example, the lesbian lover in a relationship where one partner not only did not give birth, but where she, with her lover's agreement, took over the financial responsibility for the family? What if her responsibility to her family was primarily financial? Should we let the state define her as less than a mother, and therefore deny her rights to the child whom she considers her own even though she has no biological connection and has not related to the child in a way typical to women?

We all know such families in the lesbian and gay community. We know nontraditional heterosexual families as well. The problem here is that the deviant mother is let in the back door in Fineman's scheme by imposing a "must be" on fathers, which inevitably demands that we define how much care it takes to be a mother. As we will see shortly, my own guidelines for family law reform would define these "must be's" as narrowly as possible.

Although Fineman seeks to denaturalize the heterosexual family, she still privileges the biological family in her scheme of intimacy. This privilege has imposed untold suffering on gays and lesbians who, because they had no biological connection to their child, lost "custody" when their beloved partner died, in spite of the explicitly stated contractual desires of the departed lover.[23] This is the case not only for gays and lesbians. Many straight couples use marriage as a shield to shut abusive biological transgenerational relatives out of their child's life, insuring that custody will go to the lover or spouse upon death and not to the biological family.

Dependency is undoubtedly a reality in the rearing of children and in the care of the ill. But there are many transgenerational members of family, spry men and women in their seventies and eighties who would not be adequately described as "dependents." What can make grandparents, biological or adopted, so special is that they do not give the same kind of care as parents. In many societies the aged are viewed as a source of wisdom and valued for their role in moral education. Even when an older person becomes ill and in need of care, she is still not reducible to the status of a child. The dependency of an ill adult and that of a child should be differentiated in part to preserve the dignity of the adult, who needs to be recognized and respected for their maturity despite the fragility imposed by age. Thus, I would argue against Fineman's analogizing all dependency through the figure of the child.

Children should also be recognized as persons with rights and responsibilities appropriate to their age. I am aware of the appropriation of children's rights rhetoric in the fathers' movement. Still, children should be recognized as persons and as members of the moral community from birth, with the scope of their rights increasing with maturity. Some rights, especially what Amartya Sen has called "capability rights"[24]—the rights to develop the basic skills necessary to become an individuated person—would be given to the child so that she can set out on life's way as her own person.

The mother/child dyad exists only in fantasy. The fantasy, if taken as truth, corrodes the possibility of a mother/child relationship, since the very idea of a relationship demands two differentiated beings. Traditional psychoanalysis suggests that the dyad as fantasy is perpetuated by both infantile and feminine narcissism.[25] Fineman argues that it is only because of the degradation of the mother that most schools of psychoanalysis define individuation as against the mother, rather than with the

117

mother's support of her daughter's personhood. However, the beginning of a *relationship* between mother and daughter, and the celebration of our symbolic distance that makes recognition possible, can occur only once the fantasy that we ever were a dyad is dissolved. Trying to simply reenact the dyadic fantasy gets us nowhere new. That is why I disagree with Fineman's enactment of the mother/child dyad as a metaphor for what loving care might be in a transformed society.

Sex cannot be legislated out of families because it is irreducible to literal sex acts between adult lovers. In efforts to combat sexual abuse within the family, feminist reforms have at times fallen short by failing to acknowledge the presence of eroticism in familial relationships. Relationships in families are erotically charged; awareness of that eroticism is what makes sexual responsibility on the part of the adult possible. Unlike Fineman, I suggest that it is only through acknowledgment of this eroticism in the family that transformation is possible.

In poems that seem daring 2700 years later, Sappho writes of her erotic celebration of her daughter's "magnificence" and joys in her daughter's stride as it expresses a freedom she has never known and mourns for as lost to herself. Sappho's erotic appreciation of her daughter is inseparable from the celebration of her daughter's physical freedom, her strength. Sappho sings of the distance between the two that makes a mother's joy in her daughter's singularity possible. The daughter "whose skin of burnished gold pales the magnificence of the sun"[26] is uncapturable by the mother who cannot keep up with her daughter as she runs down the beach. This mother joys in the stride that takes her daughter into her own future as she stays behind marveling at the play of lights illuminating her daughter's beauty.

The most profound lore of heterosexuality may well be that daughters and mothers are sexual rivals: the mother wanting to hold her daughter to her or subject her to the plight of femininity. Our feminist lore should at least begin with the other tale, with the affiliations with, rather than appropriations against, the daughter's freedom.

I agree with Jacqui Alexander when she writes,

> One would urgently need an emancipatory praxis that decon-
> structs the power of heterosexual lore that positions women as
> their own worst erotic enemies and rivals, that might explode
> mothers' inherited discomfort with the emerging, restless sexu-
> ality of their own daughters, a sexuality that is often viewed as
> threatening and anxious to usurp. We might have to speak the
> unspeakable and name the competitive heterosexuality, an un-
> named homosexual desire between mother and daughter, its
> complicated, as yet unspecified origins, and its contradictory so-
> cietal sanctions and approbations.[27]

Eroticism is what gives "life" to intimacy. Yes, there is work to
be done to provide the necessary care for young children, lots of
it—lots and lots and lots of it—but there is also sometimes a
joyous, often frustrating, frequently heart-wrenching passionate
engagement in the cooperative, interactive endeavor I would
call a family.

Luce Irigaray's entire program of legal reform is rooted in the
need for women to achieve a legally recognizable civil identity
so that they can transmit to their daughters the symbolic meaning of being a woman precisely so that the two will not be col-
lapsed in a fantasized dyad. That is certainly the strength of her
program, for Irigaray argues that we need to reinterpret the
great myths of creation:

> The daughter's words to the mother may represent the most
> highly evolved and most ethical models of language, in the sense
> that they respect the intersubjective relationship between the two
> women, express reality, make correct use of linguistic codes and
> are qualitatively rich.[28]

For Irigaray, the story of Hades is the mythical expression of
the condition of mothers and daughters who are forbidden to
symbolize their erotic joy in one another. As for modern patriarchical cultures, Irigaray writes:

119

For little girls, education, the social world of men-amongst-
themselves and the patriarchal culture function as Hades did for
Kōrē/Persephone. The justifications offered to explain this state
of affairs are inaccurate. The traces of the story of the relationship between Demeter and Kōrē/Persephone tell us more. The
little girl is taken away from her mother as part of the contract
between men-gods. The abduction of the daughter of the great
Goddess serves to establish the power of the male gods and the
structure of patriarchal society. But this abduction is a rape, a
marriage with the consent of neither the daughter nor the mother,
an appropriation of the daughter's virginity by the god of the
Underworld, a ban on speech imposed on the girl/daughter and
the woman/wife, a descent for her (them) to the invisible, oblivion, loss of identity and spiritual barrenness. (p. 111)

Irigaray then finds patriarchy symbolically inseparable from the
sacrifice of the virgin and the mother's submission or banishment if she resists. Hades represents the spiritual oblivion of a
placated masculine sexuality that is the compensation for men's
acceptance of their inevitable castration. But this compensation
demands sacrifice:

Patriarchy has constructed its heaven and hell upon this original
sin. It has imposed silence upon the daughter. It has dissociated
her body from her speech, and her pleasure from her language. It
has dragged her down into the world of male drives, a world
where she has become invisible and blind to herself, her mother,
other women and even men, who perhaps want her that way.
Patriarchy has thus destroyed the most precious site of love and
its fidelity: the relationship between mother and daughter, the
mystery which is guarded by the virgin daughter. (p. 112)

To Irigaray, a new culture, a new symbolic peace between the
sexes, would exist thanks to Aphrodite's female *philotes,* which
Aphrodite interpreted as "the spirit made flesh" (p. 95). A new
civil law that could recognize women's sexual difference would
begin then with the explicit reversal of the mythological founda-

tion of patriarchy. It would do so first by granting to the girl the right to her virginity and the right to the mother to defend her children against any unilateral decision based on men's law. Patriarchy in its most traditional sense made the girl's virginity a "thing" owned by the father. The civil law would break with its patriarchal origins by giving virginity as a right to an identity to the girl, and giving the right to protect her to the mother as her guardian.

But Irigaray's new civil law is not against men or fatherhood. For her, the recognition of the right of the daughter to her virginity is the law that "civil" men would want, because only such a law would end the "thingification"[29] of women and so could be the basis for a possible reciprocity between the sexes. The granting to women of a civil identity objectified in law is the beginning of a peaceful civilization between the sexes.

Further, the cost to women of a legally recognized civil identity should not be the forced repudiation of their sexual difference:

> Women must obtain the right to work and to earn wages, as civil persons, not as men with a few inconvenient attributes: menstrual periods, pregnancy, child rearing, etc. Women must not beg or usurp a small place in patriarchal society by passing themselves off as half-formed men in their own right. Half the citizens of the world are women. They must gain a civil identity with corresponding rights; human rights, as well as rights respecting work, property, love, culture, etc.[30]

Men will no longer be cast into "incivility" either. A new "balance" has to be created. Irigaray takes Hegel's insight to the conclusion he would have reached if he had not been blinded in his vision of love by patriarchical assumptions. Until the law recognizes that there are *two* sexes, each recognized as having a civil identity with rights and duties, proper to the recognition of their sexual difference, the law makes true love impossible. To quote Irigaray,

The fact that the girl as a minor becomes an adult "through marriage" manifests yet again the female gender's subjection to existing institutions and customs rather the girl's civil recognition as an autonomous person.

Therefore, the law has to be changed for love. So that lovers remain two in love, woman and man have to be civil adults and their alliance has to be guaranteed by words that have a value for both of them.[31]

For Irigaray, following Hegel, sexuate rights turn on the recognition of sexual difference as a universal. The law has to be made appropriate to the natural reality of human beings in the sense of their sexed identity:

By virtue of this law: Universal and particular are reconciled, but they are two. Each man and each woman is a particular individual, but universal through their gender, to which must correspond an appropriate law, a law common to all men and to all women. (p. 51)

I strongly disagree with Irigaray that our sexed identity is a natural reality and that our particularity as a person can be adequately expressed through legally defining gender as a universal. Thus, I reject her conceptualization of sexuate rights in spite of the advance she has made by insisting on women's right to a civil identity that recognizes the inviolability of their persons. The problem, philosophically, is found in Irigaray's own appropriation of Hegel. Although women would be given a civil identity, the attempt to give rights, thought through gender difference as a universal, denies women the freedom to reimagine their sexual difference. For Irigaray, there are naturally two sexes. Her ontologization of the two denies that women live their biology in infinitely different and original ways. In the imaginary domain, sexes cannot be counted because what we will become under freedom cannot be known in advance. As Ursula Le Guin has beautifully written, "it is in our bodies that we lose or begin our freedom, in our bodies that we accept or end our slavery."[32]

Family Law and an Equivalent Law
of Persons

In spite of my fundamental disagreement with her, Irigaray is absolutely right to insist that family law reform must be rooted in the transformation of women's civil identity and must be rid of all traces of patriarchy as well. What would be fair family law guidelines that would encompass the equivalent law of persons and protect the full civil identity of all who fell under its governance? First and foremost, the state could not impose any form of family as *the* good family, and so could not reinforce the heterosexual and monogamous nuclear family, even if such families continued to be one way which in people organized their sexual lives and their relationships to children. Gays, lesbians, straights, and transgendered would all be able to organize their sexuality as it accorded with their own self-representation at the time.

But what about intergenerational relationships? Obviously, children need care. A considerable amount of time and devotion is needed to bring up a child. In our society the nuclear heterosexual family has been the institution assigned primary, if not the entire, responsibility for the raising of children.

One popular justification for the heterosexual family is that it is in the best interests of the child to have two parents, a man and a woman, who live together. Statistically, we know that the divorce rate means that many children of heterosexual parents do not live in such families.[33] Is there any reason to think that living as a heterosexual makes one a better parent? There is absolutely no evidence other than that grounded in homophobia that this is the case.[34] Open gay and lesbian parenting is so new that there are few studies available. Those that exist

123

show that gay and lesbian parents tend to have less conflict in the family, and that in itself may benefit children; as to why that is the case, some have guessed that there is greater ease in communication between members of the same sex. Since gay and lesbian parenting often involves access to technology and is a difficult row to plow, those parents overall are economically more stable than their heterosexual counterparts. Their children are wanted. Both the economic stability and the intense desire to parent have been noted as factors that have helped create healthy and happy children in these families.[35]

Lesbian partners show the most egalitarian patterns in sharing household responsibilities. This example of integration of work and home life has seemed to be particularly beneficial to the self-esteem and general life outlook of girls raised by lesbians.[36] These preliminary studies should certainly assuage any legitimate fears that gays and lesbians will not be committed parents. Long-term commitment to children is clearly necessary. How are we, as a society, to provide for the reproduction of the next generation, given the need young children have for stable, lasting relationships? The interests of the state would have to be consistent with the equivalent evaluation of each one of us as a free and equal person, and children would be recognized as persons whose scope of rights would mature with time. I am only describing a reform structure consistent with the limit that must be placed on family law by the recognition of our full equality as persons; I am not making specific legislative proposals. But I would argue that, to be legitimate, specific proposals would have to be guided by this structure.

First, regulation of the family should protect all lovers who choose to register in civil marriage, or some other form of domestic partnership. Many gays and lesbians have argued against the mimicry of heterosexuality inherent in the very idea of marriage.[37] I am sympathetic to this line of reasoning. Still, it is consistent to demand as a right even what you choose under your own construction of your own person never to exercise. The denial of this legal recognition is an illegitimate incorporation of moral or religious values into the basic institutions of a constitutional government. Moreover, because the government has no legitimate interest in monogamy, it cannot enforce coupling. Simply put, in the name of equality, if polygamy is to be allowed, so is polyandry, as well as multiple sexual relationships among women and among men.

Second, the government must provide a structure for custodial responsibility for children. If the government has no legitimate interest in a particular form of family life, it should also have no legitimate interest in linking custodial responsibility only to those people who are in a sexual relationship. Thus, Fineman's goal of separating parental responsibility from its inherent intertwinement with the heterosexual couple would be achieved: two women friends who were not sexually involved could assume parental responsibility for a child; three gay men could assume parental responsibility for a child; and finally, a traditional heterosexual couple could also assume parental responsibility for a child. The difference would be that custody would not be a given fact of their sexual unit. In other words, a man skittish about becoming a parent could choose to stay married to his partner and yet also choose not to share full custodial responsibility for his child, leaving his partner to take on custodial responsibility with another friend or, for that matter, a woman lover rather than himself.

To achieve the needed stability for children, the assumption of custodial responsibility would carry with it all that it does now—financial support, limits on movement, and so forth. Parents would be legally established at the time they assumed custodial responsibility; each child would have a legally recognized family. If there were others who, because of sexual affiliation with one of the custodial parents, wanted to assume legal status as a parent, it would be up to the initial group to decide whether or not they should be allowed to do so. The procedure would be similar to that of current step-parent adoptions. Custodial responsibility would remain for life; legal responsibility to custodial children would continue regardless of the sexual lives of the members of the custodial partnership or team. From my stand-point as a mother, I would prefer a "team," but I understand that to be only my preference.

Those persons who have recently argued against divorce have done so because the stability of children is often profoundly undermined in divorce, let alone in an ugly custody battle.[38] Divorce, or an end to a sexual liaison of one of the partners in the team, would not in any way affect custodial responsibility. The only reason for a partner or a team to legally sue to terminate someone else's custodial responsibility in the partnership, or team, would be what we now call the doctrine of extraordinary circumstances, for example, sexual or physical abuse. Children could also sue to separate themselves from one custodial partnership or team, but under the same doctrine. If minors, the only requirement would be that they choose another custodian. Would adults owe financial support to other adults in this arrangement, if for example one member of the partnership or the team chose to stay home during the early years of the child's life? My answer would be only by contract.

Once you have signed on, you have signed on for life, which is why I believe that this conception of custodial responsibility meets the state's as well as the children's interest in stability. But could you add on? I have already advocated that you should be able to do so. For example, could you, as an adopting mother, embrace the birth mother in a relationship of shared custody? Could it be the other way around? It already is the other way around in lesbian couples, where the birth mother and her lover seek joint custody together. The situation of lesbian lovers obviously demands that we reenvision the meaning of adoption, for in these cases the two lovers seek to parent together. The tortuous process of adoption has been eloquently described by lesbian parents. The birth mother is a mother by birth. Her lover is denied parental status in most states, and in states where she can achieve it, the birth mother must give up her rights in order for her lover to adopt. This case forces us to confront how difficult it is for our society to conceive of two mothers raising a child together. We keep imposing one choice, which is the last thing the mothers want.

The problem is inseparable from a culture that imposes monogamous heterosexuality, because it is only in that culture that the existence of two mothers is such a problem.[39] Patriarchy, as Irigaray eloquently describes, lets the man, not the woman, determine his line. The existence of two mothers causes a problem only when a society is organized around patrilineal lineage. If both women are to be accorded civil status, then it follows that they are free as persons to assume custody together. This would end the pain associated with lesbian adoption.

Lesbian mothers are obviously in a relationship with one another. But so are adopting mothers who never meet the birth mother. The fear of the "return of the birth mother" haunts adoptions. But why? If she has signed away primary custody, she cannot take the child back. Why wouldn't this return be envisioned as a good thing, as it turned out in the case of Lorraine Dusky? As Dusky describes, "all of us long ago made peace with our places in Jane's life. She calls me Lorraine. 'Mom' is her other mother."[40]

We cannot lose our children because they are not ours to have. That children are not property is recognized by their inclusion in the moral community of persons from birth. Obviously, this idea of custodial responsibility and children's rights demands that we stretch our imaginations. It demands that we struggle to free ourselves from the picture of the family as "Mommy and Daddy and baby makes three." But if we are truly to take seriously what it means to treat each one of us as an equal person and thus not insist on a "proper" family or "normal" sexual relations, then we have to have the courage to do so. It is what is demanded of us by our civic duty.

I have little doubt that it is in the best interests of the children. Certainly it would meet Fineman's goal of ending the horrendous tragedy of a woman losing her children because she does not live up to some fantasy conception of what her duty as a mother is. If a woman was living up to her custodial responsibility, it would not matter whether she had one lover or many. It certainly would not matter that she currently, or in the past, had another woman as lover. But rather than entitling women through the reciprocal right of mothers and children, I would do so through the reciprocal right of custodial partners and children. I would advocate this conception of parental entitlement because any state regulation based on normalized conceptions of femininity, including those of the mother as caretaker, is inconsistent with the equal protection of the imaginary domain.

The third legitimate state interest is equitable distribution of the burdens of reproduction and the equal protection of the health of young children. Obviously, we would have to have provisions for health care for children. I would also argue that we would have to have income maintenance for families. Mothering should no longer be a class privilege. In order to support oneself beyond the level of a guaranteed income, people have to work. Therefore, we would need to provide some kind of publicly funded child care as part of parental entitlement.

The structure of these reforms would provide stability to children and sexual freedom to adults. Since there would be no state-enforced normalized family, children who fell outside the norm would not be stigmatized. There would be no normal family, as if such a thing has ever existed. Part of the difficulty for adopted children is that they have fallen outside of the norm. By lifting the norm, we lift the stigma.

BRAVE NEW FAMILIES?

Are these brave new families? In *Brave New World* Aldous Huxley fantasized about the totalitarian horror of the state outlawing families as dangerous sites of intimacy. In Huxley's tale, embryos were processed in many duplicate prints to stamp out beings individuated enough to be persons. Love was outlawed, and indeed, the hero's great crime against the state was that, as a sign of individuality, he fell in love.

Like all totalitarian states, the brave new world fought valiantly to defeat the imaginary domain, the place of retreat that kept the person uncapturable, individuated from the regime. The torture of the regime, imagined in *1984* as well, articulates the centrality of defeating the imaginary domain in a totalitarian state. The state reaches into that sanctuary, breaking the divide between fantasy and reality, by actualizing the victims' worst nightmares. The message is clear—there is no sanctuary from the state.

A family law that insists that this sanctuary is crucial to the protection of our inviolability clearly and firmly rejects the state control of persons of the brave new world. That state fears eros. In contrast, an equivalent law of persons that would allow us to initiate and set forth our own lives as lovers and parents celebrates eroticism.

For some, the realization of their desire to parent demands reliance on technology: lesbian couples frequently rely on sperm banks; many gay and straight men have turned to surrogates. Straight couples have also sought out reproductive technology. This kind of technology is extremely costly, and economic class limits who has access to it. Dusky worries that human beings born of this new technology are missing a piece: "like androids out of science fiction, they lack a full human parentage, that connection with our past that forms such a large part of our present. They fill the hole in their identity with rage."[41]

But what is "full human parentage"? Isn't it better that we leave it to each of us to work through what it means to be lovers and parents, rather than have the state impose limits that will exclude some from representing their own sexuate being? Children born into love are the lucky ones. But I would at least hope that no one in this day and age would argue that sexual intercourse is necessarily loving. Can the act of artificial insemination be a loving act, as joyous to the lovers as any sex that transpires between heterosexual couples? The answer is of course. It is not the body parts that makes the love. I find nothing "out of kilter" about planning babies.

The question of technology brings us back to an old argument in feminism that should be confronted. Over the last two hundred years, numerous feminists have contended that naturalized motherhood is the enemy. State enforced denaturalization should then be *the* demand of feminism. Shulamith Firestone made that argument in the 1970s.[42] Less extreme feminists like Simone de Beauvoir simply advocated the avoidance of motherhood in the name of freedom.[43] Cultural feminists have responded strongly that this is just more of the same degradation of women and everything they stand for.[44] But the equal protection of our imaginary domain insists that the individual woman be given the space to grapple with what motherhood means to her. State-imposed denaturalization would clearly controvert the imaginary domain.

Families are special because they offer a space for eroticism in which love and life can flourish.[45] Whether they are created through biology or adoption, or some combination of both, the specialness of erotic connection will obviously make families different from other associations in civil society, in and out of which people move freely.

I have argued strongly that adopted children and birth mothers should have access to each other if they seek it. The idea of the birth mother and an adopting mother living together as lovers is still obviously a brave new family to some. And yet this is exactly what lesbian lovers seek to do. Indeed, the demand for open records has been deeply controversial because it challenges the patriarchal concept of entity privacy that Fineman so eloquently criticizes. All the imaginary domain can do is give us the space to try to dream up and live out love in our relationships to other adults and with our children. This recognition would be a big step toward the dissolution of the myth of Hades, where those who have been denied their right to represent their own sexuate being have been banished.

What and How Maketh a Father?
Equality versus Conscription

THE PROGRAM OF THE FATHERS' MOVEMENT:
"THE CARROT AT THE END OF THE STICK"

The Stick

IN THE United States there is a growing movement of primarily heterosexual white men who advocate a return to their paternal responsibilities. According to the movement two main impediments keep men from becoming Fathers. The first is their nature. Few women, even in their worst fantasies and fears about what men are really like, view them as bleakly as David Blankenhorn, author of *Fatherless America: Confronting Our Most Urgent Social Problem.*[1] For Blankenhorn, whose description of men is echoed throughout the fathers' movement, men are by nature irresponsible, slovenly, murderously aggressive, rapacious, and polygamous, if one can even dignify their need to spew their sperm as widely as possible by identifying it with such an institutional structure. Such ribald creatures, if left to themselves, will desert their families, inevitably yielding to their licentious sexuality and socially disruptive impulses. Of course, then, the problems of fatherlessness and all other social ills resulting from this pernicious reality need to be solved; stern direct and indirect measures must be taken to curb the urges men cannot control by themselves.

No matter this grim analysis; there is reason for optimism, for we as a people can lay down the law and conscript (*conscript* is the word Blankenhorn uses) men into fatherhood and monogamy. The historical view offered by the movement is of a past in which religion and other social forces played a much greater role in reigning men in than is the case now. Because men have been effectively forced into the role of father before, they can be so forced again. But to do this, we will need to change our licentious cultural environment. Therefore, according to the movement, we must press for law that either prohibits or at the least limits access to divorce. We must take action, both legal and otherwise, to track down deadbeat dads and bring them back home. Men will have to learn that unmarried "sex" is something that will carry a heavy cost. The fathers' movement has backed welfare reform legislation that demands that a single mother provide the state with the name of the biological father of her child as a condition of receiving benefits. The movement argues that the state should bring paternity proceedings against these men, imposing the duties of fatherhood on them, like it or not. Then, knowing that they are going to have to pay for their children, they will have been given a strong economic incentive to become "responsible reproducers."[2] But state enforcement of male responsibility for the children they father needs women to go along with the program. Once we have rounded these fathers up, women will need to educate them as to their proper role in the good family.

Crucial to the success of actually keeping men in place once they are conscripted into family life is their feeling that women *really* need them as *men*. According to movement organizers, women have unfortunately gotten used to men being out of the picture, and indeed, some even seem inclined to continue life without the father. If the state should do its best to force men into responsible fatherhood, then it should also clamp down on the alternative lifestyles that have developed. Lesbianism is always perceived as a particularly dangerous threat—the "image" of two women reproducing without a man represents the culminating nightmare of our purportedly licentious culture where "anything goes." The simple answer is to circumscribe homosexuality and to make sure "underground" lesbians do not continue to show the way to male-free reproduction. Other steps will have to be taken to keep them from getting around the laws. As a recurring figure in the writings of the movement, the lesbian is not only a woman who enjoys sexual relations with other women; she represents all the horrible modern women who have extramarital sex, abortions, or have children as if men were *unnecessary* in their lives. Moreover, it is not just lesbians using sperm banks, but single mothers who challenge masculinity by having children out of wedlock.

On this account then, the sperm banks must be closed so that all women will have to have a "real" man if they want to get pregnant. And since men are to be needed as fathers, not just sperm donors, the state should either outlaw divorce altogether or at least end no-fault divorce, because a man who leaves his family is definitely the one at fault.

The Carrot

The fathers' movement is clearly convinced that if we are vigilant and take the measures necessary to circumscribe alternatives to the 1950s television model of the nuclear family, we will get men to comply with the role of the good family man. After all, we have had success in conscripting men for war even though, as literature and historical memoirs teach us, their nature was as often as not to run away from, rather than into, the line of fire.

But the movement wants to use a carrot as well as a stick and so, if men are to take it on, the role of the good family man has to be made so attractive that men's enthusiasm and energy are aroused. Here, again, is where women come in, needing to make men feel big in their role. The father is not just to be another parent immersed in all the nitty-gritty day-to-day tasks of parenting, but the Father with all the authority and power that word is supposed to inspire. William Safire has described what fathers want: "we want our own intrinsic authority back. This essential prerogative of fatherhood has been stolen from us by children who want us to be their friends and by these children's mothers who insist on shared paternalism."[3] This is the man's role, and other members of the family are to recognize that only a real man can play it well; and it is this recognition that provides the fundamental psychological incentive men must be given if they are to be willing to be brought back into the fold. Again, to quote Safire: "Beyond the pleasure of watching their seed miraculously develop, fathers who make the family effort need recognition as 'head' of a household. Frequent challenges to that authority are affirmations, not denials, of its existence. The expectation of paternal authority—freely, if grudgingly given—goes with family territory."[4] According to the fathers' movement, rigid gender division in the family is necessary to make the father's role manly and dominant enough for men to want to play it.[5] There is a simple idea here: if men are to be fathers, women must be mothers in the traditional sense.

Long Live the King

The insistence on rigid gender division within the family pits the fathers' movement against feminists, although one school of feminism within psychology seems to be as vehement as the fathers' movement in its insistence on the importance of the man's role in parenting to the creation of a happy family life and to the development of the well-being of its members.[6] Of course, the goal of objects-relation, or relational, psychology is to analyze the psychoanalytic source of the separation of masculinity from the care and intimacy associated with parenting.[7] Objects-relation theory does not accept the fathers' movement's claim that men are by nature rakish creatures who must be ruthlessly trained. Rather, the theory finds that the source of the separation of masculinity from qualities associated with mothering lies in the perpetuation of rigidly defined gender roles within the family. The individuation of young children becomes conflated with differentiation from the mother only because mothers, both in fantasy and to some extent in life, are the ones contained by the home while the father is the parent engaged with the outside world. Young children, then, attracted to the ever-expanding world to which they are exposed by the ages of two or three, come to see their father as representing this larger world. The feminist hope is that mothers, remaining free persons, could represent this "new world," and so its exploration would no longer be solely identified with a fantasized figure of the father.[8]

Objects-relation analysts provide clinical support in defense of a diversity of masculinities and femininities that belie the fathers' movement's claims about men's nature.[9] Raising children in freely formed families that would allow for alternative and extended kinship relationships would expose children to a much more complicated version of masculinity and femininity within the family and so would offer new forms of identification for themselves. Thus feminists' divergence from the fathers' movement is over what makes a father, *not* over the desirability of men playing a much more active role in child care, whether or not they are members of a heterosexual nuclear family. Because feminists purportedly want to rid families of men and encourage women to take their children and run, the fathers' movement attacks feminism. As should be evident from the last chapter, this is clearly not the case of the feminism I advocate.

Most of us who are mothers want any help we can get; of course, we do not want to lose the right to our children because that help is absolutely necessary if we refuse to live lives in accordance with the fantasy of "the good mother."[10] The question then is, if this is our view, why is the fathers' movement so hostile to all feminists? The answer is obvious: the fathers' movement is not out to encourage men to be parental. Indeed, the movement is hostile to the extended kinship systems many of us are creating that let men be more engaged in caring for young children than were the men in the 1950s television programs so cherished by the fathers' movement. By "the good family man," the movement does not mean that the man should get up in the middle of the night as often as the woman, or that he should change as many diapers or even come close to that; and certainly he is not meant to take his daughter to ballet class while his partner works. That is to say, the fathers' movement does not want men to parent—they want them to Father, and they have very specific ideas about what fathering entails. First and foremost, the persistent reinforcement of the rigid gender divide in the family must be maintained so that men can rest assured that they will not be "femmed" by their acceptance of the role of the good family man. Indeed, the carrot to entice men back to the family is the promise that as Fathers, men can be little kings in their own domains. Clearly, then, feminists are seen as the enemies of this movement and for good reason: women have endured horrible suffering in the "castles" of these little kings, who have been legally allowed to indulge their fantasies of what it means to rule their families without threat of outside invasion.

THE SUBJECTION OF MEN AND THE FEMINIST CRITIQUE OF PATRIARCHY

Two Stories

The fathers' movement has focused almost exclusively on men, with organizers paying no attention to the feminist analysis of the link between male violence and the carrot offered by the movement that each man as a father can be king in his own "castle." But the movement has at the same time given no attention to the toll that the masculinity imagined by the fathers' movement takes on men. The fathers' movement's premise is that men desert their families because it is their nature to do so, so that without a legal and cultural framework of coercion and encouragement, there will be further erosion of the family structure. But is the problem to be identified solely as a cultural one? Of course not. And to underscore my answer, here are the true stories of two male auto workers who both finally left their families.[11]

Jim Nelson was fifty-three years old and a skilled electrician in a Michigan auto plant for twenty-five years before he was laid off in 1995.[12] By then, he was earning $52,000 a year, partly from the overtime he often took. He had children ranging from thirteen to twenty-seven; he had put his two oldest children through college; his wife had stayed home when the children were young. To help out with college expenses, she had taken part-time work as a secretary. Nelson's union benefits supplemented his unemployment check so that with the help of his wife's earnings they still made ends meet, and then his wife took on full-time work to help out further. But the fact that his wife was the one who went out to work now while he had to take over the "feminine" household responsibilities humiliated him. He confided in friends that he no longer felt like a man. For months after he was laid off he vigilantly—but without success—looked for work that was close to the level of skill and pay of his position as an electrician. Finally, in defeat, he began to look for much less skilled jobs offering considerably less pay, and he still had no luck. He was given different reasons for why he was not right for the jobs: either he was too old and/or overqualified. Finally, he gave up and he began spending his days in bars. Often when drunk, he physically abused his wife. Although the couple went into counseling, Nelson was in such deep despair over what he saw as his failure to fulfill his role as a man that he could not be helped. After twenty-nine years of marriage, his wife felt she had no other choice but to leave him. One year to the day from when he was laid off, he turned the gun he used for hunting against himself.

Nelson's tragic story gives a human face to the economic reality reported in *The State of Working America*,[13] published by the Economic Policy Institute. Workers making over $50,000 counted for twice the percentage of lost jobs at the end of the 1980s that they had at the end of 1970s. In 1995, 3 million workers were affected by layoffs, a figure that is 50 percent higher than the number of people affected by violent crime. Since 1979, 49 million jobs in the higher-skill range, such as the one Nelson held, have been lost to the economy. In one-third of all the households in the United States, one family member has lost a job in the last five years. One in ten adults reports that the loss of a job has caused both a financial and a personal crisis leading to estrangement or divorce in the case of both the unemployed partner and his or her spouse.

My second story is that of Sam Morris. Morris was a friend of Nelson's. They worked at the same plant for almost the same number of years. Due to an affirmative action policy, Morris, an African American, was allowed to train as an electrician in 1972. He also was laid off in 1995. The year he was laid off, Morris made $48,000. Like Nelson, Morris was at first determined to find a comparable job; he admitted to becoming increasingly depressed as the months dragged on without any hope of skilled employment. His wife had worked for more than ten years as a waitress at a local restaurant. Like many African American couples, she worked nights while he worked days because they could not afford adequate after-school care. Morris joked that maybe being forced to see each other led to their separation. About one year after Morris had lost his job he moved out. Morris began looking for jobs at every possible level of skill and pay. When his sixteen-year-old son, who worked at McDonald's, gave him a tip that there might be a job opening up there, he applied for it. In a recent study Katharine Newman and Carol Stack show that for every job at McDonald's, there are fourteen applicants.[14] Morris was not one of the lucky ones. Recently, he found a job as a part-time busboy.

For both Nelson and Morris, work was not only, or even primarily, about money. The capacity to be the breadwinner in the family was deeply tied in with the sense of their worth as men. Morris's position in particular had provided him with security to which most African Americans still cannot hope to aspire because of continuing discrimination. After his layoff Morris was diagnosed with hypertension. A recent study has shown that hypertension among African Americans is the leading cause of heart attacks.[15] A study further traced a connection between hypertension and economic insecurity, an economic insecurity that is part of the reality of discrimination that has African American workers suffering twice the unemployment rate of whites.

Parenting and Economic Hope

Neither Morris nor Nelson prior to his suicide could maintain their marriages, although both had prided themselves on being good family men. But because both had identified their primary role as that of the breadwinner, the major change in their economic lives affected them deeply in their views of themselves as husbands and fathers. The impact of the downsizing of the workforce of the United States on men in their family lives has been completely ignored by the fathers' movement.

Martha Fineman notes that there is a second kind of fathers' discourse, which focuses more on these issues, and she rightly points out that this discourse is connected to movements among African American and Hispanic men. Still, she observes, this discourse *too* accepts the male role as head of household without question, wanting those suffering race and class prejudice to be helped economically toward regaining that role. As Fineman writes, "In this discourse, fatherhood is a window into the 'real' or hard issues of unemployment. Fathers must have access to jobs and training programs in order to 'be' fathers, but their status as fathers remains unexplained. The concerns are still economic and the competitive focus is still the relationship between the sexes in the arena of the family."[16]

But studies show that both men and women connect their capacity to parent with economic security. More specifically, parenting introduces the need for economic planning; the most obvious example for those who can afford it is "saving for college." But children have innumerable day-to-day needs: medical costs have to be covered; food, clothing, and a secure place to be raised in have to be provided. An ability to maintain a child even if one loses a job demands that a financial plan for savings has been followed before. But the downsizing of America has

139

wreaked havoc with people's economic expectations. More and more young people express concern that they will not be able to afford children, and so it follows that the capacity to set forth one's own life as a sexuate being, particularly when parenting is involved, demands that we address the just *scope* of access to goods and resources, with the understanding that a degree of economic security is necessary for those who would be parents.

The stories of Nelson and Morris represent the worst nightmares of many workers. There were simply no jobs at their skill or compensation level. Work was so much part of their identity that they came to be willing to do any sort of work; thus, Morris jumped at the chance to work as a busboy. Although the centrality of work to men's lives has long been documented,[17] the fathers' movement fails to grasp how the vision offered by the movement of what makes a man a man could play a role in the terrible tragedy of Jim Nelson's life. The economic facts of life are that many men in this society cannot match up to this idealized patriarchal figure; the problem for both Nelson and for Morris was not that they were not trying to meet it—it was that they were. Nelson certainly was not an irresponsible drifter, and he was not a womanizer. Outlawing divorce, closing sperm banks, and cutting single mothers off of welfare certainly would not have helped him. The "education" Nelson needed was an alternative vision of masculinity that would have let him retrieve some of his pride and dignity after he was laid off. True, crucial to his sense of well-being would have been finding a job that would have used his skills and allowed him to feel like a productive member of society. As persons, we all need access to decent jobs. Any program that took families seriously and that, like the fathers' movement, purportedly wanted to make men responsible parents, would have to address the economic realities undermining family life. Job retraining, an increase in the minimum wage law (a bill that Congress recently passed), and health insurance should all be viewed as central to any encompassing program to enhance families. Clearly, neither Morris nor Nelson needed the stick to be "good family men."

THERE'S NO SUCH THING AS FATHER, AND IT'S A GOOD THING TOO

The so-called carrot of paternal authority, in which a man is established as the little king of his family, did not do Nelson or Morris much good.[18] Nelson's unemployment brought on an identity crisis that drove him to suicide. Does the analysis of men offered to us by the fathers' movement help us in any way to understand the depths of these men's despair, especially because their supplementary unemployment benefits kept them from having to face immediate financial devastation? (Note that the union fought to ensure these benefits.) The fathers' movement argues that men need at least an illusion of power over women and children because only this will allow them to rein in their aggression and sexual licentiousness. This argument does not explain the despair both Morris and Nelson experienced. After all, they could have used their free time for screeching around on motorcycles and getting laid every afternoon. Instead, they desperately looked for work, day in and day out.

Clearly, the patriarchal family organization, with its set qualities for what makes a father, imposes a great burden on men. Jacques Lacan's tale of how men became civilized points to why the carrot and the stick are inseparable.[19] According to Lacan, entrance into our culture and the acquisition of our unique status as speaking beings is based on our radical wrenching away from the maternal body and the bliss she represents—that is, that we are driven into language when, as infants, we grasp the fact that the Mother does not exist solely for ourselves alone. The initial fantasy of the infant is that in their dyadic unity the infant and the Mother are one. Where she goes, so goes the infant. Her breast is the child's breast. But of course this fantasy cannot last (nor, as I have argued in the last chapter, should we try to mourn its loss). The Mother *is* a separate person. She has her own life. She leaves. We have to call out to her, literally scream for her, to bring her back into the room. That Mommy can and does leave causes great anxiety in the infant, and so the infant begins to resist this traitor for taking away this imagined total security—of course, absolute security is a fantasy. A condition of this fantasy is that the Mother is not a sexual being with her own desires. The fantasy figure on whom the infant is totally dependent is the Phallic Mother, who contains everything in herself and so cannot be driven away from the infant by any need of her own. Once the fantasized mother/child dyad is shattered, the Phallic Mother "remains" in the imaginary as all powerful, and threatening, in her power both to bestow and take away life. She returns to us in cartoons; like the character of the Sea Witch in Disney's *Little Mermaid,* this scary Phallic Mother is unconsciously contrasted to the actual Mother, who is now found to be incomplete, a being split in affections by desire. The "scar of the navel" is not only actual in birth; it is also a symbolic tear ripping us away from the imagined cocoon of the pre-Oedipal relationship.

The introduction of the child into the "rules" of adulthood, that which Lacan calls the symbolic order, is at the expense of the Mother/Other and all that she represents, and this symbolic castration is actualized in the institutional structures and laws of patriarchal culture. The phallus, the signifier for this law, bars us from the Mother, and in mythology, we see the dire effects imposed upon anyone who breaks the law. But, for Lacan, breaking the law—the literal incest taboo—becomes the sweeping metaphor for resistance to the patriarchal order. Therefore, Lacan finds the ultimate cultural law to be that imposed by the Oedipus complex, a law that, in the name of the Father, bars both sexes from returning to the fantasized maternal other and all she has come to represent in patriarchal culture.

The anxiety generated by the loss of the Phallic Mother dyad turns the child toward the Father because, in the Oedipal crisis, he is recognized as the one the Mother desires. The narcissistically wounded infant turns toward the Father because the Father is whom "Mommy" desires. But what singles out the Father? Or, in other words, what is it that Daddy has that

Mommy desires? The simple answer is the penis, but Lacanians would never put the answer so simply. To them, identification with the Father is inseparable from the projection of the power to control the Mother, to literally give her a name, and in that sense guarantee that she and, correspondingly, the infant are spoken for. Thus, surely, it is the name of the Father, his representation as the source of blood ties, that is the basis for identification with him, and not the simple fact that he has the penis. The biological penis takes on the significance for the little boy because he has one himself, and this is identified with the power to take his place as an equal among men in society, a power established by patrilineage. In fact, only very recently has a child who was not given the father's name not been ostracized as a "bastard" and rendered a social outcast. Some current Republican politicians, as well as organizers of the fathers' movement, would have us return to those days.

In this Lacanian account, therefore, the penis is identified with the phallus as the symbol of potency and the representation of family continuity because of the infant's idealization of the actual Father. If not read through the context of patriarchy and the legal power it gives to the Father, a penis would be just a penis. A little boy can identify himself through his projection of his likeness to the Father who has the penis. It is this unconscious identification of the phallus with the penis that allows the little boy, at least on the level of fantasy, to compensate for the fundamental loss of the dream of bliss he has to endure in order to enter civilized order. Psychically, those who become men have their subjectivity organized around this promise that they can become men like Daddy and control women so they will not go away. This position over women purportedly compensates for the burdens of civilization.

The "bad news" for the little boy is that this fantasy leaves him in a constant state of anxiety and terror that what makes him a man can always be taken away from him by the (imaginary) Father with whom he unconsciously identifies. Moreover, the endless substitutions for this father, in the form of deans,

CEOs, politicians, and other figures of powerful men, keep him in unconscious subordination. That his masculinity is always on the line explains the gesture mandated by the pecking order among men: "Just don't take it away from me and I'll work sixteen hours a day and never talk back." This account of male insecurity is responsible for a man's need for the fantasy that he is superior to women.

The cultural analysis of the fathers' movement echoes the need for men to have power over women in order to accept their real roles in society. Yet real, living, breathing men are psychologically imprisoned by the very patrilineal masculinity that purportedly gives them their status as men. Clearly, the Lacanian account of masculinity affords a basis for an alliance between men and feminists to challenge gender structures and expand the meanings of sexual difference. This in turn would free men from attributes of masculinity that become fixed by identification with the idealized father whom they eventually fail to measure up to since the ideal phallic man is not real. Loss of a job can be understood as a terrible failure to measure up to this ideal. The carrot of masculine power is inseparable from the freezing of gender traits deemed appropriate. In our two stories neither man could see unemployment, even when it was not accompanied by immediate financial threat, as an opportunity to spend more time with his children or to develop sides of himself that had been forced to lie dormant because of the pressures of having to be the breadwinner. When women rise against the law of patriarchal culture they are, indeed, on the side of men. This is the deep truth in the union song "Bread and Roses" that begins this book: "the rising of the women means the rising of the race." Nelson did not feel he was worthy of his family or, indeed, that he deserved to continue to live because he did not measure up as a man. If fatherhood were not loaded with all the heaviness of patriarchal meaning it could be taken up with much more joy. The fathers' movement does not even consider the possibility that they are making fatherhood terribly scary by insisting that men be Fathers with a capital *F*. Insensitively, they turn away from tragedies such as Nelson's suicide. The carrot of masculine domination in the family should better be understood as a killing weed, and not just for women.

ARE MEN REALLY AS BAD AS ALL THAT?

The fathers' movement describes men as "burdened" with such great sexual prowess that they must be tamed; that is why the carrot of male domination is necessary, and why women must treat men as if they were the head of the family. This description of men is drawn in such broad outlines that it appears as a caricature. Of course, one could respond that all men are not like that. The Lacanian analysis of masculinity, however, could supply us with another analysis of the fathers' movement's description of men. The description can itself be understood as a compensatory fantasy and, more specifically, as a defensive reaction against the fear of castration. Work alone can be taming. It would be hard to run around with women and work as hard as Morris and Nelson did. The day-to-day humiliations many men have to endure at the hands of employers undermine their feeling that they are "real" men. Better to imagine oneself as a great stud than as Walter Mitty or the beaten-down Willy Loman of Arthur Miller's *Death of a Salesman*. Perhaps no playwright has more eloquently shown the devastating effects on individual men of castration games played out at work than David Mamet in *Glenngarry Glen Ross*.[20]

In these stories, the losers end up fired. By taking their places in sales competitions, they put their "dicks" on the line. And, as would be expected, some lose it. Those who fail in the sales competition are "fucked." The compensatory fantasy of the all-powerful stud allows one to find a different image of oneself as a man. Women do not fare well in these fantasies because now they have to be the ones who get it "in the ass," showing that there is still something left of the man despite his loss at work. The fantasy does hold out the promise that women should be available to make the man feel manly. Indeed, some porno-graphic images portray women as both the source of and the proper targets of pent-up aggression. Women, in other words, become the displaced object of rage for the high price the world of work demands of men. The description of men in the fathers' movement can normatively backfire, unconsciously being read as what men should be. There is then a double message in the way men are portrayed by the fathers' movement. After all, who wants to be the good family man, leaving the stud to have all the fun with all those women? The stud, man that he is, will prove himself by fighting the "draft" of marriage. It is only the wimp who will capitulate. The man's man will take his prowess and go with it where he will.

MEN'S EQUALITY AND LEGAL REFORM: PERSONHOOD FOR ALL

If one analyzes the reasons for the description of men in the fathers' movement, the effect is to banish men to the realm of the phenomenal.[21] If this movement can be dignified as having a philosophical basis, it is clearly Hobbesian. For Hobbes, men in a state of nature are truly scary beings, much like those creatures described by the father's movement.[22] But even these creatures driven violently by aggression are rational enough to pursue their own self-interest to the point of agreeing that some kind of coercive political structure is needed to rule over their own worst tendencies. But the regulations to be agreed to in the Hobbesian social contract would be those only absolutely necessary for men, for the protection of their person or their properties. If monogamy could be justified within a Hobbesian framework, it would be because too much violence to themselves would result from the constant "natural" desire for men to steal each other's women so as to have as many as possible. Certainly, under a Hobbesian social contract, the kind of extensive interference in men's lives advocated by the fathers' movement would not be acceptable. Yet the theory of equivalent persons I advocate has to remain "agnostic" to the Hobbesian account of men's nature as well as to all other accounts that justify one form of repressive social organization over another. Whatever their nature supposedly is, men must be recognized as free and equal persons.

What kind of legislation could be consistent with that recognition? Here we are returned to my argument in the last chapter that once children are involved, the state can enforce stabilized representations of who a man has become if he impregnates a woman and she chooses to carry the pregnancy to term. Like it or not, he takes on some responsibilities when he takes on a sexual relationship. If he does not wish to become a parent, then he is responsible to do everything he can to see to it that his sexual relations do not lead to that result. The state can surely pass legislation to *encourage* responsibility without undoing a man's freedom to represent his sexuate being. We clearly need extensive sex education programs in all our schools to encourage sexual responsibility in the first place.

This of course is just one example. The key distinction is between legislation that encourages responsibility but does not conscript men and therefore undermine the idea that they are responsible for their own lives. The kinds of job programs I advocated earlier could be tailored so as to more directly encourage men to be responsible to their children. Other economic incentives for responsibility could include legislated access to low-income housing and tax breaks to the father who provides parental support.

Paternity proceedings should also be allowed if the woman seeks to enforce the man's responsibility to the child. But the reasons given for these proceedings must be tailored to be consistent with the freedom of the woman to go it alone or hook up with another partner, male or female, if she chooses. In other words, without the consent of either of the parties, the state cannot initiate paternity proceedings in the name of the enforcement of the heterosexual family so as to effectuate economic efficiency.

Currently, paternity proceedings have been justified as part of welfare reform and the rhetoric of family values. The first justification is well known. If fathers would "step up to the plate," then many fewer women and children would be left in poverty. One way of lowering welfare costs is by forcing men to take up the support for their children whether women want the tie or not. The second justification is that families need fathers to produce "normal" children. This has been the central call of the fathers' movement. There is a solid evidence that this is not the case.[23] The state also cannot coerce women who are unwilling to go into proceedings for sanctions or for support because, for example, they fear for their lives. More generally, if they are forced to keep the relationship with the man, this coercion would violate their imaginary domain.

I sympathize with the pain so evident in the writings of Maggie Gallagher, a strong advocate of many of the coercive measures promoted by the fathers' movement.[24] Gallagher was herself a single mother—one more of those women done wrong by an irresponsible man. She clearly suffered the worst kind of disillusionment when her lover did not marry her when she found she was pregnant. There may be no worse pain than disillusionment. Gallagher's particular response is to argue for laws against divorce. Gallagher herself did not have to pursue the lover who left her because her parents supported her, both emotionally and economically. She finished her education, married, and, as a married mother, has a thriving career. More power to her. Gallagher and her new lover entered into vows that contain an explicit commitment to never get divorced. Given her history, this expression of her own imaginary domain is hardly surprising.

I do not want to trivialize her heartbreak or the heartbreak of the millions of other women who have endured so much suffering because of out-of-wedlock pregnancy. But the answer cannot be to end divorce by forcing others to follow Gallagher's path. The emotional and economic suffering imposed by an unwanted pregnancy is inseparable from the impositions of patriarchy. Currently, as the story goes, women can turn only to a man or to the state. Under our new welfare "reform," she is certainly implicitly condemned for her irresponsible behavior in getting pregnant without a provider in tow.

The family law reforms I advocated in the last chapter, which would be consistent with both men's and women's freedom, would give unmarried pregnant women of every age many more options than "man or state." But the reforms would also give more options to men than the patriarchal regimes of family organization have offered.

As I argued earlier in this chapter, both men and women need economic security if they are to take on the responsibility of parenting. The kind of economic legislation I advocate is a good example of the difference between reforms that primarily encourage responsibility rather than coerce support. Sometimes we need paternity proceedings for the women who need support, and then we should be consistent and serious about the enforcement of the order of support that results from these proceedings. But there is always a down side to such proceedings because you can make a man give money but the state cannot force him to be a father. Some things, certainly love, simply cannot be forced.

Throughout the centuries parenting has obviously been many a woman's "burden." And, as with other burdens socially imposed, it has brought with it a deep undercurrent of resentment. It is tempting to let that resentment form into a consolidated view of men that demands their constraint. If they are to be recognized as *free* sexuate beings, so are women, and that is undoubtedly what has the fathers' movement so unnerved.

Given the new technologies that seemingly "favor" women's reproductive capacity—with the help of a turkey baster and a sperm bank, a woman can have a baby on her own—it is not surprising that many heterosexual men feel anxious about their chance at fatherhood. What if we really do not need them? How are they going to know who their own children are, let alone claim their right to them?

In truth, these are old problems that new technology makes seem more pressing now. Complaints would undoubtedly arise between men and women recognized as free to set forth lives consistent with their own particular representations of themselves as sexuate beings. The best solution to conflicts within families freed from enforced sexual choices and economic deprivation is love, and love cannot be legislated.

* CHAPTER SIX *

Troubled Legacies: Human Rights, Imperialism, and Women's Freedom

Is THE IMAGINARY DOMAIN necessarily a Western ideal, premised on the central value of the individual? The question of whether or not this ideal, as well as others associated with Western rights, should be universalized is no longer simply academic. In the last ten years a worldwide feminist movement has pressed hard for a human rights agenda that would not only force human rights organizations to address the problem of discrimination against women, but also would promote the idea that since women make up half the human race, women's rights are human rights. Any concept of rights that does not include women's rights makes a mockery of the idea of human rights. This claim should be understood as a demand for inclusion of women in the moral community among nations established by the very idea of human rights.

In 1993, at the Convention on the Elimination of All Forms of Discrimination against Women (CEDAW), a treaty was signed by 130 countries.[1] Three principal networks emerged from this: the Latin American Committee for the Defense of Women's Rights, the Asia-Pacific Forum on Women, Law, and Development, and Women in Law and Development in Africa.[2] The demand of CEDAW is clear: the equivalent evaluation of women must itself be considered a basic human right.

This enthusiasm for including women in "rights talk" has also come under serious attack. Given the brutal legacy of imperialist domination that obliterated subjugated peoples' language and culture, it is hardly surprising that many of the world's postcolonial nations view any legal, political, or cultural practice associated with the West with suspicion, or even as treasonous.

As for women in particular, some avowed nationalists have sought to revive traditional practices that were either outlawed or culturally disparaged by the colonizers. One classic example is female genital mutilation, which church missionaries and the nations that sent them on their so-called civilizing missions sought to suppress by law and force if necessary.[3] The struggle to maintain practices that certainly seem to violate CEDAW has persistently been defended by some leaders in developing countries as crucial to a new nation's reclaiming the culture and the traditions of which it had been robbed.

Among politically concerned academics and human rights activists from the former colonial nations of the "first world,"[4] the question of the form and scope of human rights has added immediacy to the debate over the questions of universalism versus relativism. Whose concept of right, the person, and reason should be used in the advocacy of a human rights agenda? Given the relationship between imperialism and the imposition of the so-called white man's burden, attempts to answer that question have to be politically loaded. The "white man's burden" was not only that his were the civilized standards to be taken up by all peoples, but that he had the responsibility to impose them. "The heart of darkness" drummed out its message in a horror show of violence hailed by the colonizers as the salvation of "savages."[5] This legacy has haunted the debates over whether or not there are universal moral norms that can inform an agenda of human rights, particularly when these norms are used to justify economic sanctions or other means of enforcement against nations that will not go along with the rights program.

THE TENSION BETWEEN POLITICAL LIBERALISM AND THE FEMINIST HUMAN RIGHTS AGENDA

For John Rawls, questions of international law, including human rights, present liberalism with a test of its fidelity to its own principles: political liberalism must find a way to justify a liberal and thus tolerant attitude toward nonliberal, yet decent, nations. Otherwise, political liberalism can rightly be charged with being illiberal because it imposes a view of the good associated with Western ideals of democracy that other countries and cultures do not accept.[6] For Rawls, standards of tolerance in a fair law of peoples could be justified only if the nation demonstrated some commitment to human rights, but the concept of human rights in such a law need not be "Western."

As a result, human rights must not

> depend on any particular comprehensive moral doctrine or philosophical conception of human nature, such as, for example, that human beings are moral persons and have equal worth or that they have certain moral and intellectual powers to a minimum sufficient degree that entitle them to these rights. To show this would require a philosophical theory that many if not most hierarchical societies might reject as liberal or democratic; or else in some way distinctive of Western political tradition and prejudicial to other cultures.[7]

For Rawls, basic human rights can be defended on a neutral basis, in the sense of not incorporating any Western ideals, as long as these rights are connected to the basic immunities that would be inherent in a system of law guided by a common, good conception of justice.[8]

The big problem for feminists is that this "neutral" conception of human rights has over and over again proved to be useless in defending women against even those abuses that it should clearly cover, such as death by execution for refusing to wear the veil. Thus, human rights activists have convincingly argued that hierarchical definitions of women's place in society are inseparable from human rights violations.[9] As Ruth Anna Putnam has also rightfully noted, for many women throughout the world, the real struggle is for freedom from religion, not tolerance of it.[10] The feminist response within the human rights community has been that the only solution is to demand women's treatment as equals as a basic human right. This demand for equality un-

153

doubtedly disrupts one of the central tenets of hierarchical societies and certainly flies in the face of the dominant interpretations of many religious traditions. Rawls does not address the feminist critiques of a "neutral" human rights agenda, adding fuel to the accusation that so-called tolerance of national cultures becomes one more justification for ignoring the horrendous violence millions of women endure on a daily basis. But then what is the feminist response to Rawls to be? Is the demand for treatment as equals hopelessly disrespectful of decent, yet hierarchical cultures? If not, how are we to reconcile the recognition of women's basic human right to be included in the moral community of nations constituted by human rights treaties and conventions with a politically liberal tolerance of national and cultural difference?

NATIONAL LIBERATION AND CULTURE

Before attempting to answer that question, we need to examine some of the assumptions about nationalism and culture that have seemingly led political liberalism into this quandary. Assumptions about nationalism and culture have promoted the identification of feminism with the West, an identification that belies the significant work of "third world" feminists.[11] Of course, not all feminism is rights oriented, even when focusing on the demand for the treatment of women as equals or for an equivalent evaluation of sexual difference. But the assumption that demands such as that for "erotic autonomy"[12] are both Western and individualistic have deeply influenced the tenor of the debate over a feminist human rights agenda.[13] Feminism is simplistically defined as *in opposition* to the traditions and kinship structures of many third world countries. Thus, feminist activism and respect for cultural and national difference come to seem incompatible with one another. But exactly what is meant by a nationalism that cannot be reconciled with feminism?

154

First, we need to distinguish between a nationalism that hails itself as a revival of the old ways before socialism and/or the cultural and economic invasion of the West and nationalistic struggles that self-consciously define themselves as for liberation from all forms of recolonization. Both are present in today's world. Nationalist revivals seek to do just that, to "revive" what has purportedly lost life: the culture, history, race, spirit, and institutions of the national community that were buried under Western or socialist domination. Revival of tradition turns this kind of nationalist movement toward an often mythologized past, to the reestablishment of national boundaries and cultural practices that have been pushed under. Revival of the nation's traditions is viewed as crucial for the break with the West or with the morally bankrupt "socialism" of the Soviet Union.[14]

But other movements that are also nationalist, in the sense that they seek to establish the new nation's sovereignty, argue strongly against either the possibility or normative desirability of cultural revival. What *should* happen when national liberation struggles break up the old strata of culture of the colonized nations while "renewing forms of expression and the rebirth of imagination"?[15] Frantz Fanon, for example, argues strongly:

Is the national struggle an expression of a culture? . . . Ought one to say that the battle for freedom however fertile *a posteriori* with regard to culture is in itself a negation of culture? In short, is the struggle for liberation a cultural phenomenon or not?

We believe that the conscious and organized undertaking by a colonized people to re-establish the sovereignty of that nation constitutes the most complete and obvious cultural manifestation that exists. It is not alone the success of the struggle which afterward gives validity and vigor to the culture; culture is not put into cold storage during the conflict. The struggle itself in its development and in its internal progression sends culture along different paths and traces out entirely new ones for it. The struggle

155

for freedom does not give back to the national culture its former value and shapes; this struggle which aims at a fundamentally different set of relations between men cannot leave intact either the form or the content of the people's culture. After the conflict there is not only the disappearance of colonialism but also the disappearance of the colonized man.[16]

Fanon provides normative, political meaning to national liberation that separates it from struggles for independence from the West that seek revival of the former culture. Forcibly imposed cultural conservation should not be confused with national liberation. Yet it is precisely a return to such forms that some "revolutions" in the third world have hailed as evidence of their break with all that is Western. Iran is a classic example— forcing women to wear the veil or face brutal persecution or even death clearly crushes the imagination and absolutely forbids new forms of expression.[17]

Fanon's understanding of national liberation and culture is an important reminder that both cultural and natural difference are not static realities. In the political effort to constitute a new nation, the struggle to reshape cultural forms is integral to how a colonized people come to imagine their freedom as a *new* nation in which they are no longer defined by their oppressors. Freedom is given content as part of the attempt of the colonized to politically, ethically, and culturally shape themselves as representatives of their own future.

The protection of the space "for the rebirth of imagination" cannot be separated from the nitty-gritty efforts to establish sovereignty and develop an independent economy. The need for this "space" is intertwined with, as Fanon's analysis points out, the way colonization captures the psychic and symbolic life of the colonized. This understanding of the relationship between culture and national liberation provides powerful arguments against state repression during the process in which a country makes way for individual and collective, artistic, and political efforts to represent freedom. Feminism in the third world has often manifested itself as one of the experiments in the representation of freedom in national liberation movements.[18]

When confronting arguments for respect for cultural difference used as an argument against women's human rights, an analysis of what is at stake in the human rights movement cannot proceed clearheadedly unless there is an understanding that *which* cultural forms will prevail is part of the political struggle in any new nation. What respect for cultural difference means is obviously one thing if one is an outsider—a "first world" human rights activist—and something different if one is a national liberation fighter within the struggle for independence. But Fanon's point goes deeper. He sees that national liberation demands there be no going back, that these attempts at "return" run counter to the nation's liberation by thwarting the rebirth of the imagination necessary to it.

Within newly constituted nations, the repression of feminist attempts to enact completely new relations between "men" is a form of recolonization of the sort that Fanon warns against. Let us consider M. Jacqui Alexander, who describes the relationship between recolonization and the suppression of lesbian and gay citizens of the Bahamas:

Heteropatriarchical recolonization operates through the consolidation of certain psychic economies and racialized hierarchies and within various material and ideological processes initiated by the state, both inside and beyond the law. These actions can be understood clearly as border policing, in this instance, the unequal incorporation of the Bahamas into an international political economy on the basis of serviceability (e.g., tourism). Attempts to guard against the contamination of the body politic by legislating heterosexuality are contradictorily bolstered by state gestures that make borders permeable for the entry of multinational capital. Making the nation-state safe for multinational corporations is commensurable with making it safe for heterosexuality for both

157

can be recodified as natural, even supernatural. Tourism and imperialism, through multinational capital production are now as integral to the national order as heterosexuality.[19]

Thus, Alexander concludes that the struggle for "erotic autonomy" and the cultural forms in which it can be expressed lie at the heart of the struggle against recolonization and for national liberation. Feminist and gay and lesbian movements serve the cause of national independence. The Western ideal meant to bolster tourism is state-imposed heterosexuality that seeks to bring order to the more relaxed, unregulated family forms that before had been accepted in the Bahamas.[20] Alexander shows us how law became one of the means by which the state sanctified its political norms to rid itself of the "decadent"—all those sexually other to "normal" heterosexuality. The law became the sign of the "new" civilized order of the purportedly liberated nation-state.[21]

What Alexander means by erotic autonomy is very close to what I have defended as the right to represent one's own sexuate being. The connection Alexander draws between decolonization and erotic autonomy undermines the fantasy that only Western women can indulge in the luxury of sexual freedom. Furthermore, Alexander challenges the notion that sexual freedom is "merely cultural," an aside to the nitty-gritty work of economic development.[22] Her analysis also demands that we distinguish between cultural "revivals" dressed up as national liberation, which serve only the purpose of recolonization, from the struggles Fanon describes for forming cultures that would aspire to the freedom promised to the people by a reconstructed independent nation.

Alexander's suspicion of law is rightfully part of a feminist suspicion of rights talk. Thus, even if we do not fall under the sway of the fantasy that it is only "first world" feminists who have the time to dream about "the roses," we are still left with serious questions about what role law should play in the struggle for our freedom as sexuate beings. To insist that the demand for sexual freedom is not simply a "first world" ideal does not mean that to defend it as a matter of right is not to fall back into Western formulations of the person or the subject.

Is the Demand for Treatment as an Equal as a Human Right a Western Demand?

Certainly the central argument I have made in this book in defense of the imaginary domain does turn us back to what Rawls would call a philosophical conception of our equal worth as persons; this is the case for both uses of the imaginary domain, since they take us back to Kant's idea of our freedom as moral persons. The imaginary domain does this first by insisting that it is the failure to initially evaluate women as free and equal persons that has made the inequality between men and women so difficult to address in proceduralist conceptions of justice. Therefore, the demand put upon a theory of justice is that women must be imagined and evaluated as free persons, and that all forms of egalitarian legislation must be tailored so as to be consistent with their freedom.

The further recognition of the imaginary domain as the political and ethical basis of the right to self-representation of one's sexuate being, at least as I have argued for it in this book, clearly does turn us back to the Western tradition in that it foregrounds the subjective aspect of right. And the subjective aspect of right returns us to the fundamental Kantian idea that my most precious right is to my freedom, and thus, I must be legally allowed to coerce you into harmonizing your freedom with mine.[23] This subjective aspect of right has perhaps been the most controversial in traditional human rights discourse because it most obviously seems to threaten community by replacing it with the Western capitalist notion of the possessive individual.

I will return to the question of whether or not feminists can be satisfied with anything less than inclusion of the subjective aspect of right in human rights discourse shortly. For now let me stay with the problem of the feminist demand for the treatment of women as equals, with tolerance for a decent national culture in which women are still not considered of equal worth to men because of the place they are given in either a religious or cultural hierarchy. As we have seen, equality does demand some basis of comparison. If not simply to be reduced to a demand for what men get on average, equality seems also to need a philosophical conception of equal worth; otherwise, what is the basis of the claim that treatment as anything other than equal to men is unjust? So the question becomes, can we have this strong political demand for equality without justifying it on the basis of a Western philosophical conception of the person or subject? Third world feminists have already clearly shown us that we can.

In Suriname, Renate Druiventak, one of the leading women activists of a group called Mofina Brasa, which, crudely translated, means "the poor must embrace each other," found her inspiration to struggle for women's equality in the Afro-Surinamese Winti religion. The program she advocates is for equality for women in all aspects of life, from land distribution to education. *Winti*, which means "wind," are spirits, but as Gloria Wekker describes, they are not "conceptualized as external, transcendental beings or entities, but as integral parts of the self."[24] Druiventak describes the roots of her activism for women:

> We Creoles have an enormous advantage because we have Winti who transmit knowledge to us. Winti come upon you in your dreams, they give you strength and push you in a particular direction. I wasn't consciously thinking of a political party for women but in my dream, Mama Aisa (Mother Goddess of the Earth) came to me and told me to do something for women to help them cope in these difficult times. Afterwards I prayed, *mi ben tak'nanga mi 'ik' nanga mi skin* (I talked to my I, to myself). Gradually the idea of a woman's action group shaped itself and I asked, how do I go about this? Whom do I ask to help me? (p. 334)

The phrase "I talked to myself" is part of the plethora of terms that refer to the self as a site of many possibilities that are third person expressions of one's Winti. The understanding of the self is "more profitably conceived of as a kaleidoscopic, ever-moving sequence than as a unique, bounded, static essence" (p. 336).

This understanding of the self also rejects any rigid separation of the masculine and the feminine because each human being has both within the Winti cosmology. Again, to quote Wekker:

> Within this cosmological system, human beings are understood to be partly biological and partly spiritual beings. The biological side of humans, flesh and blood, is supplied by earthly parents. The spiritual side is made up of three components, two of which are important here. All human beings have a *kra* or *yeye* (soul) and *dyodyo* (parents in the world of the gods). The *kra* and the *dyodyo* together define a person's mind, intellect, consciousness, personality, characteristics and mentality. A human being is integrated into the world of the gods by his or her godly parents, who look out for and protect their child throughout life. At birth, the *dyodyo* bestow a *kra* with an immortal "soul," with male and female components, upon a human being. Both *kra* and *dyodyo* consist of male and female being and both of these pairs are conceived as human beings, with their own personality characteristics. (p. 335)

The integration of masculine and feminine as part of the kaleidoscopic self undermines any cultural practices that attempt to purify masculinity by cleaning out its feminine other.

A third challenge to stable sexual or personal identity is embodied in the mati work. *Mati* is the Creole word for "friend." Mati work is a celebratory culture of feminine sexual difference that unabashedly involves sexual relations between women. Women who engage with mati work may also have stable relationships with men. Working-class Creole men accept mati work. Many of the women involved in mati work are spiritual leaders in their community due to their knowledge of herbal medicines and healing practices. The mati networks, although explicitly sexual, also involve support for mothers through actual child care and shared knowledge about pregnancy and birthing rites. There is explicit celebration in mati work of women's desire for sexual expression. Mati work is the collective space where women find pleasure in each other. The mati do not, however, claim to have stable identities as lesbians or bisexuals, but instead accept "themselves as carried by a strong male winti, Apuku, who cannot bear to see his 'child,' the woman, engaged in a long-term relationship with a flesh-and-blood male. It is the Apuku who is sexually attracted to women, and thus no innate sexual identity needs to be claimed" (p. 338).

From within the spirituality of her own culture, including mati work, Renate Druiventak found "the basis" for the demand for equivalent evaluation of women, precisely because men are not the only ones with "the balls":

> One hundred members of the party were invited to the vice-president's, seventy-five women and twenty-five men. Who do you think did all the talking? Only three of the men. At a certain point I could not stand it anymore, I got up and said what a disgrace this was. There is no place for women at the table, we are only being used. I told all of those *bigiston nenge* (men with big balls) off; they are neglecting women's interests. It is time to do things differently now, male politicians have not accomplished anything. I want to start a women's action group or political party. The group has to be so strong that men will come begging on their knees for us to cooperate with them. Then I will put my demands on the table: at least three or four female ministers in the Cabinet. (p. 347)

In Suriname, middle-class women who have separated themselves from Creole culture and embraced Western notions of the "proper" family and sexuality have been much more terrified of the demands of Mofina Brasa that women be treated as equals to men (p. 349). Their demands have accordingly been much more "modest," in keeping with a decent heterosexual woman's place within a patriarchal society. The working-class and peasant women in Mofina Brasa see this middle-class movement with its moderate demands for "family law" reform as a Western implant. The embrace of the disenfranchised, on the other hand, is to support each other in freedom from all forms of sex, gender, and class hierarchies. They find this freedom in the practices of mati work. Mofina Brasa took these practices onto the national stage of politics to make a strong demand for equality, including actual political representation. Here we find a culture in which the "I" of Western individualism has no place; the mati practice that supported the demand for equality is explicitly collective. Duiventak did not find her inspiration in a Western philosophical conception of the person, but instead in the mother goddess. Yet Mofina Brasa has been relentless in the demands for women's treatment as equals. It should be obvious by now that a militant demand that women be treated as equals need not bolster itself by an appeal to Western concepts of the subject or the person. It should be equally evident that the cosmology of the Winti religion provides a "tradition" from within which the demand for equivalent evaluation and the recognition of women as free and equal to men sexually, politically, and ethically, can be rooted.

The Possibility of an Overlapping Consensus

There are many other examples besides Suriname of feminists demanding equality in their own countries from within their cultural practices, drawing on background conceptions of human nature, religion, and the ultimate meaning of life that diverge sharply from Western notions.[25] Thus, there certainly is a basis for optimism that nations could reach an overlapping consensus that one of the universals that must be recognized by all cultures is the equivalent evaluation of feminine sexual difference.

The idea of an overlapping consensus comes from John Rawls,[26] and Charles Taylor has forcefully argued that politically effective human rights agendas would more than likely proceed through something like an overlapping consensus.[27] The idea is that people from very different cultural, religious, and ethnic backgrounds could reach agreement on norms of behavior that we can call human rights, and could promote these norms, and their legal enforcement, as universal for all cultures without attempting to agree on a philosophical or theological justification for these rights. The demand for equivalent evaluation of sexual difference is more likely to promote the overlapping consensus than the demand for formal equality because many women in very different cultures, including the Western democracies, have sharply contested the idea that the feminist demand for equality should turn either on any appeal to our likeness to men or on our desire to be like them. Nothing in the program of Mofina Brasa is based on women showing that they are like men, precisely because the Winti cosmology does not recognize the kind of stable sexual identity that would make that demand comprehensible, let alone politically desirable.

Universal equivalent evaluation should be measured by answers to the questions of whether or not legal institutions, laws, education, particular cultural practices, or other basic structures of society, operate in a manner consistent with the equivalent evaluation of women. The precise form of these questions and their answers, particularly those raised in specific political battles in any one country, would have to refer to the cultural, political, ethical, and religious norms of that society. What equivalent evaluation would mandate would remain a matter of political contest. But the human right would have to demand that women, gays, lesbians, and all other forms of sexuate being be able to ask that question, no matter their own traditions or religions.

This, then, is the connection between the imaginary domain

broadly construed and the human right to equivalent evaluation of women in the moral community that is constituted by an overlapping consensus on human rights. Women, gays, and lesbians must be given the moral space to reimagine and reinterpret their religious traditions and cultural practices. Thus, the human right to be included as an equal has to protect freedom of conscience and tolerance of competing interpretations of all facets of each society.

This demand for moral space is not the same as an insistence that all societies embrace the Western separation of church and state. Rather, particular forms of legal institutionalization should be thought of as only a way to provide the moral space. For example, Islamic women could deeply disagree with the separation of church and state, and yet argue strongly that nothing in the Koran mandates that women wear the veil or deny themselves a college education.[28] Horrifyingly, in recent years, many Islamic women who have made this argument have been murdered. The human right to equivalent evaluation and the political, moral, and psychic space it demands would allow women to enter the contest of interpretation without risk of execution.

Obviously, it goes against the interpretation of some religions by some powerful members, including, unfortunately, some who are heads of state, that women be allowed to enter the contest of religious debate. Indeed, these members' interpretation of their religion is that if women claim the standing to challenge religious authority, that alone is enough reason for them to be executed. It is this kind of behavior that the human rights community clearly should seek to end. Obviously, it is irreconcilable with the equivalent evaluation of women as members of the moral community constituted by human rights.

Religions throughout the world are in upheaval due to the contest between varied interpretations of sacred texts and religious practices, in part because of women, gays, and lesbians insisting on their place in the religious community. There are now gay rabbis and female Episcopal priests. The pope may think that sodomy is a mortal sin, but many gays and lesbians

165

remain devout Catholics and now practice openly in some parts of the world. Often, respect for religious difference begins with the same faulty assumption we already noted about culture. Religions are no more static than are cultures, and all the great religions throughout the world are now being challenged on their views of sexuality. These challengers argue for their own interpretations of sacred texts. Moreover, nothing in the demand for political, moral, and psychic space takes away the respect for religion. Instead, what these demands do is undermine the right of some members of a religion to use brute force to ensure the dominance of their particular interpretations.

WHY THE IMAGINARY DOMAIN DOES NOT NEED A SUBJECTIVE CONCEPTION OF RIGHT

This concept of equivalent evaluation and the protection of freedom of conscience does not have to turn on the subjective concept of right I have defended in this book, which gives to the individual person the legal power of coercion to force others to harmonize their freedom with hers. As Charles Taylor rightly notes,

> This [subjective concept of right] seems to give pride of place to autonomous individuals, determined to demand their rights, even (indeed especially) in the space of widespread social consensus. How does this fit with the Confucian emphasis on close personal relationships, not only as highly valued in themselves but as a model for the wider society? Can people who imbibe the full Western human rights ethos, which (in one version anyway) reaches its highest expression in the lone courageous individual fighting against the evils of social conformity for his rights, ever be good members of a "Confucian" society? And how does this ethic of demanding what is due to us fit with the Theravada Buddhist search for selflessness, for self-giving, and *dana* (generosity)?[29]

166

Although feminists within both these religions have contested the confluence of sacred values and religious enlightenment with the religious patriarchal organization,[30] I agree with Taylor that for many of the world's peoples, for either religious or other reasons, Western individualism is ethically undesirable, and therefore they will be reluctant to accept a model of rights that has to be based on it.

But I do want to note a specifically feminist reason for advocating subjective rights. Subjective rights do not position the legal claimant as a victim who looks to the law to shield her from the state; instead, the state has to articulate the equality before the law of a woman's power to coerce others to harmonize their freedom with hers. Due to the Kantian emphasis on freedom that I have used to defend a subjective concept of right, these rights empower persons. That is, I am contesting the idea that a right so conceived reinforces "wounded attachments."[31] To give a woman equal coercive power to force others to harmonize their freedom with hers, even only before the law, does not sit easily with traditional patriarchal norms, which continue to dominate so many aspects of our legal system. This demand for subjective rights is then part of what in a Western country equivalent evaluation means. Because this demand is infused with the idea of right, it continues to present a challenge to legal institutions of the West.

But, as I have argued throughout this book, the challenge to patriarchal norms frequently masquerading as those of the community, even when made through the advocacy of subjective right, is neither anthropologically individualistic nor individualistic in its ethical aspirations. Rather, the importance of community and of close personal relationships is recognized as crucial for most human beings at every turn in this book. The right to represent one's sexuate being legally allows intimate associations that have historically been foreclosed by the law. This right can at the least promote a society where no one is isolated or closeted because of sexuality, as long, of course, as it does not involve nonconsensual violence or violation of the degradation

167

prohibition. The desire for freedom may arise because a person wants to live out her days with her lesbian lover as an open family, not because she wants to break apart social consensus.

But because feminists in many countries are dismantling the patriarchal norms of cultures and religions, this rebellion against patriarchy is often identified, by those who are against it, as an attack on community. But the women in rebellion are struggling to reconstitute their community into one that includes themselves as equal members. We could argue as well that patriarchy has disrupted the community or the developing nation, and that by rebelling against patriarchy, women are serving the community or nation, rather than the other way around. The reason so many feminist and women's movements seem to be against community is because the community and/or the nation is identified with patriarchal ordering.

Some feminists in the human rights movement have pressed for an approximation of the subjective concept of right because in so many countries women seem to need these rights to protect themselves against their kin or their religions: for example, countries where women are not allowed access to collective land or, in other cases, are prevented from owning it. In these instances, subjective right is the only way of conceiving the feminist political or even legal demand for equitable land distribution. When women in large numbers are demanding land with or without the right to own it, the "consensus" that they should not work it or own it has broken down, and new possibilities for the reconstitution of the community with women as farmers and landowners open. For some women activists, the struggle will be articulated as an appeal to the "true" interpretation of their religion or culture. For others, the struggle will be against the old values of the colonies in the name of the newly liberated nation-state. For some of us in the West and in other countries throughout the world where the struggle for rights has been foregrounded—for example, in the "socialist" states, what we used to call Eastern Europe—these struggles will be articulated through an appeal to rights.[32]

Again, unless patriarchy and community are conflated, these struggles need not be thought of as undermining nation or community. I want to emphasize the danger of such conflation because it has helped justify the condemnation of feminism as necessarily Western and anticommunity. Taylor is right that in our complex world we can only hope for an overlapping consensus on universals if we allow norms of behavior, even as we call them human rights, to be loosened from their connection to Western notions of the individual. But this overlapping consensus will not deserve its name if it compromises women's basic right to be included in the moral community that is constituted by human rights.

What of women who believe deeply that their own faith leads them to take their place in the religious hierarchy, for example, to wear the veil or to enter into a polygamous marriage? The space allotted to them by the imaginary domain would allow them to practice their faith in a way many feminists would consider inconsistent with their own equality.[33]

Of course, I believe that feminists are right to argue that many women have so deeply internalized their own degradation that they have lost the ability to imagine themselves as equal.[34] Their continual degradation is their only intelligible reality, but even so, on the level of human rights they must be respected as possessors of their own imaginary domain. The dilemma of "false consciousness" is an old one. If a "right consciousness" is imposed from the outside by "right thinking" feminists who know what women should want, then the degraded status of those upon whom it is imposed is affirmed rather than challenged. This "corrective" to false consciousness perpetuates the cycle it tries to break and, ironically, reinforces the intractability of women's position in society. The imaginary domain as an ideal poses an inherent challenge to the symbolic intractability of any sexual identity by demanding that all such positions be left open for reinterpretation. The political and ethical struggle to make the imaginary domain accessible to women at least psychically is obviously going on throughout the world and will undoubtedly continue for a very long time.

The Monitoring and Enforcing of Human Rights by International Organizations

How far should the feminist human rights community go in advocating the use of human rights for outlawing certain practices, such as female genital mutilation, which some women sincerely believe is part either of their faith or of the cultural recognition of their sexual difference? The use of the words *genital mutilation* obviously gives my view away, as I can see no way to reconcile this practice with an equivalent evaluation of our sexual difference. But many women argue to the contrary, insisting that as a Western woman, I just don't get it. But I have not changed my mind. And I strongly believe that feminists within the human rights community should continue to achieve an overlapping consensus that female genital mutilation is inconsistent with the equivalent evaluation of our sexual difference—this, not least because the vast majority who have undergone genital mutilation are female children who had no moral space to consider or contest what was done to them. And what was and is done is extreme indeed, hardly adequately described by the phrase "female circumcision":

> This term however, implies a fallacious analogy to nonmutilating male circumcision in which the foreskin is cut off from the tip of the penis without damaging the organ itself. The degree of cutting in female circumcision is anatomically much more extensive. The male equivalent of clitoridectomy (in which all or part of the clitoris is recovered) would be amputation of most of the penis. The male equivalent of infibulation (which involves not only clitoridectomy but also the removal or closing off of all of the sensitive tissue around the vagina) would be the removal of all the penis, its roots of soft tissue, and part of the scrotal skin.[35]

Given the gravity of the bodily harm, it is hardly surprising that many African women's organizations have focused on ridding their countries of this practice. Some African women have pressed for laws to outlaw the practice outright. Others have used political and educational tools because of the difficulty of changing a cultural practice that for some women is associated with the dignity of their sex and the "liberation" of their countries (p. 226).

What should Western feminists within the human rights community do? We should clearly follow the debates between different women's organizations within each country about this issue and, for now, advocate a human rights agenda that would make space for that debate. Obviously, the way in which women view the role of law in a particular struggle is often shaped by class. The modifications of law in a specific country will depend on how deeply the practice is rooted in the culture and, more importantly, the meaning given it by the women who perpetuate it.

"First world" women are not the most knowledgeable about female genital mutilation, and should not pretend to be so, which does not mean that we should not be fearless in lending support against the practice in whatever ways we can. We should understand that feminists in the third world do not need us a saviors, particularly as the United States has one of the highest incest and rape rates in the world. Moreover, the United States government has a long, brutal history of intervention in other countries. Given this history, feminist human rights activists within the United States and other Western countries do have to proceed with care when they seek outside monitoring of any country's norms by established human rights organizations, some of which are independent from the rich "first world" nations, including the United States, in name only. The questions concern which international human rights organizations we should support, as well as what kind of monitoring or what manner of sanctions of another country's laws are crucial for first world feminists in the human rights community. Too, we must remember that projecting a "savagery out there" is often easier than facing the glaring wrongs in one's own culture.

The Reform of Asylum Status in U.S. Immigration Law

One thing we should do immediately is make it much easier for women seeking to escape female genital mutilation to find refugee status in the United States. For the first time ever, a woman was granted asylum in the United States in 1996 based on her fear that if she returned to her country, she would be "persecuted" by being forced to undergo female genital mutilation.[36] The form of mutilation she would have been subjected to was relevant to the decision that the harm this would have done to her was serious enough to constitute persecution. Thus, the court left open the possibility that less invasive forms of female genital mutilation might not constitute persecution. Furthermore, the court took into account the fact that the young woman involved belonged to a social group opposed to female genital mutilation. Although a legal victory of sorts, *In Re: Fauziya Kasinga* clearly refused to recognize any kind of female genital mutilation as enough to constitute persecution.[37]

A person claiming asylum in the United States must bear the burden of proof that she or he meets each of the four separate elements stipulated in the Immigration and Naturalization Act (INA). These are:

1. The alien must have a fear of persecution;
2. The fear must be well-founded;
3. The persecution must be on account of race, religion, nationality, membership in a particular social group or political opinion;
4. The alien must be unable or unwilling to return to the country of origin.[38]

I do not mean to add to the already substantial feminist literature that has effectively argued that these so-called neutral standards, when interpreted by the INS, have effectively disadvantaged women because women are not found credible and therefore their fear not well founded, or because the harm they fear is judged trivial, or because women do not constitute a "social group" for the purposes of the INS.[39]

Feminists in the human rights movement have forcefully argued that gender should be added to the second prong of the test, or at the very least, that being a woman should be understood as "a membership in a particular social group."[40] But should we add gender to the list of what persecution must be based on if it is to be a valid claim for asylum? If we do, we will simply be repeating on an international level the exclusions and confinements that have come with the dominant legal interpretation of sex-as-gender within our own domestic constitutional and discrimination law.[41]

The Universal Declaration of Human Rights uses sex, rather than gender, and we should follow suit in U.S. immigration policy.[42] Thus, gays and lesbians, and the transgendered, as well as straight women, would be able to pursue their claims for asylum. Violations of bodily integrity such as rape, severe beating, or execution because a person is either a woman or a gay man would clearly be persecution because of one's "sex."

Part of the problem with the use of gender as a legal category or legal designation of a social group is that, paradoxically, it reinforces the logic of persecution. What do I mean by this? Take, for example, enforced wearing of the veil. The attempt to make all women be women in one particular way is part of the "external cohesion" women are rebelling against. In other words, persecution is an attempt to make sure that women are a cognizable social group that can both be recognized as such and be put in its proper place in the social hierarchy. Crucial to allowing women the moral space to contest the interpretations of their "sex" imposed by religious and cultural traditions is a challenge to their external cohesion, and thus the cognizability of their existence as a social group.

Feminism, Utopianism, and the Role of the Ideal in Political Philosophy

THE CHARGE AGAINST FEMINISM

THAT FEMINISM frightens some people, challenging many established religious, traditional kinships, and cultural norms, is only too evident. That these challenges produce anxiety is hardly surprising. But the root charge against feminism—that we are totalitarians, hence "feminazis"—is deeply disturbing ethically. There are no feminist death squads, let alone concentration camps, so that the effect of the term is to trivialize the human devastation Nazism left in its wake. Yet despite the glaring inappropriateness of the comparison, the term continues to have a certain credibility in our public culture, the charge implying that if they could, feminists would forcibly impose their own vision of a sexually egalitarian society, stomping on people's basic freedoms and intimate associations.

IS THE IMAGINARY DOMAIN A BAD UTOPIAN IDEAL?

In other words, feminists are "bad utopians" in that their blueprint for a good society is wholly out of touch with what is possible for actual human beings to live out in their daily home, work, or public lives. Perfectionists, feminists would reshape our natures no matter what it took, so as to transform us into creatures without gender or sex. Given the "perfectionist" experiments associated with socialist states in the twentieth cen-

174

tury, it is hardly surprising that many people would be wary of another. More broadly speaking, the charge against utopianism is meant to indicate that the writer is simply out of touch with reality rather than armed to change it.

But can a charge of bad utopianism be made to stick against the ideal of the imaginary domain, either in the sense that it is out of touch with reality or is the ideological arm of the feminist police? I think not. Thomas Nagel has argued that the problem of utopianism almost inevitably arises in political philosophy because it "presents an ideal of collective life, and it tries to show people one by one that they should want to live under it."[1] As he points out, if political philosophy is to accomplish both tasks, the psychology of what reasonable people can be expected to accept has to be part of the justification of any ideal of political life.[2] Since a mere appeal to the badness of people cannot in and of itself be given moral weight as an argument against change without completely undercutting the ideal function of political philosophy, the key is what *reasonable* people can be expected to accept. As Nagel recognizes, this is most particularly the case because people change, indeed become ethically better or worse depending on their political, economic, and social circumstances. Thus it is that people will be able to change enough to accept a political ideal, and this changing can be part of what it means to include psychological motivation in the justification of the ideal itself.

The question then becomes: Can we expect reasonable people to accept the ideal of the imaginary domain? Currently, the basic idea of reasonableness in political liberalism is that each of us accords each other the recognition that each is to be treated as a free and equal person before both the law and within the other basic institutions of our society. The heat generated by the dispute over "family values" and the attacks on feminazis show that the vast majority of heterosexuals feel very strongly about their right to orient themselves to their own sexuality and establish intimate associations in their own way. They stress over and over again how important their families are to them, how important it is to them that they be the ones to give meaning to the place of love and sex in life, not some outside political or moral authority. The one real exception to this desire to be free of outside political and moral authority is the fathers' movement, which has based its argument in part on men's incapacity to be reasonable. Arguing with heterosexual men won't help, so the story goes, since they can't hear the reasons through the roar of their hormones. This argument was answered in chapter 5, so I will only note here my acceptance of the Kantian ethical presupposition that all human beings, including straight white men, have the capacity for reasonableness.

The question then becomes, is it reasonable for people to deny to others what they insist upon as a matter of right for themselves? The answer to that is of course no. It cannot be reasonable to degrade those who have chosen a sexuality and family life that does not match some norm that others hold dear by treating them as something less than free and equal persons. Thus, if lesbian couples are not allowed to be parents, they are clearly being compelled to live out lives in ways not of their own choosing.

Here again, the value of an interpretative approach to the discontinuity thesis is seen to allow us to distinguish between those who want to impose their view of what appropriate sex is on everyone else and those who argue that as sexuate beings all of us have to be accorded treatment as free and equal persons.[3] I need to stress this point. The discontinuity thesis demands that we separate our own individual concepts of the good from what we can impose on all of us as a matter of right, given our equal standing as persons. To read the imaginary domain as an endorsement of one kind of sexual life or intimate association misses the philosophical basis on which it is defended. The separation of the right from the good is crucial for the recognition of our equal personhood precisely because our own deeply held convictions about what is good for us sexually may push us in the direction of thinking that our way is the only way. A lesbian couple taking on parenting does not in any way interfere with a heterosexual couple's right to parenthood; rather, both couples should have the right to set up their intimate lives in the way they imagine is best for them.

Some heterosexuals have argued that the open existence of gays and lesbians violates their "right" to live out their lives as they see fit—a life free of the presence of gays and lesbians. But what in fact they are claiming is the right to control access to public space in accordance with what they define as "good" sexuality.[4] In a politically liberal society, such discrimination would violate the rights of others to be treated as free and equal persons. Moreover, the presence of openly gay and lesbian persons in no way denies equal personhood to anyone, nor does it create hierarchical gradations of sexual difference that mark some as persons less worthy of happiness. We are all to be left with the right to orient ourselves sexually and make our families as we see fit.

To argue that the privileging of one form of sexuality or family is inconsistent with equal treatment of persons seeks only to end the *privilege* of heterosexual families, not that form of family.[5] To confuse the two positions is to fail to see that political recognition of the right in matters of the heart demands discontinuity between what any one of us thinks is good sexually for us or for other people, including our children, from what can be imposed by the laws and basic institutions of society. The right of each adult person to self-representation of his or her sexuate being is what is reasonably to be expected in a politically liberal culture because without it, public recognition of each one of us as a free person would be seriously undermined if not altogether denied. Here we should note that the imaginary domain is neither out of touch with the ideals of a politically liberal culture nor does it explicitly endorse, or worse yet enforce, any nontraditional, non-heterosexual relationship as the "good" relationship.

In our society, some ways of seeing the world and relationships are simply not available to people deeply divided by race and class and, indeed, by our engendering into two sexes. But the experience of valuing the freedom to orient oneself sexually and live openly with loved ones is actually widely shared. Of course, homophobic denial blocks awareness of how horrific it is for a lesbian mother to lose custody of her children simply because she lives openly with her lover. Still, we can appeal to what all humans share in our struggle to have others recognize that the importance of love, sex, and family is no less important just because one is not heterosexual. That these values are widely shared affords a strong basis for our further argument against having the state interfere in the sexual lives of *any* consenting adults, of whom very few would want to have the state in their bedroom.

I do not mean to trivialize the power of denial or underestimate the role of unconscious fantasies underpinning the so-called judgments people often make condemning the sex lives of others. It is indeed difficult to reflect on one's sex or on one's sexual desires, which draw us into the deepest recesses of our unconscious fantasy life. Sex and desire are common denominators, and by valuing them for themselves, people can see the freedom that should be given to all others in the name of the fundamental public values of a politically liberal culture.[6]

In the last fifty years families in the United States have changed drastically. A lesbian baby boom would have been unimaginable in the 1950s. The ideal of the imaginary domain gives form to what is actually happening. People are claiming the space, both psychic and public, for a self-representation of their sexuate being. One aspect of Stonewall was the absolute refusal on the part of gay men and lesbians to concede that just being gay made someone an outlaw.[7] To give symbolic form to what is being claimed in actuality is part of the role of *ideals* in political philosophy.

THE DESIRABILITY OF STABILIZATION

To demand the imaginary domain as a matter of right is to seek stabilization of the political recognition of the moral status of gays, lesbians, women, and other forms of sexuate being that are being dreamed up around the world. For some activists and theorists, the demand for stabilization inherent in the concept of right makes all "rights talk" suspect.[8] Better to do without stabilization, to give up fighting for the right, in the name of keeping all possibilities for struggle open. For example, the labor movement in this country long disputed the question of whether or not it was desirable for unions to seek legal recognition.[9] The argument is that laws can always be used against those who advocate them, and rights are only so much paper unless there is someone or some movement to demand their enforcement.

While appreciating the valid political worry about the double edged sword of the role of enunciated rights in limiting what can be open to political contest, I do not believe it is applicable here. It is helpful to frame this distinction in the terms of temporality. Insofar as they are lasting, enunciated rights fix a desirable present into the future, thus closing out future possibilities for liberation and potentially reinforcing existing power structures they were meant to challenge. But in the end, what is stabilized is the right of the person to claim herself as her own design. Rather than freezing the present, it asserts the right to future possibilities. This protection of the future inherent in the definition of the ideal can help free our political struggle from the burden of past identities, both singular and collective, as the only truth of who we are. Of course this freedom will be sought within the symbolic material that shapes the imaginary domain, symbolic material that consists of representational forms, unconscious fantasies, and prohibitions through which we have been gendered. Our right to our imaginary domain does not disavow the material constraints of how we are sexed, but is a right to imagine, represent, and symbolize the meaning of the material constituents of sex and gender as we lead our lives as sexuate beings. So defined, the ideal does not endorse any theory of the truth of women's identity. Thus, it cannot easily be charged with reinforcing what it seeks to challenge—women's identity as the unequal sex.

Of course, the demand for this right is deeply destabilizing in societies, including our own, in light of what has not been granted, which is why many Western feminists have historically been ambivalent about the political possibilities in a demand for equal rights.[10] But to demand rights provides a rallying call precisely because it can give form to political struggle and, at least in the West, can tie feminism to some of the most fundamental concepts of social order in modern Western democracy.[11] As I have argued throughout this book, a person's right to the self-representation of her sexuate being is a conclusion logically drawn from the politically liberal understanding of what the recognition of us all as free and equal persons means; moreover, it is inconsistent with privileging any one form of the family as good and so to be imposed upon us all by the state or by the basic institutions of society.

WHAT IS LEGITIMATE STABILITY IN KANTIAN POLITICAL PHILOSOPHY?

No doubt the institutionalization of this right would be destabilizing to those who have been brought up to expect that women and gays and lesbians would not and should not have it. But this kind of destabilization cannot morally count against change since it turns on the expectation that some of us, because of our sexuate being, will continue to be graded down, treated as less than free and equal persons. As Rawls has argued, only a just society can claim any legitimate basis for stability, and as we have seen, the principles of a just society can be generated only through a representational device that postulates all persons as free and equal.

The demand that women be evaluated as free and equal persons is thus a condition for legitimate stability. No use of the imaginary domain is utopian in the sense that Nagel describes: "A project of transformation is often condemned as utopian if it will not lead to a result which is stable in this sense—a result which generates its own support by calling forth new possibilities of mutual respect and recognition of moral equality through adherence to co-operative institutions."[12] If women were recognized as free and equal persons, our current form of social organization would clearly be shaken up. People would undoubtedly be called upon to change, since certain social forms could no longer be assumed as just in the normal course of things—for example, that men would have wives who did most of the child care. Of course, men could still be free to try to set up their lives in this way, and nothing would prevent women from seeking out and valuing a traditional family life. But it would be foolish to say that the changes would not be far reaching, since patriarchal social, political, and cultural forms have been a mainstay of what we think of as civilization.

But the changes demanded by the political recognition of the ideal of the imaginary domain would not controvert anyone's freedom. What kinds of psychic and ethical changes would actually take place would be left to us. Moreover, these kinds of changes would take time. More important, no one would be legally, let alone violently, forced to change. Supposedly, the fear of feminism has been that it forces people into one sexual model because that is the only way to end male domination. But the imaginary domain insists, on the contrary, that as a matter of right we should not impose any model of sexual life but rather that people should be allowed to craft their own. To give people this freedom does not mean that they have to use it in any particular way. The ideal of the imaginary domain narrowly tailored in the name of the freedom it seeks to protect sharply parts ways with feminist projects of transformation that try to give content to what sex can mean by enforcing legal definitions of either femininity or masculinity, so as to end male domination.[13] The degradation prohibition that I defend does allow for certain forms of sexual conduct to be legally regulated, but only to the extent that they controvert the recognition of all of us as free and equal persons.[14]

THE IMAGINARY DOMAIN AND GENDER
IDENTIFICATION

When the imaginary domain is politically defended as a matter of right, there is no appeal to a moral condemnation of the value of gender identification or of any particular form of family. If we stayed with Kant's moral philosophy alone, the value of gender identification would be called sharply into question. Christine Korsgaard has made this argument powerfully:

> According to an old quip, Christianity has not been tried and found too difficult, but rather has been found too difficult and so not tried. Despite some currently popular claims about the bankruptcy of the Enlightenment, I believe that this is true of Enlightenment ideals. Communitarians, champions of the family, and the promoters of ethnic and gender-identification may suppose that they have somehow discovered that the ideal of the sovereign individual is inadequate for human flourishing. But the truth is that many of them have balked when they realized how different a world that respects the ideal would have to be from the one we live in now. The centrality of gender is one of the things that would have to go.[15]

I agree with Korsgaard that if we solely remain with the Kantian ideal of freedom, it would demand that little or no value be given to gender identity; but we have learned much about the complexity of sex since Kant's time, so that we cannot dismiss easily the complexity of sexual difference.

The political and ethical justification of the imaginary domain and an understanding of what sexual freedom can be for gendered beings are tempered by the recognition of psychoanalytic insight. Thus we are conscious of the moorings of our own symbolic order, of the meanings of masculinity and femininity, and of how the deep desires human beings have are shaped by the intertwinement of real and fantasied relationships from which we can never fully extricate ourselves. This recognition of the complexity of sex and gender identifications, although in no way an argument against the Kantian ideal of freedom, does demand its reformulation. People cannot and should not be legally forced to confront, let alone revalue, identifications that have made them who they are. But people *can* be given the psychic and moral space for the exploration of new possibilities and for the chance to rework the fabric of the web of meanings out of which the self is spun. This then is what the imaginary domain offers as a legal and political ideal.

On the other hand, a full-blown feminist ethical justification for the imaginary domain clearly implies doubt as to the *value* of rigid gender identification. Judith Butler has written "of the cost of articulating a coherent identity position by producing, excluding, and repudiating a domain of abjected specters that threaten the arbitrarily closed domain of subject positions."[16]

The imaginary domain as both a psychic and a moral space for recovery of "new" and "old" identifications demands that we not be subjected, as a matter of law, to an "arbitrarily closed domain of subject positions."[17] Toni Morrison captures the effect of this closed domain in her novel *Sula* when she writes, "Nobody knew my rose of the world but me. . . . I had too much glory. They don't want glory like *that* in nobody's heart."[18] The ethic that one not only can, but should, represent a range of identifications is what opens up the space for a woman with glory in her heart.

Is it utopian to argue that we can and should keep space open for the representations of "new" and "old" identifications through which we reimagine and reshape who we are? Some schools of psychoanalysis would clearly say yes, since they insist that the basic repression upon which civilization is founded is the symbolization of the relationship to the mother. According to one version of the Freudian story, human beings become adults by turning toward the father, both for an actual relationship and as the master image of the ideal human being. But what is repressed is still always "there," and the debate among psychoanalysts is what can be made with the "thereness" that is there. Again, some schools of psychoanalysis warn us off this project as dangerous to psychic and political "health."[19]

But whose health? And at what cost? The cost to us is that, as women, we are denied a symbolizable relationship with the Mother and to the feminine. We are left with a dearth of symbolizations of the feminine and of sexual difference, not the least because these images are presented to us with racial stereotypes already in the picture. The feminine escapes us because its meanings cannot be pinned down, except for the elusive ideal of the desirable Woman ever present in the media. But these ideals project an object of desire, not a person who can reimagine herself through reidentification while keeping the meaning of who she is in motion. Heterosexual white men, seemingly privileged ones, have an established ideal that is held out for them to meet—thus, they do not seem to be buried under a slew of contradictory images of what it means to be "sexy"—but what does their privilege amount to? The little boy can identify with masculine cultures through his likeness to the Father—both have the penis—but only by subjecting himself to the codes of masculinity.[20] The psychic organization of the masculine subject is guaranteed a fixed position in the realm of phallic reference. But the price paid for this position is that all other forms of identification, particularly with the feminine other, must be abjected. For almost every man, the fantasy that he has the phallus is always belied by his relations with actual men in the hierarchical world of work. Thus, he can always lose what gives him identity by being pushed out of the boys' club, by being exposed as a "sissy" and one who "can't cut it."

Of course, the story of civilization and its discontents is highly speculative and has been sharply challenged for so being.[21] But it has become part of our shared cultural knowledge and, indeed, even our sense of reality, that gender identity cannot be challenged because it psychoanalytically grounds the possibility of adulthood. The Kantian argument defended in this book is that no matter how seemingly rooted in social reality gender identification might be now, this reality cannot be used to exclude women from the moral community of persons. As a moral and political matter, women must be left free.

A deontological theory can seem utopian because it insists on the separation between right and reality. But it is just this separation that makes a broad deontology so powerful in feminist theory. First, it shifts the grounds on which critics can challenge feminism as unrealistic: on the level of right, it does not matter whether or not "in reality" women have ever been free or not. Second, it foregrounds the centrality of freedom in feminist politics because it does not begin its argument for equality through an appeal to our likeness to men but to our political recognition as free persons who must be given the moral and psychic space to represent how women see themselves as sexuate beings. The role of the imaginary domain, as of any ideal, is to represent the separation of right from reality, and to maintain the critical edge that delimits the conflation of the two.

Feminism also challenges the idea that rigid gender identity is so firmly rooted in reality that we cannot imagine new ways of being "sexed" that are less costly to both men and women.[22] A good definition of *utopian* is that what is possible cannot be known in advance of social transformation. This is the sense of *utopian* I have consistently defended[23] because of the pride of place given to the imagination, including its function as fundamental to reason.

Let us not forget that Rawls's hypothetical experiment in imagination allows him to represent the rationality of the principles of justice. I agree completely with Rawls that we need representational devices in political philosophy;[24] and indeed, that the imaginary domain should be understood to help us represent what the original position demands in terms of the equivalent evaluation of sexual difference. My only disagreement with Rawls, at least the Rawls of *A Theory of Justice,* is that the form of justice, including the principles of justice, cannot and should not be figured once and for all.[25]

As with the principles of justice, so with ourselves. How we know who we are and how we have been formed sexually is part of a complex process through which we formulate a self with a personal story. Because who we could become in a society in which women were fully recognized as free and equal persons is not yet possible for us to experience, the process of reimagining ourselves does not have an end point.

Utopianism has always been tied to the imagination, to visions of what is truly new. A world in which we could all share in life's glories would be one radically different from our own society. Yet what is possible always changes as we change with the transformations we try to realize. Is it then utopian to think that we could share in life's glories? Is it a mere fantasy, or is the presence of the dream *itself* not proof enough that it might be possible? At last it is up to us to turn yesterday's utopia into a new sense of reality.

* *Notes* *

CHAPTER ONE

1. See Marcia Cohen, *The Sisterhood: The Inside Story of the Women's Movement and the Leaders Who Made It Happen* (New York: Fawcett Columbine, 1988).

2. Several Title VII cases illustrate the difficulties gays and lesbians face when challenging discriminatory actions against them on the basis of sexual orientation rather than gender. See *Dillon v. Frank*, 952 F.2d 403 (6th Cir. 1992), in which the court found that congressional intent dictated against interpreting Title VII causes of action to include those claiming discrimination on the basis of sexual orientation; *deSantis v. Pacific Tel. & Tel. Co.*, 608 F.2d 327 (9th Cir. 1979), in which the court disallowed a class action suit on behalf of gays and lesbians claiming discrimination on the basis of sexual orientation; *Ulane v. Eastern Airlines, Inc.*, 742 F.2d 1081 (7th Cir. 1984), in which the court disallowed a female transsexual to proceed on claims of discrimination either on the basis of gender or on the basis of transsexuality.

3. "Equality of what?" is one of the two questions that Amartya Sen has argued is central to any ethical analysis of equality. The other is "Why equality?" See *Inequality Reexamined* (New York: Russell Sage Foundation; Cambridge: Harvard University Press, 1992), p. 12.

4. See *Romer v. Evans*, 116 U.S. 1620, 1634 (1996) (Scalia, J., dissenting). Justice Scalia asserts "The problem is that, because those who engage in homosexual conduct tend to reside in disproportionate numbers in certain communities . . . have high disposable income . . . and of course care about homosexual-rights issues much more ardently than the public at large, they possess political power much greater than their numbers, both locally and statewide."

5. See generally *The World's Women, 1995: Trends and Statistics* (New York: United Nations, 1995) for a comprehensive analysis of the status of women worldwide. See also Claudia Goldin, *Understanding the Gender Gap: An Economic History of American Women* (New York: Oxford University Press, 1990).

6. Amartya Sen, "Gender Inequality and Theories of Justice," in

Women, Culture, and Development, ed. Martha Nussbaum and Jonathan Glover (Oxford: Oxford University Press, 1995), p. 259.

7. Amartya Sen and Martha Nussbaum have eloquently defended a development ethic that can be used to judge societies as to whether or not they have met at least a minimum threshold of basic capabilities, most markedly the capability to survive. (introduction to *The Quality of Life* [Oxford: Clarendon Press, 1993]) The capabilities approach is not a theory of formal gender equality, although it can be effectively deployed to measure the extent of women's inequality before that threshold and can focus the demands of justice on these inequalities. Unlike formal equality, it focuses on a human being's actual freedom, by which is meant the capability to function. As a theory of equality of well-being and capability, it is not restricted to the provision of a minimum threshold; the measure is not based on men in some idealized setting, but on individual achievements in the actualization of freedom. To quote Sen:

> I have argued in favor of judging individual advantage directly in terms of freedom to achieve rather than in terms of primary goods (as in Rawls, 1971), incomes (as in standard welfare economic discussions), resources (as in Dworkin, 1981), and other proposed spaces. The "capability perspective" involves concentration on freedoms to achieve in general and the capabilities to function in particular. Individual achievements in living could be seen in terms of human functioning, consisting of various beings and doings, varying from such elementary matters as being adequately nourished, to such complex functions as taking part in the life of the community, achieving self-respect and so on. (From "Gender, Inequality, and Theories of Justice," pp. 266–67)

As we will see throughout this book, the "broad deontology" I offer can be easily attached to the capabilities approach when what is required is either a provision of a measure of gender inequality or of the demands put on the basic institutions of society to address the realization of fundamental liberties that must be offered to all citizens in the name of their freedom.

8. See, for example, Martha Fineman, *The Neutered Mother, the Sexual Family, and Other Twentieth-Century Tragedies* (New York: Routledge, 1995).

9. Ibid.

10. Let me remind the reader again that even using gender as the standard of critique of gender inequality is itself problematic because it is unclear which men are to serve as the measure. Thus, as I have already suggested, we need to defend an adequate development ethics by which we highlight the glaring cruelty of the inequality of women before life's barest chances to justice. This is best viewed by Nussbaum and Sen's minimum threshold (*Quality of Life*).

11. I borrow the phrase from Charles Taylor, *Sources of the Self* (Cambridge: Harvard University Press, 1989), p. 31.

12. See Judith Butler, *Bodies that Matter: On the Discursive Limits of "Sex"* (New York: Routledge, 1993), chap. 1, for a compelling critique of the sex/gender distinction in feminist theory. See also Moira Gatens, *Imaginary Bodies: Ethics, Power, and Corporeality* (New York: Routledge, 1996) for an excellent discussion of how we cohere as a body only by having a bodily ego that we internalize and project as an imaginary and ever reimagined unity. For my own discussion of the body as a projected unity, see *The Imaginary Domain* (New York: Routledge, 1995), pp. 38–43.

13. Simone de Beauvoir, *The Second Sex,* trans. H. M. Parshley (New York: Vintage Books, 1974), p. xviii.

14. For a fuller discussion of what I mean by "recollective imagination," see *The Imaginary Domain*.

15. bell hooks, *Outlaw Culture: Resisting Representations* (New York: Routledge, 1994), p. 238.

16. hooks, *Bone Black: Memories of Girlhood* (New York: Henry Holt, 1996), p. 171.

17. Virginia Woolf, *A Room of One's Own* (London: Harcourt Brace and Co., 1929). For Woolf, femininity is intertwined with confinement and exclusion from both real and imaginary places of exploration. In the famous fable "Shakespeare's Sister," Woolf imagines the devastating effects of exclusionary confinement and the very real violence that is brought down on women who break out of the roles allotted them as women. Shakespeare's imaginary sister was kept from going to school, and so she stole her brother's books. She is reminded to stick to her proper role, just because, as Woolf imagines her, she is loved by her parents and they know the price of a woman going astray. Betrothed to a young man that her father finds appropriate, she finds that the torment of her rebellion finally leads her to take action.

Like her brother, she has a taste for the theater, a gift for "the tune of words," but she is told "no woman could possibly be an actress." There is no safe place for her to be taken in, "yet her genius was for fiction and lusted to feed abundantly upon the lives of men and women and the study of their ways. At last—for she was very young, oddly like Shakespeare the poet in her face, with the same grey eyes and rounded brows—at last Nick Greene the actor-manager took pity on her; she found herself with child by that gentleman and so—who shall measure the heat and violence of the poet's heart when caught and tangled in a woman's body?—killed herself one winter's night and lies buried at some cross-roads where the omnibuses now stop outside the Elephant and Castle" (*Room of One's Own,* p. 48).

For Woolf, Shakespeare's sister would have in truth been destroyed in the streets of London if she had not committed suicide. She would never have made it far in London without being raped. She would have been shut out from owning her own gifts. "For it needs little skill in psychology to be sure that a highly gifted girl who had tried to use her gift for poetry would have been so thwarted and hindered by other people, so tortured and pulled asunder by her own contrary instincts, that she must have lost her health and sanity to a certainty" (p. 49). Femininity is imagined here as a living torment. The writers Woolf describes have been bravely trying to dig themselves out. The imaginary domain demands that we lift the prohibitions that prevent us from freeing ourselves.

18. Patricia J. Williams, *The Alchemy of Race and Rights* (Cambridge: Harvard University Press, 1991).

19. Ibid., p. 154, emphasis added.

20. Joan Wallach Scott, *Only Paradoxes to Offer: French Feminism and the Rights of Man* (Cambridge: Harvard University Press, 1996).

21. Ibid.

22. Amartya Sen's capability perspective may best be situated for the second level of equivalent evaluation because it is tailored to analyze how differences have to be taken into account from the perspective of actual freedom in order to achieve equality. In "Gender Inequality, and Theories of Justice," Sen contrasts the capability perspective to John Rawls's defense of primary goods as follows:

One of the features of gender inequality is its association with a biological difference which has to be taken into account in understanding the demands of equality between men and women. To assume that difference away would immediately induce some understanding of correspondence between the space for primary foods and that of freedoms to achieve. For example, with the same income and means to buy food and medicine, a pregnant woman may be at a disadvantage vis-à-vis a man of the same age having the freedom to achieve adequate nutritional well-being. The differentiated demands imposed by neo-natal care of children also have considerable bearing on what a woman at a particular stage of life can or cannot achieve with the same command over primary goods as a man might have at the corresponding stage in his life. These and other differences in which biological factors are important (although not exclusively so) make the program of judging equity and justice in the space of primary goods deeply defective, since equal holdings of primary goods can go with very unequal substantive freedoms. (p. 265)

23. Immanuel Kant, "On the Relationship of Theory to Practice in Political Right," in *Kant: Political Writings,* ed. Hans Reiss (Cambridge: Cambridge University Press, 1970), p. 74.

24. See John Rawls, *Political Liberalism* (New York: Columbia University Press, 1993) on how it is hard to even know what metaphysics is p. 29, n. 31.

25. Kant has lower expectations than Rawls of what can be achieved even in a lawful state that meets all three a priori principles. Law is necessarily a field of coercion, and we need coercion to be able to live out our freedom if some try to prevent us from doing so without having a legitimate cause. Due to his understanding of the inevitability of conflicts between persons who are recognized as free human beings, Kant puts considerably more emphasis on right as a legitimate form of coercion to protect someone's authority as a free person than Rawls does. To quote Kant,

All right consists solely in the restriction of the freedom of others, with the qualification that their freedom can co-exist with my freedom within the terms of a general law: and public right in a commonwealth is simply a state of affairs regulated by a real legislation which conforms to this principle and is backed up by power, and under which a whole people live as subjects in a lawful state (*status juridicus*). This is what we call a civil state, and it is characterised by equality in the effects and counter-effects of freely willed actions which limit one another in accor-

NOTES TO CHAPTER ONE

dance with the general law of freedom. ("Theory and Practice," pp. 75–76)

26. Rawls, *A Theory of Justice* (Cambridge: Harvard University Press, 1971), pp. 13–14.

27. Ibid., p. 13.

28. Rawls, *Political Liberalism,* pp. 5–6.

29. Kant describes his own understanding of the original contract as follows:

> This then [a civil law that meets Kant's a priori conditions] is an *original contract* by means of which a civil and thus completely lawful constitution and commonwealth can alone be established. But we need by no means assume that this contract (*contractus originarius* or *pactum sociale*), based on a coalition of the wills of all private individuals in a nation to form a common, public will for the purposes of rightful legislation, actually exists as a *fact,* for it cannot possibly be so. Such an assumption would mean that we would first have to prove from history that some nation, whose rights and obligations have been passed down to us, did in fact perform such an act, and handed down some authentic record or legal instrument, orally or in writing, before we could regard ourselves as bound by a pre-existing civil constitution. It is in fact merely an *idea* of reason, which nonetheless has undoubted practical reality; for it can oblige every legislator to frame his laws in such a way that they could have been produced by the united will of a whole nation, and to regard each subject, in so far as he can claim citizenship, as if he had consented within the general will. This is the test of the rightfulness of every public law. For if the law is such that a whole people could not *possibly* agree to it (for example, if it stated that a certain class of *subjects* must be privileged as a hereditary *ruling* class), it is unjust; but if it is at least *possible* that a people could agree to it, it is our duty to consider the law as just, even if the people is at present in such a position or attitude of mind that it would probably refuse its consent if it were consulted. ("Theory and Practice," p. 79)

30. Ibid., p. 75.

31. See Cornell, *The Imaginary Domain.*

32. See Susan Moller Okin, *Justice, Gender, and the Family* (New York: Basic Books, 1989), pp. 101–9; and Ruth Anna Putnam, "Why

Not a Feminist Theory of Justice?" in Nussbaum and Glover, *Women, Culture, and Development,* pp. 298–330.

33. Although a full discussion is beyond the scope of this book, we do need to raise the question as to whether Rawls's political concept of freedom is circumscribed because of his insistence that it must be tailored to meet the conditions of reciprocity between citizens.

34. Rawls argues, "In justice as fairness, on the other hand, persons accept in advance a principle of equal liberty and they do this without a knowledge of their more particular ends. They implicitly agree, therefore, to conform their conceptions of their good to what the principles of justice require, or at least not to press claims which directly violate them. An individual who finds that he enjoys seeing others in positions of lesser liberty understands that he has no claim whatever to this enjoyment. The pleasure he takes in others' deprivations is wrong in itself: it is a satisfaction which requires the violation of a principle to which he would agree in the original position" (*A Theory of Justice,* p. 31).

35. Rawls argues that the free citizen is not based on a strong theory of autonomy because some citizens do not accept this kind of autonomy due to their religious beliefs. As members of their religion, they might fiercely reject their right to claim their own persons. But even if this were the case, Rawls argues that when they are in their role as citizens, they are given this recognition in a solely political sense. Thus, he gives to us a political conception of what it means for each citizen to claim her own person, and to be recognized as such. To make his point as to why this recognition that, for political purposes, each citizen is recognized as free to claim her own person, Rawls contrasts the free person of liberal democracy with the condition of the slave:

> To take an extreme case, slaves are human beings who are not counted as sources of claims, not even claims based on social duties or obligations. Laws that prohibit the maltreatment of slaves are not based on claims made by slaves, but on claims originating from slaveholders, or from the general interests of society (which do not include the interests of slaves). Slaves are, so to speak, socially dead: they are not recognized as persons at all. This contrast with slavery makes clear why conceiving of citizens as free persons in virtue of their moral powers and their having a concep-

tion of the good goes with a particular political conception of justice. (*Political Liberalism*, p. 33)

As we will see throughout the book, to different degrees, depending on class and race, women are still rendered "socially dead."

36. For a fuller discussion please see chapter 3 in addition to Cornell, *The Imaginary Domain*.

37. Sherry B. Ortner, *Making Gender: The Politics and Erotics of Culture* (Boston: Beacon Press, 1996).

38. I have of course shared that difficulty. In *The Imaginary Domain*, I still justified the recognition of women's sexual freedom based on their equal citizenship, not simply as an end in itself for a human being. I will return shortly and, indeed, throughout this book to what I mean by sexual freedom. For now, I simply want to note that minimum conditions of individuation, including the imaginary domain as the legally protected space for the contestation of sexual personae and the self-representation of one's own sexuate being, still appealed to what conditions had to be realized for citizens to engage in practical reason and thus to realize the two moral capacities Rawls practically attributes to citizens. To remind the reader, these are: First, citizens are regarded as having the moral power to have a conception of the good. This moral power includes their ability to revise and criticize their own ideas of what is good on the basis of an appeal to either rationality or to reasonableness. Second, persons are to be regarded as being capable of taking responsibility for their aims and assessing them for their reasonableness.

In spite of myself, in *The Imaginary Domain* I was still "selling" our freedom by making it useful to our value as citizens (see pp. 17–20). I am now making an argument that is consistent with the central Kantian idea that freedom be ethically valued for its own sake.

39. Scott, *Only Paradoxes to Offer*, pp. 32–36.

40. Rawls, *A Theory of Justice*, pp. 289–93.

41. Kant, *Political Writings*, p. 74.

42. Rawls, *Political Liberalism*, p. 32.

43. Scott, *Only Paradoxes to Offer*, pp. 97–99.

44. Of course, much has changed in the Western political democracies. Women are now recognized as being capable of representing themselves in the public arena. They can vote. They can run for office. They can get divorced. They can claim their own inheritance. They can

open their own businesses and compete for desirable professional jobs. But in our political culture, do we truly recognize women as free and equal persons in the Kantian sense? The legislation to regulate women—for example, fetal protection laws—shows that we are far from having "reflective equilibrium" on the basic proposition that women are inviolable as free persons. See my discussion in chapter 3.

45. Rawls, *Political Liberalism,* p. 33.

46. Kant, *Political Writings,* p. 74.

47. It needs to be noted here that Kant's concept of right is not purely negative. Of course, part of a Kantian concept of right turns us to the conditions of rightfulness to which subjects must agree so as to accept principles of justice and then actual laws and legislation. For Michel Foucault, at least in some of his writings, it is precisely this saying "yes" to authority, even if only to certain hypothetical conditions of rightfulness, that is a form of subjection. To quote Foucault:

> This reduction of power to law has three main roles: (i) it underwrites a schema of power which is homogenous for every level and domain—family or state, relations of education and production, (ii) it enables power never to be thought of other than in negative terms: refusal, limitation, obstruction, censorship. Power is what says no. And the challenging of power as thus conceived can appear only as transgression, (iii) it allows the fundamental operation of power to be thought of as that of a speech-act: enunciation of law, discourse of prohibition. The manifestation of power takes on the pure form of "Thou shalt not." ("Power and Strategies" in *Power/Knowledge: Selected Interviews and Other Writings, 1972–1977,* ed. Colin Gordon [New York: Pantheon Press, 1980], pp. 139–40)

But Kant's concept of right does not neatly follow Foucault's schema. The power to coerce others through right is not just the power to restrict. It is the power one has to coerce others to harmonize their freedom with hers. Let's take the example of sexual harassment and, more specifically, my own definition, which would replace the traditional understanding of quid pro quo harassment. Quid pro quo harassment has been traditionally defined as unwanted or unwelcomed sex in the context of unequal power relations. "Unequal power relations" has usually been construed to mean those between employers and employees.

Critics of sexual harassment regulation have agreed that this definition defines women as victims, as the helpless woman who cannot deal with her employer on her own. On at least one Foucauldian interpretation, sexual harassment allows women only the right to censor the behavior of others. But they get this right only if they show that they made themselves into the proper subject, one who does not "want" or "welcome" the advances. Thus sexual harassment cases are only too often rehearsed as horror stories in which women try to show that they are good enough girls who deserve to censor the behavior of men. Not surprisingly, the combination of the subjugation to law's imposition of a definition of what it means to be a victim and the legally demanded demonstration that one is "a good girl" has made some feminists wary of the whole legal edifice of sexual harassment (See Wendy Brown, *States of Injury: Power and Freedom in Late Modernity* [Princeton: Princeton University Press, 1995], pp. 55–56).

But now let's take the first piece of *my* definition of sexual harassment, which attempts to foreground freedom and the right to coerce others to harmonize their freedom with mine. My definition is unilaterally imposed sexual requirements in the context of unequal power (for my full definition, see *The Imaginary Domain,* p. 170). Here, a woman would not have to show that she was a victim, even in the simplest sense. She would not have to show that she could not get the guy to stop, nor would she have to show that she was a "good girl" because "unwanted or unwelcome" would no longer be at issue. Instead, we are demanding freedom in the workplace for women to dress the way we like, and so forth, without being held responsible for "readings" of what we wear. If a man persists in trying to impose his readings of what I am doing or wearing, then he can be coerced to harmonize his freedom with mine. If I wear short skirts and black stockings to work, it is my business to do so without some man thinking that I want him in my face. Part of the demand for freedom is that we will no longer be held responsible for the fantasies men have about us that force us to circumvent our freedom in the workplace. Under this definition, we are not simply asking the man to stop; we are demanding that the workplace be one where my freedom as a worker is not undermined by having the space in which I represent myself curtailed.

The demand to be freed from sexual harassment can then be understood as an *affirmative* power to demand that others harmonize their freedom in the workplace with mine. This interpretation of sexual harassment should also satisfy liberal critics of feminist sexual policing (see, for example, Thomas Nagel, "Personal Rights and Public Space," *Philosophy and Public Affairs* 24 no. 2 [Spring 1995]). This affirmative power and the coercion that goes with it does not put a woman in the position of victim, but instead in the position of authority over her sexuality in the workplace.

48. Kant, *Political Writings*, p. 76.

49. The advocation of our equal intrinsic value—which I join in this book—has usually been justified by an appeal to a concept of objectivity. For example, Thomas Nagel has argued that if we adopted an impartial perspective—the view from nowhere—we would see that there could be no claim to the inherent superior value of one human being over another because such a claim would necessarily rest on the viewer's partiality toward his own group, religion, sex, and so forth. We all care deeply about our personal commitments, but, so the argument goes, there are some basic aspects about human life that will have impersonal value because they are the "raw data provided by the individual desires, interests, projects, attachments, allegiances and plans of life that define the personal points of view of the multitude of distinct individuals, ourselves included" (Nagel, *Equality and Partiality* [New York: Oxford University Press, 1991], p. 11). This recognition that certain "raw data" have value to us all—impersonal value, because they are a part of what makes personal value possible— allows us to adopt such a view and deploy it more generally. In other words, it helps explain why it is psychologically credible for us to adopt such a viewpoint. When we take up the impersonal viewpoint, it challenges the idea that the basic values in other lives do not matter as much to them as yours do to you. The impersonal view does not single you out over anyone else.

50. This is the fundamental insight in Hegel's normative philosophical history of the meaning of modernity. See *Phenomenology of the Spirit*, trans A. V. Miller (Oxford: Clarendon Press, 1977). See also Niklas Luhmann, *Love as Passion: The Codification of Intimacy*, trans. J. Gaines and D. Jones (Cambridge: Harvard University Press, 1986). Following thinkers such as Hegel, Luhmann argues that the historical period we think of as "modernity" is defined by the replace-

ment of stratified differentiations with functional differentiations. Hegel was the first to explicitly recognize that the normative significance of this historical change was the political and moral establishment of the person. Secondly, Hegel recognized that the person, freed from a substantive definition of hierarchical standing, would *necessarily* have to be defined by an abstract conception. Any filling in of the person would deny her ideal freedom from the constraints of social and political hierarchies.

51. See Scott, introduction to *Only Paradoxes to Offer*. Eighteenth-century universal rights debates opened up a space for French feminists to demand that the state grant women full citizenship. That citizens' rights were not extended to women was the Revolution's great "lie" that French feminists sought to articulate and remedy (p. 11).

52. I borrow this phrase from Nikol G. Alexander. Alexander and Cornell, "Dismissed or Banished? A Testament to the Reasonableness of the Simpson Jury," in *Birth of a Nation'hood: Gaze, Script, and Spectacle in the O. J. Simpson Case,* ed. Toni Morrison and Claudia Brodsky Lacour (Pantheon: New York, 1997).

53. For an excellent discussion of social death, see Orlando Patterson, *Slavery and Social Death: A Comparative Study* (Cambridge: Harvard University Press, 1982).

54. Henrik Ibsen, *A Doll's House and Other Plays,* trans. Peter Watts (1910; reprint, London: Penguin Classics, 1965).

55. See, for example, bell hooks, *Ain't I a Woman? Black Women and Feminism* (Boston: South End Press, 1981).

56. Recent developments regarding granting gays and lesbians the legal right to marry highlight the complexities of the struggle to allow individuals their full standing as persons. See *Baehr v. Miike,* 65 USLW 2399 (Cir. Ct. Hawaii 1996), for an example of the legal battles same-sex couples face with regard to marriage. Gay and lesbian couples should have access to whatever civil laws are currently available to heterosexual couples, as a matter of equivalent right. As I argue throughout this book, the state cannot violate the sanctuary of the imaginary domain and individual representations of sexuate being. The state therefore cannot privilege certain kinships over others. For example, the Defense of Marriage Act, which narrowly defines marriage, clearly should not be admissible state policy. The act defines "marriage" and "spouse" as follows: "In determining the meaning of

any Act of Congress, or of any ruling, regulation, or interpretation of the various administrative bureaus and agencies of the United States, the word 'marriage' means only a legal union between one man and one woman as husband and wife, and the word 'spouse' refers only to a person of the opposite sex who is a husband or a wife" (H.R. 104–664 [1996]).

57. But this recognition that women are citizens has not been coincident with the recognition of women as equivalent persons. For an excellent historical discussion of why not, see Joan Wallach Scott, "Citizens but Not Individuals: The Vote and After," in *Only Paradoxes to Offer,* chap. 6.

58. See Fineman, *The Neutered Mother.*

59. For example, Catharine A. MacKinnon's theory of state cannot be granted moral credibility in that given her theoretical analysis of what a woman is, it has to deny that women are equivalent persons *now,* with the capacity for self-representation. Mackinnon's substantive theory of equality pits itself against women's freedom because she denies that women as constructed under male domination can be representatives of themselves. See *Toward a Feminist Theory of the State* (Cambridge: Harvard University Press, 1989).

60. Ronald Dworkin and Catharine A. MacKinnon, "Pornography: An Exchange—Comment/Reply," *New York Review of Books* 41, no. 5 (March 3, 1994).

61. Simone de Beauvoir, *The Second Sex.* De Beauvoir used the word *second* to highlight the asymmetrical positioning of the feminine in relation to the masculine. The feminine, and thus woman, is always relegated to the position of the other. She writes, "man represents both the positive and the neutral, as is indicated by the common use of *man* to designate human beings in general; whereas woman represents only the negative, defined by limiting criteria, without reciprocity" (p. xviii).

62. Toni Morrison, *Sula* (New York: Knopf, 1973).

63. Thomas Nagel, "Justice and Nature," *Oxford Journal of Legal Studies* 17 (1997).

64. See Okin, *Justice, Gender, and the Family.*

65. De Beauvoir, *The Second Sex.* She writes, "There is one feminine function that it is actually almost impossible to perform in complete liberty. It is maternity" (p. 774).

66. Ronald Dworkin was the first to develop a two-tiered theory of equality as necessary if each one of us is to be treated as an equal rather than just granted equal treatment. For an excellent recent summary of Dworkin's position see, "Why We Are All Liberals." Although Dworkin does not use reproduction as an example, his argument is structurally similar to the one I have made here. He effectively argues that equal concern for our person demands some theory of distributive justice that would address the gross inequalities of our current distributional arrangements. His theory to address the scope of rights and claims demanded by the first tier of treatment as an equal is equality of resources. See also "What Is Equality? Part 2: Equality of Resources," *Philosophy and Public Affairs* 10 no. 4 (Fall 1981).

67. Irigaray's writings on sexuate rights seemingly contradict her philosophical work, in which the question of sexual difference is left as a question. In her writing on sexuate rights, Irigaray conceives of the individual as either man or woman, and argues that each individual lives a natural reality that corresponds to his or her sexual difference. She goes on to call for a law capable of recognizing lived sexual difference as a universal. In doing so, however, she restricts definitions of personhood by remaining in a system of sexual difference made up of two, and only two, kinds—male and female. I further discuss Irigaray's recent work in chapter 4. See Luce Irigaray, *I Love to You: Sketch of a Possible Felicity in History,* trans. Alison Martin (New York: Routledge, 1996).

CHAPTER TWO

1. My argument is structurally similar to what Hegel means by conscience: "Conscience is the expression of the absolute title of subjective self-consciousness to know in itself and from within itself what is right and obligatory, to give recognition only to what it thus knows as good, and at the same time to maintain that whatever in this way it knows and wills is in truth right and obligatory. Conscience as this unity of subjective knowing with what is absolute is a sanctuary which it would be a sacrilege to violate." Georg W. F. Hegel, *Philosophy of Right,* trans. T. M. Knox (Oxford: Oxford University Press, 1967), p. 91.

2. Ronald Dworkin, "Foundations of Liberal Equality," in *The*

Tanner Lectures on Human Values (Salt Lake City: University of Utah Press, 1990).

3. Sigmund Freud, *The Ego and the Id,* trans. Joan Riviere (London: Hogarth Press, 1962).

4. Oliver Sacks, "The Disembodied Lady," in *The Man Who Mistook His Wife for a Hat and Other Clinical Tales* (New York: Summit Books, 1970), p. 42.

5. There are, of course, philosophers who have challenged that there is a coherent self that develops from self-perception. Hume was the notable example. Sacks describes what a Humean person looks like when a clinician meets him in person and not just in philosophical speculation:

> Hume, as we have noted, wrote:
>> I venture to affirm . . . that (we) are nothing but a bundle or collection of different sensations, succeeding one another with inconceivable rapidity, and in a perpetual flux and movement.
>
> Thus, for Hume, personal identity is a fiction—we do not exist, we are but a consecution of sensations or perceptions.
>
> This is clearly not the case with a normal human being, because he *owns* his own perceptions. They are not mere flux, but *his* own, united by an abiding individuality or self. But what Hume describes may be precisely the case for a being as unstable as a super-Touretter, whose life is, to some extent, a consecution of random, or convulsive perceptions and motions, a phantasmagoric fluttering with no centre or sense. To this extent he *is* a "Humean," rather than a human, being. This is the philosophical, almost theological, fate which lies in wait, if the ratio of impulse to self is too overwhelming. It has affinities to a "Freudian" fate, which is also to be overwhelmed by impulse—but the Freudian fate has sense (albeit tragic) whereas a "Humean" fate is meaningless and absurd. (*The Man Who Mistook His Wife for a Hat,* p. 119)

6. Jacques Lacan, "The Mirror Stage," in *Ecrits: A Selection,* trans. Alan Sheridan (New York and London: W. W. Norton, 1977), pp. 1–7.

7. In recent decades, feminist activists have effectively applied the concept of "post-traumatic stress" to describe the psychological impact of sexual assault.

8. See Nancy V. Raine, "HERS: Returns of the Day," *New York Times,* October 2, 1994, sec. 6, p. 34.

9. Living in a culture in which rape is so prevalent has an effect on all women since no woman can truly project a future in which she is safe. On the one hand, the message functions to convey to women that we must be prepared to defend ourselves from the inevitable attack. Yet the seeming inevitability of this attack makes clear just how vulnerable we are. A woman is thus in the position of constantly anticipating an attack, anticipation that is coupled with the anxiety of being incapable of defending herself. See Sharon Marcus, "Fighting Bodies, Fighting Words: A Theory of Politics and Rape Prevention," in *Feminists Theorize the Political,* ed. Judith Butler and Joan W. Scott (New York: Routledge, 1992). See also Peggy Reeves Sanday, introduction to *Fraternity Gang Rape: Sex, Brotherhood, and Privilege on Campus* (New York: New York University Press, 1990); and Isabelle V. Barker "Feminism without 'Women': A Theory for Anti-Rape Politics" (1994, manuscript on file with author).

10. Although bodily integrity involves a representation of ourselves as integral persons, the realization of what our bodily integrity *means* will undoubtedly vary in accordance with the different situations we face. Moreover, we will sometimes need help from others in realizing our representations of who we are, particularly when we face traumatic situations in which our most basic sense of ourselves is challenged or undermined. As I argued earlier, bodily integrity turns on the primordial creation of a bodily ego. Obviously, the body as proper to the self is severely challenged by serious illnesses. In fact, the body can come to be perceived as other to the self, or in the case of a terminal illness, as a hostile "agent" that is killing the self. When bodily integrity is so brutally challenged we can only consciously recollect it by trying to give a different meaning to it in its new condition. We have to be allowed to represent what this condition means and how we choose to live and/or die with it. Faced with no hope of recovery, how to die with one's sense of self intact becomes an issue of great weight. We know that some people diagnosed with a terminal illness see nothing in front of them but anguish and degeneration and so appeal for help in speeding the process of dying. For some, a desperate condition may lead them to seek a doctor's help in committing suicide. Obviously, such a person cannot be left alone in her privacy if she can die only with the a doctor's help. For a defense to the right of assisted suicide, see Ronald Dworkin, Thomas Nagel, Robert Nozick, John Rawls,

Thomas Scanlon, and Judith Jarvis-Thomson, "Assisted Suicide: The Philosophers' Brief," *New York Review of Books* (March 27, 1997), pp. 41–47.

Justice Blackmun's historic decision in *Roe v. Wade*, 410 U.S. 113 (1973), recognized a woman's choice to abort as hers to make with her doctor, at least in the first trimester. Implicit in the decision is that a woman who seeks an abortion cannot be alone in her privacy. Even in the first trimester, abortion involves either a medical procedure or a doctor's involvement after a pill or injection to induce abortion has been administered. Blackmun recognized, as he did in *Bowers,* that the privacy line of cases begun in *Griswold* did not fit easily with the right to abortion:

> The pregnant woman cannot be isolated in her privacy. She carries an embryo and, later, a fetus, if one accepts the medical definitions of the developing young in the human uterus. See Dorland's Medical Dictionary, 478–479, 547 (24th edition 1965). The situation therefore is inherently different from marital intimacy, or bedroom possession of obscene material, or marriage, or procreation, or education with which *Eienstadt* and *Griswold, Stanley, Loving, Skinner* and *Peirce,* were respectively concerned. (*Roe v. Wade,* at 158)

Blackmun's concern was with both the state's interest in protecting the embryo, an interest that becomes more pressing when the pregnancy reaches the second trimester, and the state's interest in the health of the mother. Obviously moved by the bloody horror stories of unattended abortions, Blackmun was particularly concerned with the provision of safe hospital facilities for the performance of later-date abortions. In the majority's post-*Roe* decisions, the state's interest in protecting the health of the woman was completely dropped from the discussion as justification of the right to an abortion. In his dissents in the post-*Roe* cases, Blackmun aimed his argument at the majority's erasure of this interest. In dissent after dissent, he stressed women's health and women's need for safe medical facilities to carry out abortions, particularly in the second trimester.

Justice Blackmun recognized that privacy, at least as interpreted as "the right of solitary individuals to be left alone," could not easily be applied to the right of abortion. But he also saw how basic and fundamental the right to abortion was to women's freedom to make the intimate decisions in her life. My defense of the right to abortion as crucial to bodily integrity and to the equal protection of minimum conditions of individuation were discussed at length elsewhere. For now I want to return to the "public" nature of abortion. Abortion, like the right to die, clearly involves the deepest recesses of one's being. Such a decision is obviously personality defining and a clear candidate for protection by any meaningful concept of conscience. Yet, as in the case of the right to intimate sexual association, the right to abortion demands actualization, not just expression. The exercise of the right to abortion is to have an abortion, and so puts a demand upon the state to make having an abortion as safe as possible. Justice Blackmun's difficulty in his post-*Roe* decisions was to reconcile the need for regulating the provision of medical care with the right to privacy. Simply put, complete deregulation of abortion made no sense to him, and yet that was what the privacy line of cases seemed to call for.

11. See Nancy Chodorow, *Reproduction of Mothering: Psychoanalysis and the Sociology of Gender* (Berkeley: University of California Press, 1978); and Jessica Benjamin, *Like Subjects, Love Objects: Essays on Recognition and Sexual Difference* (New Haven and London: Yale University Press, 1995).

12. Kant, for example, justified the possibility of moral freedom by making the metaphysical distinction between the noumenal and the phenomenal self.

13. I agree with Rawls that political liberalism does not imply a view of the subject in spite of all the confusion about what metaphysics even means. See *Political Liberalism* (New York: Columbia University Press, 1993), p. 29 n. 31.

14. The "privacy right" was established by the following Supreme Court cases: *Griswold v. Connecticut*, 381 U.S. 479 (1965); *Roe v. Wade*, 410 U.S. 113 (1973); *Carey v. Population Services International*, 431 U.S. 678 (1977).

15. 15.381 U.S. 479 (1965).

16. Ibid.

17. In *Griswold*, marital privacy is established: "Would we allow the police to search the sacred precincts of marital bedrooms for telltale signs of the use of contraceptives? The very idea is repulsive to the notions of privacy surrounding the marriage relationship" (pp. 485–86). In his concurring opinion, Justice Brennan appeals to "the entire

fabric of the Constitution and the purposes that clearly underlie its specific guarantees demonstrate that the rights to marital privacy and to marry and raise a family are of similar order and magnitude as the fundamental rights specifically protected" (p. 495). Some years later, gays and lesbians are explicitly denied the "sacred precinct" of the marital bedroom in *Bowers v. Hardwick*, 478 U.S. 186 (1986): "No connection between family, marriage or procreation on the one hand and homosexuality on the other has been demonstrated . . . by the respondent." See also Morris B. Kaplan, *Sexual Justice: Democratic Citizenship and the Politics of Desire* (New York: Routledge, 1997), chap. 1, for an excellent summation of the cases on privacy and how they have used the state interest in the protection of marriage to deny that gays and lesbians have privacy.

18. See for example Andrew Sullivan, *Virtually Normal: An Argument about Homosexuality* (New York: Alfred A. Knopf, 1995).

19. See for example Elizabeth Schneider's writing on privacy as a cover for abuse: "Particularity and Generality: Challenges of Feminist Theory and Practice in Work on Women-Abuse," *New York University Law Review* 67, no. 3 (June 1992).

20. Recent policy regarding gays in the military distinguishes speech from conduct. The infamous "don't ask, don't tell" policy authorizes the discharge of a military member who "has stated that he or she is a homosexual or bisexual or words to that effect" *unless* "the member has demonstrated that he or she is not a person who engages in, attempts to engage in, has a propensity to engage in, or intends to engage in homosexual acts" (10 U.S.C. Section 654[b][2]). Litigation surrounding the policy has for the most part reinforced this distinction. For example, in *Able v. United States,* the government argued that the military's policy was directed at "conduct" rather than speech, and therefore did not violate the First Amendment rights of gay and lesbian military personnel. For an excellent discussion of the politics of speech and conduct that informs these discussions, see Judith Butler, *Excitable Speech: A Politics of the Performative* (New York: Routledge, 1997), chap. 3.

21. Judith Butler has effectively shown how self-representations of sexual difference have historically been caught up within "the obligatory frame of reproductive heterosexuality." She writes that "acts and gestures, articulated and enacted desires create the illusion of an inte-

rior and organizing gender core, an illusion discursively maintained for the purposes of the regulation of sexuality" (p. 136). The imaginary domain is a means to dismantle the "gender core." Judith Butler, *Gender Trouble: Feminism and the Subversion of Identity* (New York: Routledge, 1990), see in particular "From Interiority to Gender Performatives," pp. 134–41.

22. The First Amendment reads: "Congress shall make no law respecting an establishment of religion or prohibiting free exercise thereof; or abridging the freedom of speech, or of the press, or the right of the people peaceably to assemble, and to petition the government for a redress of grievances."

23. Martin Luther, "95 Theses or Disputation on the Power and Efficacy of Indulgences (1517)," in *Luther's Works: Career of the Reformer,* ed. Harold J. Grimm and Helmut T. Lehmann (Philadelphia: Muhlenberg Press, 1957), 31:25. See also Hegel *Philosophy of Right,* pp. 86–104, and Rawls, *Political Liberalism* as to why freedom of religion has been the freedom on which many of our ideals of freedom of personality are modeled.

24. See Kaplan, *Sexual Justice,* chapter 4, for an excellent discussion of how the meaning of "queer" as a political identification has informed and shaped the manner in which the demand for the right to marry is defended.

25. The issue of freedom of intimate association was at stake in *Baehr v. Miike,* 65 USWL 2399 (Cir. Ct. Hawaii 1996).

26. See Wahneema Lubiano's discussion regarding the trope of the "welfare queen" in "Black Ladies, Welfare Queens, and State Minstrels: Ideological War by Narrative Means," in *Race-ing Justice, Engender-ing Power: Essays on Anita Hill, Clarence Thomas, and the Construction of Social Reality,* ed. Toni Morrison (New York: Pantheon Books, 1992), pp. 331–34. In addition, see Sanford M. Dornbusch and Myra H. Strober, eds., *Feminism: Children and the New Families* (New York: Guilford, 1988). From 1970 to 1984 there was a 500 percent increase in the number of never-married mothers. Moreover, poverty among single-parent families headed by minority women has worsened. In 1986, while the median income for a white female-headed household was $22,500, the median income for African American female-headed households was only $7,000 (see "Wealth in Black and White," Bureau of the Census, 1986).

27. See for example, Benjamin L. Weiss, "Single Mothers' Equal Right to Parent: A Fourteenth Amendment Defense against Forced-Labor Welfare 'Reform'" in *Law and Inequality* 15 no. 215 (Winter 1997); and Christopher Jencks, "The Hidden Paradox of Welfare Reform," *American Prospect* no. 32 (May–June 1997): 33.

28. California Governor Pete Wilson recently attempted to prohibit unmarried individuals from adopting children. Legislative efforts on the part of Assembly Democrats have prevented Wilson's proposals from going into effect; however, the existence of this kind of political debate reflects the degree to which gays and lesbians have not been guaranteed rights to set forth their own lives. Mark Vanzi, "Panel OKs Bill That Would Let Gay Couples Adopt: Legislation Would Undo Rules Backed by Wilson," *Los Angeles Times* (April 3, 1997), sec. A, p. 3.

29. See Phyllis Chesler, *Mothers on Trial: The Battle for Children and Custody* (San Diego, Calif.: McGraw-Hill, 1986).

30. 478 U.S. at p. 199 (Blackmun, J. dissenting).

31. Ibid.

32. Morris Kaplan, *Sexual Justice*, p. 224.

33. For example, during the recent debate in the New York State Senate regarding the elimination of rent regulations, Republican Majority Leader Joseph Bruno set forth legislation to deny succession rights to unmarried domestic partners. He subsequently withdrew his efforts; however, the debates highlighted the tenuous nature of housing rights for gays and lesbians.

34. See Judith Stacey, *In the Name of the Family: Rethinking Family Values in the Postmodern Age* (Boston: Beacon Press, 1996), chap. two.

35. Ibid.

36. See Stephanie Coontz, *The Way We Never Were: American Families and the Nostalgia Trap* (New York: Basic Books, 1992).

37. See for example, Allan David Bloom, *The Closing of the American Mind* (New York: Simon and Schuster, 1987).

38. See *Richenberg v. Perry*, 97 F.3d 256 (8th Cir. 1996). The court held that among other things, the "don't ask, don't tell" policy did not violate the First Amendment because speech may be used as evidence to establish elements of the crime: "A servicemember's statement that he or she is a homosexual evidences the propensity toward homosexual acts."

39. Alain Corbin, "Commercial Sexuality in Nineteenth Century France: A System of Images and Regulations," in Catherine Gallagher and Thomas Laqueur, eds., *The Making of the Modern Body* (Berkeley: University of California Press, 1987), p. 211.

40. Jana Matlock, *Scenes of Seduction: Prostitution, Hysteria, and Reading Difference in Nineteenth-Century France* (New York: Columbia University Press, 1994), p. 31.

41. Judith Walkowitz, *Prostitution and Victorian Society: Women, Class, and the State* (Cambridge: Cambridge University Press, 1980).

42. Ibid., p. 93.

43. Ibid., p. 143.

44. Quoted in Matlock, *Scenes of Seduction,* p. 113.

45. Judith Walkowitz, "Male Vice and Female Virtue: Feminism and the Politics of Prostitution in Nineteenth-Century Britain," in *Powers of Desire: The Politics of Sexuality,* ed. Ann Snitow, Christine Stansell, and Sharon Thompason (New York: Monthly Review Press, 1983), p. 256.

46. Some feminist activists in nineteenth-century Western Europe sought out a sexual utopia as a means to end women's subjugation. For example, nineteenth-century feminist Olive Schreiner wrote, "Always in our dreams we hear the turn of the key that shall close the door of the last brothel; the clink of the last coin that pays for the body and soul of a woman; the falling of the last wall that encloses artificially the activity of woman and divides her from man; always we picture the love of the sexes as once a dull, slow-creeping worm; then a torpid, earthy chrysalis; at last the full-winged insect, glorious in the sunshine of the future" (quoted in Elaine Showalter, *Sexual Anarchy: Gender and Culture at the Fin de Siècle* [New York: Penguin Books, 1990], p. 56). In France, utopian Charles Fourier had a significant impact on sexual radicals. See Joan Wallach Scott, *Only Paradoxes to Offer: French Feminism and the Rights of Man* (Cambridge: Harvard University Press, 1996), pp. 57, 62. For more recent voices reflecting this perspective, see Ellen Willis, "Feminism, Moralism, and Pornography" and Joan Nestle, "My Mother Liked to Fuck," in *Powers of Desire: The Politics of Sexuality,* ed. Ann Snitow, Christine Stansell, and Sharon Thompson (New York: Monthly Review Press, 1983).

47. See, for example, Kathleen Barry, *Female Sexual Slavery* (New York: New York University Press, 1979).

48. Catharine A. Mackinnon, *Feminism Unmodified: Discourse on Life and Law* (Cambridge: Harvard University Press, 1987).

49. Drucilla Cornell, *The Imaginary Domain* (New York: Routledge, 1995).

50. Interview with Ona Zee Wiggers, on file with the author, p. 5.

51. Ibid.

52. Ibid.

53. Andrea Dworkin and Catharine A. MacKinnon, *Pornography and Civil Rights: A New Day for Women's Equality* (self-published, 1988).

54. Rosalind Pollack Petchesky, "The Body as Property: A Feminist Re-vision," in *Conceiving the New World Order: The Global Politics of Reproduction,* ed. Faye D. Ginsburg and Rayna Rapp (Berkeley: University of California Press, 1995). Petchesky argues that this intertwinement of making a claim to oneself by joining in common struggles for freedom is frequently found at the heart of slave narratives. In her reading of *Incidents in the Life of a Slave Girl,* Petchesky insists that "the self emerges as ethical subject but always embedded in the communal context of the suffering of other slaves and their efforts to achieve freedom. It is never just the story of an 'individual' and in this way contrasts . . . with the male-heroic structure of Frederick Douglass' *Narrative*" (p. 399).

55. In "Why We Are All Liberals," Dworkin succinctly describes the "discontinuity thesis" as follows:

> The most influential liberal theories insist on a methodological discontinuity between what they describe as the right (which in a political context means considerations of justice) and the good (which includes ethical and other non-moral values). Liberal theory aims at a theory of justice that is independent of any comprehensive ethical system, and can therefore be accepted by all—or almost all sectors in an ethically pluralistic society. (paper presented at the Program for the Study of Law, Philosophy, and Social Theory, New York University School of Law, Fall 1995), p. 23

56. Ronald Dworkin, *Taking Rights Seriously* (Cambridge: Harvard University Press, 1977). Dworkin distinguishes between "treatment as an equal" and "equal treatment." The former is fundamental, consisting of the right to be treated with respect and concern equal to anyone else. Equal treatment, in contrast, is the equal right to an opportunity, resource, or burden.

57. I first discussed the degradation prohibition in *The Imaginary Domain,* introduction and chap. 3.

58. For my discussion of how and why laws against sexual harassment can be defended consistently with the protection of the imaginary domain, see *The Imaginary Domain,* chap. 4.

59. In 1995, the U.S. Supreme Court unanimously upheld the exclusion of the Irish American Gay, Lesbian, and Bisexual Group of Boston (GLIB) from Boston's annual St. Patrick's Day Parade. The Court ruled that the parade organizers had a First Amendment right to exclude groups whose message they disagreed with (115 S.Ct. 2338 [1995]). In turn, this ruling had effects on Gay Pride Parades: a group calling themselves "Normal People" commenced a lawsuit seeking inclusion in the 1995 San Diego Gay Pride Parade. When the Supreme Court ruling came down, they dropped their lawsuit. I argue that the government should not enter into these disputes to begin with. The degradation principle that I have outlined, however, would apply in the San Diego case, because, simply by denoting themselves "normal" this group "grades down" gays and lesbians as "abnormal."

The litigation surrounding defining "Irishness" has continued without satisfactory outcomes. The New York Irish Lesbian and Gay Organization (ILGO) was excluded from parades in past years. So in 1996, ILGO applied for a permit to hold its own parade, which was to take place before the official New York City St. Patrick's Day Parade. The city denied them a permit. ILGO sued the city and lost (*ILGO v. Giuliani* WL 91633 [S.D.N.Y., March 4, 1996]). The District Judge found that the city would have denied a second permit for any applicant because of logistical problems and therefore concluded that ILGO had not been discriminated against.

60. As I have argued elsewhere, I am unconvinced that it would be politically desirable to try to overcome value pluralism. See Cornell, "Pragmatism, Recollective Imagination, and Transformative Legal Interpretation," in *Transformations* (New York: Routledge, 1993).

61. See Dworkin, "Do Liberty and Equality Conflict?" p. 3, (unpublished manuscript on file with author). To quote Dworkin,

The second principle insists that this special relationship is best understood as one of special responsibility, that living is an assignment we can execute well or badly. The assignment includes an intellectual challenge to live out a conception of what makes a life successful, that is personal in the sense that the agent has embraced it, rather than political in the sense that it has been thrust upon him. Living well, on this view requires both personal commitment and a social environment in which commitment is both encouraged and respected.

62. See Hegel, *Philosophy of Right,* pp. 33–35.

63. For a longer discussion of the imaginary domain and the Western concept of the individual, see chapter 6.

64. Dworkin, "The Roots of Justice," pp. 28–29, unpublished manuscript on file with author.

65. See Charles Taylor, "The Politics of Recognition," in *Multiculturalism: Examining the Politics of Recognition,* ed. Amy Gutmann (Princeton: Princeton University Press, 1994). Taylor explains:

> For Kant, whose use of the term *dignity* was one of the earliest influential evocations of the idea, what commanded respect in us was our status as rational agents, capable of directing our lives through principles. Something like this has been the basis for our intuitions of equal dignity ever since, though the detailed definition of it may have been changed.
>
> Thus, what is picked out as of worth here is a *universal human potential,* a capacity that all humans share. This potential, rather than anything a person may have made of it, is what ensures that each person deserves respect. Indeed, our sense of the importance of potentiality reaches so far that we extend this protection even to people who through some circumstance that has befallen them are incapable of realizing their potential in the normal way—handicapped people, or those in a coma, for instance. (p. 41)

66. Jürgen Habermas has eloquently argued that we must thematize both the vulnerability of modern human identity and discover how it can be normatively reconstructed in a uniquely modern conception of personhood. While I do not accept Habermas's own construction of generic moral identity, I agree with him that we must thematize the vulnerability of individuation, a political and social problem that haunts modernity, and also defend a normative reconstruction of the person. See Jürgen Habermas, *Between Facts and Norms: Contribution to a Discourse Theory of Law and Democracy* (Boston: MIT Press, 1997), chaps. 1 and 2.

67. Kaplan, *Sexual Justice,* chap. 2.

CHAPTER THREE

1. *Geduldig v. Aiello,* 417 U.S. 484 (1974). Congress rarely exercises its constitutional power to overrule a Supreme Court decision. But in this case, it did.

2. Ibid.

3. Ibid.

4. See, for example, Sue Headlee and Margery Elfin, *The Cost of Being Female* (Westport, Conn.: Praeger, 1996) for a comprehensive discussion on women's continuing disadvantage in the workplace, in politics, and in receiving adequate education and health care.

5. See, for example, Marjorie Jacobson, "Pregnancy and Employment: Three Approaches to Equal Opportunity," *Boston University Law Review* 68 (November 1988): 1019–45.

6. Cynthia R. Daniels, *At Women's Expense: State Power and the Politics of Fetal Rights* (Cambridge: Harvard University Press, 1993), chap. 3. See also C. Daniels, M. Paul, and R. Rosofsky, "Family, Work, and Health Survey," Massachusetts Department of Health and University of Massachusetts Medical Center, 1985.

7. Daniels, "The Politics of Vengeance: The Case of Jennifer Johnson," in *At Women's Expense,* chap. 4.

8. Thomas Nagel, "Justice and Nature" *Oxford Journal of Legal Studies* 17 (1997): 304.

9. See Joan Wallach Scott, *Only Paradoxes to Offer: French Feminism and the Rights of Man* (Cambridge: Harvard University Press, 1996), pp. 58–70. See also Susan Moller Okin's discussion of how political theorists of the "tradition" have justified putting sexual difference and family organization beyond the reach of political philosophy, in "The Family: Beyond Justice?" in Okin, *Justice, Gender, and the Family* (New York: Basic Books, 1989), chap. 2.

10. Okin, *Justice, Gender, and the Family,* chap. 2.

11. Scott, *Only Paradoxes to Offer,* pp. 58–70.

12. Sigmund Freud, *The Complete Introductory Lectures on Psychoanalysis: Femininity* (New York: W. W. Norton, 1966).

13. For a summary of this disagreement and the contending positions as to how to justify abortion, see Cornell, *The Imaginary Domain* (New York: Routledge, 1995), chap. 2.

14. Wendy W. Williams, "Equality's Riddle: Pregnancy and the

Equal Treatment/Special Treatment Debate," in *Feminist Legal Theory,* ed. D. Kelly Weisberg (Philadelphia: Temple University Press, 1993). Williams argued that women could not have it both ways—they could not demand to be considered like men all the while demanding that pregnancy be deemed special.

15. Robin West, *Narrative, Authority, and Law* (Ann Arbor: University of Michigan Press, 1993), chap. 5.

16. See, for example, Sandra Harding and Merrill B. Hintikka, *Discovering Reality: Feminist Perspectives on Epistemology, Metaphysics, Methodology, and the Philosophy of Subject* (Dordrecht: D. Reidel, 1983); Allison Yagger and Susan Bordo, eds., *Gender/Body/Knowledge: Feminist Reconstructions of Being and Knowing* (New Brunswick, N.J.: Rutgers University Press, 1989).

17. West, *Narrative, Authority, and Law;* see also Carol Gilligan, *In a Different Voice: Psychological Theory and Women's Development* (Cambridge: Harvard University Press, 1982); and Carol Smart, *Feminism and the Power of Law* (New York: Routledge, 1989).

18. Sara Ruddick, *Maternal Thinking* (Boston: Beacon Press, 1989).

19. Sherry B. Ortner, *Making Gender: The Politics and Erotics of Culture* (Boston: Beacon Press, 1996); see particularly chap. 4, "Rank and Gender," and chap. 6, "Gender Hegemonies."

20. Ortner, *Making Gender.*

21. See Michele Rosaldo's article in which she disagrees with her earlier position that the universal relegation of women to the domestic realm is either universal or can be simplistically used to explain gender hierarchy. Rosaldo, "Women, Culture, and Society: A Theoretical Overview," in *Women, Culture and Society,* ed. Michele Rosaldo and Louise Lamphere (Stanford, Calif.: Stanford University Press, 1974).

22. Judith Butler, *Gender Trouble: Feminism and the Subversion of Identity* (New York: Routledge, 1990).

23. Ibid. See in particular, "Identity, Sex, and the Metaphysics of Substance," pp. 16–25.

24. Many feminists have felt that we need a subject of woman in order to have feminism and have refuted Butler's work for undoing the subject. Clearly, I agree with Butler.

25. See Cynthia Daniels's excellent discussion in *At Women's Expense,* chap. 1, "Fetal Animation: The Political and Cultural Emer-

gence of Fetal Rights." Hereafter, citations to Daniels's work are denoted by page number within the text.

26. See Cornell, *The Imaginary Domain.*

27. Daniels, *At Women's Expense,* p. 63.

28. "Johnson Controls Company Document E-3/90," quoted in Daniels, *At Women's Expense,* p. 63.

29. "Brief Amicus Curiae of the American Civil Liberties Union, et al.," submitted in *UAW v. Johnson Controls,* No. 89–1215 (1990), pp. A-37–38, quoted in Daniels, *At Women's Expense,* 87–88.

30. See Cynthia Daniels's excellent analysis of the narratives of the women affected by Johnson Controls's policy in *At Women's Expense,* pp. 86–87.

31. OSHA lead guidelines, quoted in Daniels, *At Women's Expense,* p. 76.

32. See also Cornell, *The Imaginary Domain,* chap. 2, where I argued that when a pregnant woman is imagined solely as a conduit or an environment for the fetus, the seriousness of the wrong in the denial of the right to abortion is "disappeared."

33. Seventh Circuit Court of Appeals decision quoted in Daniels, *At Women's Expense,* p. 78.

34. See Daniels's discussion regarding *Muller v. Oregon* 208 U.S. 412 (1908), in *At Women's Expense,* p. 60.

35. Nancy F. Cott, *The Grounding of Modern Feminism* (New Haven, Conn.: Yale University Press, 1987), chap. 4.

36. Daniels, *At Women's Expense,* p. 93.

37. Ibid., pp. 123–26.

38. bell hooks, *Sisters of Yam* (Boston: South End Press, 1993), p. 72.

39. Marie Anna Jaimes Guerrero, "Civil Rights versus Sovereignty: Native American Women in Life and Land Struggles," in *Feminist Genealogies, Colonial Legacies, Democratic Futures,* ed. M. Jacqui Alexander and Chandra Talpade Mohanty (New York: Routledge, 1997), pp. 101–24.

40. Daniels, *At Women's Expense,* p. 97.

41. hooks, *Sisters of Yam,* p. 68.

42. Nagel suggests that, in general, inequalities could be the result of physical disabilities, differences in talent, or gender. But here, in my answer to Nagel, I am going to address only sexual difference. My reason for so focusing is because our sexuate being is most certainly

not a disadvantage or a horrifying disability, caused by a defective gene—an example Nagel uses to illustrate what he means by limiting the scope of justice. He does not question in his example the need to do something to help those stricken, but does question whether or not the measures to be taken can be justified by an appeal to justice. But our sexual difference, even when understood as gender, is not reducible to natural disability or oppression by male domination—as I have argued at great length elsewhere. Genetically caused illness of course gives form to a person. But maximum liberty to affirm, re-present, and re-imagine oneself is not at stake here, although I do not want in any way to disparage the role of the imagination in a person's effort to grapple with illness. Still, coming to terms with illness and playing with, representing, and affirming one's "sex" are different.

No matter what role nature may play in both, being engendered as a woman and having a gene that predisposes you to a deadly illness are simply not the same thing. Sex, for many people, is one of the greatest sources of joy and ecstasy in their lives, as it is no doubt also a source of great suffering. Playing with our sex to the limits of our dreams is pleasure par excellence in a way that illness can never be.

43. Thomas Nagel, "Justice and Nature," p. 305. Hereafter, page references to this work appear parenthetically in the text.

44. Ibid., p. 306. Nagel writes:

> We can distinguish deontological conceptions of justice according to the way they assign systematic influences on how people fare under a social system to three categories: the good, the bad, and the neutral— depending on whether the influence legitimates, delegitimates or does not affect the legitimacy of the process in question. Minimalist conceptions put much more into the neutral category. The idea is that a great deal about human life has to be regarded as part of the given, the luck of the draw, the arbitrary but morally neutral background that forms the starting point from which moral evaluation can then proceed. Free choice legitimates, and coercion or discrimination delegitimates, but a great deal else is fate or luck—the given, from a moral point of view—so that the space for justice or injustice in the operation of society is relatively small, including only certain kinds of direct human causation. (p. 313)

45. For a summary of the division of labor in heterosexual households, see Arlie Hochschild, *The Second Shift: Working Parents and the Revolution at Home* (New York: Viking Press, 1989).

46. Nagel, "Justice and Nature," p. 319.

47. John Rawls, *A Theory of Justice* (Cambridge: Harvard University Press, 1971), p. 586.

48. One example of these inequalities has come to be called the "difference principle."

49. Kant, *Groundwork of the Metaphysics of Morals* (New York: Harper and Row, 1956), p. 127. If the principles of justice are to aspire to represent what human beings would agree to in the Kingdom of Ends, then the idea of fairness is not easily removed from the original position, which for Rawls is the perspective of eternity within this world that rational persons can adopt. I do not want to say more about this here, because this reading clearly would lead to my agreement with Rawls's "in justice as fairness, men share each other's fate" (*A Theory of Justice,* p. 102)—and I would add, as Nagel seems to doubt, life's glories.

50. Nagel, "Justice and Nature," p. 319.

51. See Amartya Sen, *Inequality Reexamined* (Cambridge: Harvard University Press, 1992); and Ronald Dworkin "Why We Are All Liberals" (paper presented at the Program for the Study of Law, Philosophy, and Social Theory, New York University School of Law, Fall 1995). Both make freedom integral to their theory of equality, and so either of their theories would be consistent with my own emphasis on freedom.

52. Okin argues that

> What seems already to be indicated in these studies, despite their incompleteness so far, is that *in a gender structured society,* there is such a thing as the distinct standpoint of women, and that this standpoint cannot be adequately taken into account by male philosophers doing the theoretical equivalent of the elderly male justices. The notion of the standpoint of women, while not without its problems, suggests that a fully human moral or political theory can be developed only with the full participation of both sexes. (*Justice, Gender, and Society* pp. 106–7)

For elaboration as to why I disagree with her on this point see Cornell, *The Imaginary Domain,* introduction.

53. John Rawls, introduction, *Political Liberalism* (New York: Columbia University Press, 1993), p. xli.

54. Susan Moller Okin, "Inequalities between the Sexes in Differ-

ent Contexts," in *Women, Culture, and Development*, ed. Martha Nussbaum and Jonathan Glover (Oxford: Clarendon Press, 1995), p. 275 n. 2.

55. See generally M. Jacqui Alexander, "Erotic Autonomy as a Politics of Decolonization: An Anatomy of Feminist and State Practices in the Bahamas Tourist Industry" in *Feminist Genealogies, Colonial Legacies, Democratic Futures*, ed. Alexander and Chandra Talpade Mohanty (New York: Routledge, 1996).

56. Ruth Anna Putnam, "Why Not a Feminist Theory of Justice?" in *Women, Culture, and Development: A Study of Human Capabilities*, ed. Martha Nussbaum and Jonathan Glover (Oxford: Clarendon Press, 1995).

57. Okin, *Justice, Gender, and the Family*, p. 183, emphasis in original.

58. Ibid., pp. 180–81, emphasis in original.

CHAPTER FOUR

1. See generally the work of Lorraine Dusky.

2. Catharine A. MacKinnon, *Toward a Feminist Theory of the State* (Cambridge: Harvard University Press, 1989).

3. Diana Jean Schemo, "The Baby Trail: A Special Report; Adoptions in Paraguay: Mothers Cry Theft," *New York Times* (March 19, 1996), sec. A, p. 1.

4. Lorraine Dusky, *Birthmark* (New York: M. Evans, 1979).

5. I borrow this phrase from Carol Stack's well-known book. Stack's ethnographic study of African American families showed that "kin" was a much broader concept than that which has dominated the white middle-class community. Stack's ethnographic work showed that biological ties do not define the parameters of the family. See Carol Stack, *All Our Kin: Strategies for Survival in a Black Community* (New York: Harper and Row, 1974).

6. Ibid.

7. See Susan Klibanoff and Elton Klibanoff, *Let's Talk about Adoption* (Boston: Little, Brown, 1973), chap. 16.

8. Georg W. F. Hegel, *The Philosophy of Right*, trans. T. M. Knox (Oxford: Oxford University Press, 1967).

9. Hegel, "The Family," in *The Philosophy of Right*, pp. 110–22.

10. Please refer to chapter 2 for what I mean by "social life."

11. Dorothy Roberts, "The Genetic Tie," *University of Chicago Law Review* 62, no. 1 (Winter 1995).

12. See Drucilla Cornell, *Beyond Accommodation: Ethical Feminism, Deconstruction, and the Law* (New York: Routledge, 1991).

13. E. Valentine Daniel, *Charred Lullabies: Chapters in an Anthropology of Violence* (Princeton: Princeton University Press, 1996).

14. Luce Irigaray, *I Love to You: Sketch for a Possible Felicity within History,* trans. Alison Martin (New York: Routledge, 1996), p. 47.

15. Carol Austin, "Latent Tendencies and Covert Acts," in *The Adoption Reader: Birth Mothers, Adoptive Mothers, and Adopted Daughters Tell Their Stories,* ed. Susan Wadia-Ellis (Seattle, Wash.: Seal Press, 1995).

16. The imposition of this second-class citizenship itself needs to be reformed in the name of equality.

17. Roberts, "The Genetic Tie."

18. See generally the work of M. Jacqui Alexander.

19. M. Jacqui Alexander, "Erotic Autonomy as a Politics of Decolonization: An Anatomy of Feminist and State Practice in the Bahamas Tourist Economy," in *Feminist Genealogies, Colonial Legacies, Democratic Futures,* ed. M. Jacqui Alexander and Chandra Talpade Mohanty (New York: Routledge, 1997) pp. 76–77.

20. M. Jacqui Alexander, "Not (Any)Body Can Be a Citizen: The Politics of Law, Sexuality, and Postcoloniality in Trinidad and Tobago and the Bahamas," *Feminist Review* no. 48 (Autumn 1994).

21. Alexander, "Erotic Autonomy," p. 84.

22. Martha Fineman, *The Neutered Mother, the Sexual Family, and Other Twentieth-Century Tragedies* (New York: Routledge, 1995), p. 5.

23. The outcomes of custody battles involving gay and lesbian co-parents vary greatly state to state and according to the individual judge who hears the case. For example, in *McGuffin v. Overton* 542 N.W.2d 288 (Mich. Ct. App. 1995), the court held that the lesbian partner of a deceased mother lacked standing to challenge the father's custody petitions. The deceased mother had executed a will making her partner the guardian of the children, while the father was twenty thousand dollars in arrears in child support. The court concluded that

Michigan law and case law dictated against permitting the partner to proceed with a petition for guardianship. In *Guardianship of Aston H. v. Sofia D.*, 635 N.Y.S.2d. 418 (N.Y. Family Court, 1995), however, the court awarded custody to the lesbian life partner of the deceased mother, ruling that this was in the best interest of the child. See also "Lesbian and Gay Men Seeking Custody and Visitation: An Overview of the State of the Law" (New York: Lambda Legal Defense and Education Fund, 1996).

24. Amartya Sen, *Inequality Reexamined* (Cambridge: Harvard University Press, 1992).

25. Sigmund Freud, "On Narcissism," in *The Standard Edition of the Complete Psychological Works of Sigmund Freud*, trans. James Strachey (London: Hogarth Press, 1957).

26. Excerpts from the poems of Sappho, trans. Emma Bianchi, unpublished manuscript on file with author.

27. Alexander, "Erotic Autonomy" p. 99.

28. Irigaray, *Thinking the Difference: For a Peaceful Revolution*, trans. Karin Montin (New York: Routledge, 1994), p. 111.

29. Sheila Rowbotham, quoted in Mackinnon, *Toward a Feminist Theory of the State*, p. 124.

30. Irigaray, *Thinking the Difference*, p. 63.

31. Luce Irigaray, *I Love to You: Sketch of a Possible Felicity in History*, trans. Alison Martin (New York: Routledge, 1994), pp. 132–33.

32. Ursula K. Le Guin, *Four Ways to Forgiveness* (New York: Harper Collins, 1995), p. 280.

33. Judith Stacey, *In the Name of the Family: Rethinking Family Values in the Postmodern Age* (Boston: Beacon Press, 1996).

34. See testimony in *Baehr v. Miike*, WL 694235 (Hawai'i Cir.Ct. 1996).

35. Stacey, *In the Name of the Family*, chap. 5. See also Linnea Due, *Joining the Tribe: Growing Up Gay and Lesbian in the Nineties* (New York: Doubleday, 1996).

36. Stacey, *In the Name of the Family*; Due, *Joining the Tribe*.

37. See Morris Kaplan, *Sexual Justice* (New York: Routledge, 1997), chap. 7.

38. Maggie Gallagher, *The Abolition of Marriage: How We Destroy Lasting Love* (Washington, D.C.: Regnery Publishing, 1996).

39. Same-sex parenting seems incomprehensible only in a culture that imposes heterosexuality as the norm. Consider sociologist David Eggeben's testimony in *Baehr v. Miike:* "'same-sex marriages where children [are] involved is by definition a step parent relationship' because there is one parent who is not the biological parent of the child" (p. 7).

40. Lorraine Dusky, "The Daughter I Gave Away," *Newsweek* (March 30, 1992).

41. Lorraine Dusky, "Brave New Babies?" in *Newsweek* (December 6, 1982), p. 30. The question of whether or not surrogacy should be outlawed deeply divided the feminist movement. Some feminists argued that surrogacy should be outlawed altogether, as an illegitimate aberration of the integral person. Others agreed that it should not be banished altogether, but regulated so that surrogates would not be so easily exploited. Others have argued against such regulation because it still involves the state in morally accepting surrogacy. Instead, surrogacy should remain completely deregulated. Others have insisted that in surrogacy there is a contract like any other but that we should not resort to the remedy of specific performance, a remedy that is disfavored in contract law.

The problem of surrogacy has intensified because such arrangements often end in custody fights. In such battles, the question of the surrogate mother's rights and the sperm donor's rights demand to be resolved. In the case of Mary Jo Whitehead, a surrogate who wanted desperately to keep her baby, her surrogacy was used in the custody case as evidence that she was a bad mother. What kind of mother would initially agree to selling her baby? Ultimately, the biological father, Joseph Stern, and his wife, Betsy, were given custody of the baby. The standards for so deciding were those that have often favored men with wives over single mothers in custody disputes (see Phyllis Chesler, *Mothers on Trial: The Battle for Children and Custody* [San Diego, Calif.: McGraw-Hill, 1986]).

Some feminists argued that it should never have become a custody battle. It became such a battle only because the contract to sell the baby was not upheld in the New Jersey Supreme Court. If the contract was illegal, and Joseph Stern became a father only by contract, then he had no rights to his child simply because of his biological connection. The issue that haunted these debates was once again the question of the legal status of mothers. For example, Phyllis Chesler argued that what was denied Mary Jo Whitehead once she had changed her mind was a violent patriarchal breaking of the "sacred bond" of motherhood (See *The Sacred Bond: The Legacy of Baby M* [New York: Random House, 1988]).

Things got even more difficult when the battle was not between a biological mother and a biological father, but between a gestational mother and a biological mother. In *Anna J. v. Mark C.*, 286 Cal. Rptr. 369 (Cal. App. 1991), review granted, 822 p. 2d. 1317 (Cal. 1992), an African American woman was hired by a white couple to bear their child. After the birth, the gestational mother wanted to keep the child. The court decided in favor of genetics, saying that it was genetics, and not gestational history, that was formative to identity. The court's rhetoric mimics Dusky.

How do we decide cases when by all conventional meanings of the word, there are two mothers? Here we seem inevitably plunged into subtle judgments about what biological act is more important in the constitution of mothering. Rather than making law the determinant of whether gestation is more important than biological lineage in deciding who is the "real" mother, I would draw a simple, bright line: persons cannot be sold outright; that is slavery. An adult person can alleviate a part of herself as a representation of who she is. Many of us may view this as a bad moral judgment on the part of the individual who makes it. But a baby cannot alleviate a part of itself because she is not yet capable of making that judgment. A baby cannot represent itself. Entry into the moral community at birth means at least two things: you cannot be physically violated, let alone killed, and you cannot be sold.

Thus, the parent who does not come into its relationship to the child by buying it gets to keep the child. Contracts to sell children cannot be enforced. But at the same time, surrogacy should be allowed as one way in which people make a family.

42. Shulamith Firestone, *The Dialectic of Sex* (New York: William Morrow, 1970), chap. 10.

43. Simone de Beauvoir, *The Second Sex,* trans. H. M. Parshley (New York: Random House, 1974), p. 774.

44. See generally Sara Ruddick, *Maternal Thinking* (Boston: Beacon Press, 1989).

45. It is crucial to note that families have historically been sites of abuse and pain. See Richard J. Gelles, *Family Violence* (Newbury Park, Calif.: Sage Publishers, 1987); and Raoul Felder and Barbara Victor, *Getting Away with Murder* (New York: Simon and Schuster, 1996).

CHAPTER FIVE

1. David Blankenhorn, *Fatherless America: Confronting Our Most Urgent Social Problem* (New York: Basic Books, 1995).

2. I borrow this phrase from Martha Fineman. See her discussion of fathers and how their rights and responsibilities should be reenvisioned. Fineman, *The Neutered Mother, the Sexual Family and Other Twentieth-Century Tragedies* (New York: Routledge, 1995).

3. William Safire quoted in Fineman, *The Neutered Mother*, p. 203.

4. Ibid.

5. See generally David Popenoe, *Life without Father* (New York: Martin Kessler Books, 1996); Christopher Harding, *Wingspan: Inside the Men's Movement* (New York: St. Martin's Press, 1992); and Michael L. Schwalbe, *Unlocking the Iron Cage: The Men's Movement, Gender Politics, and American Culture* (New York: Oxford University Press, 1996).

6. Nancy Chodorow, *The Reproduction of Mothering: Psychoanalysis and the Sociology of Gender* (Berkeley: University of California Press, 1978); and *Femininities, Masculinities, Sexualities: Freud and Beyond* (Lexington: University of Kentucky Press, 1994).

7. Jessica Benjamin, *The Bonds of Love: Psychoanalysis, Feminism, and the Problem of Domination* (New York: Pantheon Books, 1980). See also Jessica Benjamin, *Like Subjects, Love Objects: Essays on Recognition and Sexual Difference* (New Haven, Conn.: Yale University Press, 1995).

8. Benjamin, *Bonds of Love; Like Subjects*.

9. See generally Chodorow, *Femininities, Masculinities, Sexualities*.

10. Feminists have effectively demonstrated that women lose under the imposition of the formal equality presupposed by joint custody. Due to continuing economic discrimination against women, men have often effectively claimed that they should be given sole custody be-

cause the woman has become unstable under the strain of trying to go it alone. Often, changed economic circumstances make it desirable for the woman to move to a part of the country where she can more easily survive on whatever money she can make plus child support. Yet under a joint custody arrangement attempts at re-location can be effectively blocked. Some feminists have concluded that the reality has been so detrimental to women that we should return to the legal presumption of custody to the mother. Others have gone beyond that, advocating that we rethink the very idea of the sexual family and the role men play in it. See Martha Fineman, *The Neutered Mother*. Fineman's conclusions that male lovers should no longer be considered part of the parental family unit unless they can show they are Mothers, would be evidence for the fathers' movement that some feminists at least do want to end the role of fathers in the family. I offer an alternative feminist reform of family law that does not advocate the exclusion of male husbands and lovers from the family. See Fineman for a succinct analysis of the debate over the move to joint custody among feminists, in part 2, pp. 66–87.

11. Internal membership report of the United Auto Workers on the state of the auto industry in the United States, 1995.

12. For the purposes of confidentiality, all names in the following stories have been changed.

13. Economic Policy Institute, *The State of Working America* (Armonk, N.Y.: M. E. Sharpe, 1990–91).

14. Carol Stack and Katherine Newman. "Finding Work in the Inner City: How Hard Is It Now?" *Russell Foundation Working Papers* (1994): 76.

15. V. L. Burt et al. "Trends in the Prevention, Awareness, Treatment and Control of Hypertension in Adult U.S. Populations," *Hypertension* 26:60–69.

16. Fineman, *The Neutered Mother,* p. 204.

17. See generally Studs Terkel, *Working* (New York: Pantheon Books, 1974).

18. I borrow the phrase that heads this section from the title of Stanley Fish's book *There's No Such Thing as Free Speech and It's a Good Thing Too* (New York: Oxford University Press, 1994).

19. Jacques Lacan, *Ecrits,* trans. Alan Sheridan (New York: W. W. Norton, 1977), chap. 4.

20. Arthur Miller, *Death of a Salesman* (New York: Viking Press, 1949); David Mamet, *Glengarry Glen Ross* (New York: Grove Press, 1983).

21. I borrow this phrase created by Nikol Alexander in our discussions about our essay. Cornell and Alexander, "Dismissed or Banished: A Testament to the Reasonableness of the O. J. Simpson Jury," in *Birth of a Nation'hood,* ed. Toni Morrison and Claudia Schaeffer (New York: Pantheon Books, 1997).

22. Thomas Hobbes, "Human Nature," in *The Collected Works of Thomas Hobbes,* ed. Sir William Molesworth (London: Routledge/Thoemmes Press, 1992), 4:1–76.

23. Judith Stacey, *In the Name of the Family: Rethinking Family Values in the Postmodern Age* (Boston: Beacon Press, 1996).

24. Maggie Gallagher, *The Abolition of Marriage: How We Destroy Lasting Love,* (Washington, D.C.: Regnery Publishing, 1996).

Chapter Six

1. Elizabeth Friedman, "Women's Human Rights: The Emergence of a Movement," in *Women's Rights, Human Rights: International Feminist Perspectives,* ed. Julie Peters and Andrea Wolper (New York: Routledge, 1995).

2. Ibid.

3. L. Amede Obiora, "Bridges and Barricades: Rethinking Polemics and Intransigence in the Campaign against Female Circumcision," *Case Western Reserve Law Review* 47 (Winter 1997): 275.

4. I put "first world" in quotation marks to indicate the obvious hierarchy that exists in the enunciation of first, second, third, etc.

5. Joseph Conrad, *The Heart of Darkness*, 1902.

6. John Rawls, "The Law of Peoples," Program for the Study of Law, Philosophy, and Social Theory, 1993.

7. Ibid., p. 26.

8. Ibid.

9. See generally Peters and Wolper, *Women's Rights, Human Rights.*

10. Ruth Anna Putnam, "Why Not a Feminist Theory of Justice?" in *Women, Culture, and Development: A Study of Human Capabilities,* ed. Martha Nussbaum and Jonathan Glover (Oxford: Clarendon Press, 1995).

11. See, for example, M. Jacqui Alexander and Chandra Talpade Mohanty, "Introduction: Genealogies, Legacies, Movements," in *Feminist Genealogies, Colonial Legacies, Democratic Futures* (New York: Routledge, 1997), xiii.

12. M. Jacqui Alexander, "Erotic Autonomy as a Politics of Decolonization," in Alexander and Mohanty, *Feminist Genealogies*.

13. See Susan Moller Okin for an example of common assumptions about third world women's inability to demand sexual freedom, in Okin, "Inequalities between the Sexes in Different Cultural Contexts," in Nussbaum and Glover, *Women, Culture and Development*. In addition, see my discussion of Okin's work in chapter 3.

14. I put *socialism* in quotation marks because I do not accept that any of the horrifying political practices and institutions of the Soviet Union were necessarily socialist. For some thinkers, such as Michel Foucault, following Nietzsche, putting *socialism* in quotation marks to distinguish between the ideals associated with socialism and the reality of its purported institutionalization simply expresses the melancholia of Western leftists. I disagree. Whether or not the Soviet Union ever was best described as a socialist or capitalist economy continues to be a question worth asking as part of the political effort to rethink what remain of the valid socialist ideals. See "Power and Strategies" in *Power/Knowledge: Selected Interviews and Other Writings, 1972–1977,* ed., trans. Colin Gordon (New York: Pantheon Books, 1980), p. 136.

15. Frantz Fanon, *The Wretched of the Earth,* trans. Constance Farrington (New York: Grove Press, 1963), p. 245.

16. Ibid.

17. Akram Mirhosseini, "After the Revolution: Violations of Women's Human Rights in Iran," in Peters and Wolper, *Women's Rights, Human Rights.*

18. Alexander and Mohanty, introduction to *Feminist Genealogies.*

19. Alexander, "Erotic Autonomy," p. 67.

20. Please refer to chapter 4 for further discussion of parenting as independent of marriage.

21. Alexander, "Erotic Autonomy," p. 82.

22. See chapter 3.

23. Charles Taylor has succinctly described the subjective aspect of right as it has been part of Western democratic institutions:

Everywhere it is wrong to take human life, at least under certain circumstances and for certain categories of persons. Wrong is the opposite of right, and so this is in some sense in play here.

But a quite difference sense of the word is invoked when we start to use the definite or indefinite articles or to put it in the plural and speak of "a right" or "rights" or when we start to attribute these to persons and speak of your rights or my rights. This is to introduce what has been called "subjective rights." Instead of saying that it is wrong to kill me, we begin to say that I have a right to life. The two formulations are not equivalent in all respects, because in the latter case the immunity or liberty is considered the property of someone. It is no longer just an element of the law that stands over and between all of us equally. That I have a right to life says more than that you shouldn't kill me. It gives me some control over this immunity. A right is something that in principle I can waive. It is also something I have a role in enforcing. ("A World Consensus on Human Rights?" *Dissent* [Summer 1996]: 16).

24. Gloria Wekker, "One Finger Does Not Drink Okra Soup: Afro-Surinamese Women and Critical Agency" in Alexander and Mohanty, *Feminist Genealogies*, p. 334. Hereafter, page references to this work appear parenthetically in the text.

25. See generally Alexander and Mohanty, *Feminist Genealogies*.

26. John Rawls, *Political Liberalism* (New York: Columbia University Press, 1993).

27. Taylor, "A World Consensus on Human Rights?"

28. See, for example, Mirhosseini, "After the Revolution"; and Ann Elizabeth Mayer, "Cultural Particularism as a Bar to Women's Rights: Reflections on the Middle Eastern Experience," in Peters and Wolper *Women's Rights, Human Rights*.

29. Taylor, "A World Consensus on Human Rights?" p. 17.

30. Rita M. Gross, *Buddhism after Patriarchy: A Feminist History, Analysis, and Reconstruction of Buddhism* (Albany: State University of New York Press, 1993).

31. Wendy Brown, *States of Injury: Power and Freedom in Late Modernity* (Princeton: Princeton University Press, 1995).

32. Renata Salecl, "Why Is a Woman a Symptom of Rights?" in *The Spoils of Freedom: Psychoanalysis and Feminism after the Fall of Socialism* (London, New York: Routledge, 1994), chap. 8.

33. See Drucilla Cornell, *The Imaginary Domain* (New York: Routledge, 1995).

34. See Drucilla Cornell, *Beyond Accommodation: Ethical Feminism and the Deconstruction of Law* (New York: Routledge, 1991).

35. Nahid Toubia, "Female Genital Mutilation," in Peters and Wolper, *Women's Rights, Human Rights,* p. 226.

36. For an excellent article summarizing the situation of women who try to gain asylum in the United States, see Regine Dupuy Mc-Calla, "Asylum in the United States: A Tough Road for Refugee Women" (manuscript, on file with author). McCalla concludes that gender should be an independent category under the test for asylum.

37. *In Re: Fauziya Kasinga,* Int. Dec. 3278 at 12 (BIA June 13, 1996) (en banc).

38. INA section 101 (a)(42)(A).

39. Charlotte Bunch, "Transforming Human Rights from a Feminist Perspective," in ed. Peters and Wolper, *Women's Rights, Human Rights.* See also McCalla, "Asylum in the United States."

40. Courts have consistently shied away from recognizing that being a woman is a self-evident "membership in a social group." See *Sanchez-Trujillo v. INS,* 801 F.2d 1571 (9th Cir. 1986) for the four-prong test. McCalla eloquently traces the circuit courts' incoherent waffling on whether or not gender is a social group and the disastrous effects this has had on women. McCalla, "Asylum in the United States," pp. 13–14.

41. I endorse Greg DeFreitas's proposal for immigration policy reform spelled out in "Immigration, Inequality, and Policy Alternatives" (working paper, on file with author). For DeFreitas, the primary goal of immigration policy should be humanitarian:

This was the stated intent of 1965 immigration reform, but it gave vastly higher priority to reunification of distant family members of U.S. residents and admission of skilled workers than to refugees in harm's way, who were left to the whims of ad hoc administrative decisions. The 1980 Refugee Act aimed at a more systematic approach and replaced the Cold War definition of "refugees" (as anyone fleeing from Communism) with that approved by the U.N.: "persons with a well-founded fear of persecution based on race, religion, nationality, membership in a social group, or political views." But in practice, the still-strong Cold War bias has continued to favor what are now largely economic migrants from Cuba, Indochina, Eastern Europe, and the former Soviet Union. Recent history has produced no shortage of genuine refugees from political and ethnic violence, and our immigration system needs to reserve an adequate number of places to provide temporary or long-term haven to as many as is feasible. This may at times mean assigning secondary priority to the other main humanitarian goal, speedy reuniting of immediate family members. Of course, no one country should be expected to accept all who claim to be refugees from anywhere in the world. And even in seemingly obvious refugee crises like that of Haiti in 1994, massive population displacements will require coordination of multinational resettlement efforts. (pp. 19–20)

Reform of immigration to focus on humanitarian goals, with the addition of sex to the United Nations definition, would greatly help women in their efforts to escape the brutality that awaits them in their own countries. Such humanitarian goals have been a priority for women who seek asylum but are not escaping from Eastern Europe and the former Soviet Union and who have been denied refugee status because the ad hoc procedure does not generally take these claims as seriously as it should. DeFreitas gives us an answer to the worry about the "floodgate." If the human rights community takes persecution by sex seriously, then it will facilitate the kind of multinational coordination necessary. I would support this kind of coordination. It clearly helps women and expresses the asylum-granting nation's strong moral and political judgment against the persecution practices based on sex, including female genital mutilation, yet it does so without interfering directly with the other nation's sovereignty.

DeFreitas also calls for further reform:

1. Federal support for cities who have the highest rates of immigrants
2. Reorganization of the INS
3. An end to making occupational skills alone a sufficient basis for admission
4. Instead of exporting high-wage jobs or professionals, "business and government must be induced to finally provide first class schooling, training, and retraining for the vast numbers of low wage and underemployed Americans"
5. Lastly the United States must end its historic pattern of creating large displaced populations through its foreign policy. (p. 22)

42. "Everyone is entitled to all the rights and freedoms . . . without distinction of any kind, such as race, colour, sex, language, religion, political or other opinion, national or social origin, property, birth or other status." UDHR, G.A. Res. 217(II), Dec. 10, 1948.

CHAPTER SEVEN

1. Thomas Nagel, *Equality and Partiality* (New York: Oxford University Press, 1991), p. 21.

2. For Nagel this intertwinement of the ideal with the persuasive functions of political philosophy is what distinguishes it from other branches of knowledge such as scientific truth. Ibid., p. 23.

3. See chapter 2 for discussion regarding the discontinuity thesis.

4. See Judith Stacey, *In the Name of the Family: Rethinking Family Values in the Postmodern Age* (Boston: Beacon Press, 1996), chap. 5 for an overview of the debates surrounding gay and lesbian families.

5. See Andrew J. Cherlin, *The Changing American Family and Public Policy* (Washington, D.C.: Urban Institute Press, 1988), for an account of the ways in which heterosexual families are privileged by state policy.

6. Maggie Gallagher, *The Abolition of Marriage: How We Destroy Lasting Love* (Washington, D.C.: Regnery Publishing, 1996).

7. See John D'Emilio, "A New Beginning: The Birth of Gay Liberation," in *Sexual Politics, Sexual Communities: The Making of a Homosexual Minority in the United States, 1940–1970* (Chicago: University of Chicago Press, 1983), chap. 12.

8. For a very sophisticated and illuminating genealogy of rights and their limits, see Wendy Brown, *States of Injury: Power and Freedom in Late Modernity* (Princeton: Princeton University Press, 1995), p. 97.

9. See Thomas Geoghegan, *Which Side Are You On? Trying to Be for Labor When It's Flat on Its Back* (New York: Farrar, Straus and Giroux, 1991).

10. Joan Wallach Scott, *Only Paradoxes to Offer: French Feminists and the Rights of Man* (Cambridge: Harvard University Press, 1996).

11. Ibid., for discussion of paradoxes that are inherent in this rallying call.

12. Nagel, *Equality and Partiality*.

13. See Drucilla Cornell, *The Imaginary Domain: Abortion, Pornography, and Sexual Harassment* (New York: Routledge, 1995).

14. For my discussion of the degradation prohibition and of sexual harassment more generally, see chap. 4 in *The Imaginary Domain.*

15. Christine M. Korsgaard, "A Note on the Value of Gender-Identification," in *Women, Culture, and Development: A Study of Human Capabilities,* ed. Martha Nussbaum and Jonathan Glover (Oxford: Clarendon Press, 1995) p. 402.

16. Judith Butler, *The Psychic Life of Power: Theories in Subjection* (Stanford, Calif.: Stanford University Press, 1997) p. 49.

17. Ibid.

18. Toni Morrison, *Sula* (New York: Knopf, 1973), epigraph.

19. See *Feminine Sexuality: Jacques Lacan and the école freudienne,* ed. Juliet Mitchell and Jacqueline Rose, trans. Jacqueline Rose (New York: W. W. Norton, 1985).

20. See Cornell, "What Is Ethical Feminism?" in *Feminist Contentions: A Philosophical Exchange* (New York: Routledge, 1995), for a longer discussion of this basically Lacanian theory of sexual difference.

21. Sigmund Freud, *Civilization and Its Discontents,* ed. and trans. James Strachey (New York: W. W. Norton, 1962).

22. For my understanding of how it is possible for us to live "beyond accommodation," see *Beyond Accommodation: Ethical Feminism and the Deconstruction of Law* (New York: Routledge, 1991).

23. This interpretation of the ethical service provided by an analysis of the limits of theoretical reason obviously breaks with the idea of utopianism associated with socialist experiments. Marx himself was a bitter foe of utopianism, seeking to displace dreams and fantasies of an ideal society with rigorous scientific analysis of the inherent contradictions of capitalism. Still, in the twentieth century, socialism came to be identified with utopianism in the sense that communist parties sought to impose that truth of the good by force, if necessary, if this good conflicted with the economic and political aspirations of the persons living in those societies. What I have defended as the moment of utopianism inherent in deconstruction counters the conflation of possibility and reality because theoretical reason is limited and thus kept from grasping the truth of what can be actualized. I argue that the impossibility of knowing what is possible is what keeps open social transformations and new realities that cannot yet be thought, because

they are inconceivable within the constraints of our current symbolic order (See Drucilla Cornell, *The Philosophy of the Limit* [New York: Routledge, 1992]).

Socialism as actualized in the five-year plans of the Soviet Union was often reduced to a utilitarian calculus in which the political and economic good was forcibly imposed. Such plans necessarily implied that the good could be theoretically calculated in advance. The irony of the scientific socialism is that it ignored the category of novelty in the name of certain truth. My argument has been, on the contrary, that what is truly new, and what the utopian aspirations are to achieve it, should not be trivialized as unrealistic, because the truth of what is possible cannot be theoretically derived from reality.

24. The ethical desirability for representational devices in political philosophy has been challenged by Heideggerians. I am well aware that many Heideggerians would not phrase the objection in that way since, for Heidegger, the ethical is also challenged as an ontic and thus not a philosophical category. "Ethically desirable" is not a Heideggerian phrase.

Of course, it is impossible to be fair in an endnote to the richness of the Heideggerian suspicion of representation. Still, I feel compelled at least to note the objection since it remains a serious challenge to all forms of Kantian political philosophy and, indeed, to the idea of political philosophy itself. In crude summary, Heidegger challenged Western philosophy for the reduction of Being to its representations, a reduction inseparable from the domination of technological reason (*The Question Concerning Technology and Other Essays,* trans. William Lovitt [New York: Harper and Row, 1977]). Political philosophy, so the argument goes, no matter how it attempts to distinguish instrumental rationality from reason, will be implicated in the eclipse of Being and the perpetuation of teleological theory since it seeks to implement the representation of political possibility that still stands in for what cannot be adequately represented.

Of course many Heideggerians understand that "representation" is inevitable, but hold strongly only that hypothetical experiments in the imagination cannot escape capture by teleological reason. (See John D. Caputo, *Radical Hermeneutics: Repetition, Deconstruction, and the Hermeneutic Project* [Bloomington: Indiana University Press, 1987], chaps. 9 and 10; and Reiner Schurmann, *Heidegger on Being and Acting: From Principles to Anarchy* [Bloomington: Indiana University Press, 1987].) The rejection of political philosophy as *necessary* "perceptual teleology" is of course not the only rereading of Heidegger. (See "Political Philosophy Today" and "Ontology of Freedom: Heidegger and Political Philosophy," in Fred R. Dallmayr, *Polis and Praxis: Exercises in Contemporary Political Theory* [Cambridge: MIT Press, 1984]).

If theoretical knowledge is claimed from these experiments in the imagination so that knowledge of political philosophy is determined by them, then I would agree that these experiments have lost their "experimental" character and have indeed become a "perceptual teleology." In this sense, Rawls's statements in *A Theory of Justice* that the hypothetical experiment in the imagination could determine the principles of justice would be a "perceptual teleology." In his later works, Rawls's insistence on the humility of philosophy imposed by political liberalism seems a significant step away from a perceptual teleology (See "The Law of Peoples" *Critical Theory* [Autumn 1993]).

My own position, again in crude summary, is that just because we are stuck with representations of ourselves and our world, we are ethically called upon to reimagine, to give form to political principles. The metaphor of the imaginary domain is obviously one example of such an effort to reimagine the legal form society should give to persons as sexuate beings.

25. Rawls may no longer hold that position in *Political Liberalism* (New York: Columbia University Press, 1993).

* Bibliography *

Alexander, M. Jacqui. "Erotic Autonomy as a Politics of Decoloniza-
     tion: An Anatomy of Feminist and State Practices in the Bahamas
     Tourist Industry." In *Feminist Genealogies, Colonial Legacies,
     Democratic Futures,* ed. M. Jacqui Alexander and Chandra Tal-
     pade Mohanty. New York: Routledge, 1997.
——. "Not (Any)body Can Be a Citizen: The Politics of Law, Sexu-
     ality, and Postcoloniality in Trinidad and Tobago and the
     Bahamas." *Feminist Review,* no. 48 (Autumn 1994).
Alexander, M. Jacqui, and Chandra Talpade Mohanty, eds. *Feminist
     Genealogies, Colonial Legacies, Democratic Futures.* New York:
     Routledge, 1997.
Alexander, Nikol, and Drucilla Cornell. "Dismissed or Banished? A
     Testament to the Reasonableness of the Simpson Jury." In *Birth
     of a Nation'hood: Gaze, Script and Spectacle in the O. J. Simpson
     Trial,* ed. Toni Morrison and Claudia Brodsky Lacour. New York:
     Pantheon, 1997.
Anna J. v. Mark C., 286 Cal.Rptr. 369 (Cap. App. 1991), review
     granted, 822 p.2d. 1317 (Cal. 1992).
Austin, Carol. "Latent Tendencies and Covert Acts." In *The Adoption
     Reader: Birth Mothers, Adoptive Mothers, and Adopted Daugh-
     ters Tell Their Stories,* ed. Susan Wadia Ellis. Seattle, WA: Seal
     Press, 1995.
Baehr v. Miike, 65 USLW 2399 (Cir. Ct. Hawai'i 1996).
Barker, Isabelle V. "Feminism without 'Women': A Theory for Anti-
     Rape Politics." Manuscript on file with author.
Barry, Kathleen. *Female Sexual Slavery.* New York: New York Univer-
     sity Press, 1979.
Benjamin, Jessica. *Like Subjects, Love Objects: Essays on Recognition
     and Sexual Difference.* New Haven: Yale University Press, 1995.
——. *The Bonds of Love: Psychoanalysis, Feminism, and the Prob-
     lem of Domination.* New York: Pantheon Books, 1980.
Blackenhorn, David. *Fatherless America: Confronting Our Most Ur-
     gent Social Problem.* New York: Basic Books, 1995.
Bloom, Alan D. *The Closing of the American Mind.* New York: Simon
     and Schuster, 1987.

Bordo, Susan, and Alison Yagger, eds. *Gender/Body/Knowledge: Feminist Reconstructions of Being and Knowing*. New Brunswick, NJ: Rutgers University Press, 1989.

Bowers v. Hardwick, 478 U.S. 186 (1986).

Brown, Wendy. *States of Injury: Power and Freedom in Late Modernity*. Princeton: Princeton University Press, 1995.

Bunch, Charlotte. "Transforming Human Rights from a Feminist Perspective." In *Women's Rights, Human Rights: International Feminist Perspectives*, ed. Julie Peters and Andrea Wolper. New York: Routledge, 1995.

Burt, V. L. "Trends in the Prevention, Awareness, Treatment, and Control of Hypertension in Adult U.S. Populations." *Hypertension* 26.

Butler, Judith. *Excitable Speech: A Politics of the Performative*. New York: Routledge, 1997.

———. *The Psychic Life of Power: Theories in Subjection*. Stanford, CA: Stanford University Press, 1997.

———. *Bodies That Matter: On the Discursive Limits of "Sex."* New York: Routledge, 1993.

———. *Gender Trouble: Feminism and the Subversion of Identity*. New York: Routledge, 1990.

Caputo, John D. *Radical Hermeneutics: Repetition, Deconstruction, and the Hermeneutic Project*. Bloomington: Indiana University Press, 1987.

Carey v. Population Services International, 431 U.S. 678 (1977).

Cherlin, Andrew J. *The Changing American Family and Public Policy*. Washington, DC: Urban Institute Press, 1988.

Chesler, Phyllis. *The Sacred Bond: The Legacy of Baby M*. New York: Random House, 1988.

———. *Mothers on Trial: The Battle for Children and Custody*. San Diego, CA: McGraw-Hill, 1986.

Chodorow, Nancy. *Femininities, Masculinities, Sexualities: Freud and Beyond*. Lexington: University of Kentucky Press, 1994.

———. *Reproduction of Mothering: Psychoanalysis and the Sociology of Gender*. Berkeley: University of California Press, 1978.

Cohen, Marcia. *The Sisterhood: The Inside Story of the Women's Movement and the Leaders Who Made It Happen*. New York: Fawcett Columbine, 1988.

234

Conrad, Joseph. *The Heart of Darkness.* 1902.

Coontz, Stephanie. *The Way We Never Were: American Families and the Nostalgia Trap.* New York: Basic Books, 1992.

Cornell, Drucilla. *The Imaginary Domain: Abortion, Pornography, and SexualHarassment.* New York: Routledge, 1995.

———. "What Is Ethical Feminism?" In *Feminist Contentions: A Philosophical Exchange.* New York: Routledge, 1995.

———. *Transformations.* New York: Routledge, 1993.

———. *The Philosophy of the Limit.* New York: Routledge, 1992.

———. *Beyond Accommodation: Ethical Feminism, Deconstruction, and the Law.* New York: Routledge, 1991.

Cott, Nancy F. *The Grounding of Modern Feminism.* New Haven: Yale University Press, 1987.

Dallmayr, Fred. *Polis and Praxis: Exercises in Contemporary Political Theory.* Cambridge: MIT Press, 1984.

Daniel, E. Valentine. *Charred Lullabies: Chapters in an Anthropology of Violence.* Princeton: Princeton University Press, 1996.

Daniels, Cynthia R. *At Women's Expense: State Power and the Politics of Fetal Rights.* Cambridge: Harvard University Press, 1993.

de Beauvoir, Simone. *The Second Sex.* Trans. H. M. Parshley. New York: Vintage Books, 1974.

Defense of Marriage Act, H.R.Rep. (1996).

DeFreitas, Greg. "Immigration, Inequality, and Policy Alternatives." Working paper on file with the author.

D'Emilio, John. *Sexual Politics, Sexual Communities: The Making of a Homosexual Minority in the United States, 1940–1970.* Chicago: University of Chicago Press, 1983.

deSantis v. Pacific Tel. & Tel Co., 608 F.2d 327 (9th Cir. 1979).

Dillon v. Frank, 952 F.2d 403 (6th Cir. 1992).

Dornbusch, Sanford M., and Myra H. Strober, eds. *Feminism: Children and the New Families.* New York: Guilford, 1988.

Due, Linnea. *Joining the Tribe: Growing Up Gay and Lesbian in the Nineties.* New York: Doubleday, 1996.

Dupy McCalla, Regine. "Asylum in the United States: A Tough Road for Refuge Women." Manuscript on file with author.

Dusky, Lorraine. "The Daughter I Gave Away." *Newsweek* (March 30, 1992).

———. *Birthmark.* New York: M. Evans, 1979.

Dworkin, Andrea, and Catharine A. MacKinnon. *Pornography and Civil Rights: A New Day for Women's Equality.* Self-published, 1988.

Dworkin, Ronald. "Foundations of Liberal Equality." In *The Tanner Lectures of Human Values.* Salt Lake City: University of Utah Press, 1990.

———. "What Is Equality? Part Two: Equality of Resources." *Philosophy and Public Affairs* 10, no. 4 (Fall 1981).

———. *Taking Rights Seriously.* Cambridge: Harvard University Press, 1977.

———. "Why We Are Liberals." Paper presented at the Program for the Study of Law, Philosophy, and Social Theory, October 19–27, New York University Law School.

———. "Do Liberty and Equality Conflict?" Paper presented at the Program for the Study of Law, Philosophy, and Social Theory, September 5, 1996, New York University Law School.

Dworkin, Ronald, and Catharine A. MacKinnon. "Pornography: An Exchange—Comment/Reply." *New York Review of Books* 41, no. 5 (March 3, 1994).

Dworkin, Ronald, Thomas Naget, Robert Nozick, John Rawls, Thomas Scanlon, and Judith Jarvis Thompson. "Assisted Suicide: The Philosophers' Brief." *New York Review of Books* (March 27, 1997).

Economic Policy Institute. *The State of Working America.* Armonk, NY: M. E. Sharpe, 1990–91.

Elfin, Margery, and Sue Headlee. *The Cost of Being Female.* Westport, CT: Praeger, 1996.

Fanon, Frantz. *The Wretched of the Earth.* Trans. Constance Farrington. New York: Grove Press, 1963.

Felder, Raoul, and Barbara Victor. *Getting Away with Murder.* New York: Simon and Schuster, 1996.

Fineman, Martha. *The Neutered Mother, the Sexual Family, and Other Twentieth-Century Tragedies.* New York: Routledge, 1995.

Firestone, Shulamith. *The Dialectic of Sex.* New York: William Morrow and Co., 1970.

Fish, Stanley. *There's No Such Thing as Free Speech and It's a Good Thing, Too.* New York: Oxford University Press, 1994.

Foucault, Michel. *Power/Knowledge: Selected Interviews and Other Writings, 1972–1977*. Ed. and trans. Colin Gordon. New York: Pantheon Books, 1980.

Freud, Sigmund. *The Complete Introductory Lectures on Psychoanalysis: Femininity*. New York: W. W. Norton, 1966.

———. *Civilization and Its Discontents*. Trans. and ed. James Strachey. New York: W. W. Norton and Co., 1962.

———. *The Ego and the Id*. Trans. Joan Riviere. London: Hogarth Press, 1962.

———. "On Narcissism." In *Standard Edition of the Complete Psychological Works of Sigmund Freud*. Trans. James Strachey. London: Hogarth Press, 1957.

Friedman, Elizabeth. "Women's Human Rights: The Emergence of a Movement." In *Women's Rights, Human Rights: International Feminist Perspectives*, ed. Julie Peters and Andrea Wolper. New York: Routledge, 1995.

Gaitens, Moira. *Imaginary Bodies: Ethics, Power, and Corporeality*. New York: Routledge, 1996.

Gallagher, Maggie. *The Abolition of Marriage: How We Destroy Lasting Love*. Washington, DC: Regnery Publishing, 1996.

Geduldig v. Aiello, 417 U.S. 484 (1974).

Gelles, Richard G. *Family Violence*. Newbury Park, CA: Sage Publishers, 1987.

Geoghegan, Thomas. *Which Side Are You On? Trying to Be for Labor When It's Flat on Its Back*. New York: Farrar, Straus and Giroux, 1991.

Goldin, Claudia. *Understanding the Gender Gap: An Economic History of American Women*. New York: Oxford University Press, 1990.

Griswold v. Connecticut, 381 U.S. 479 (1965).

Gross, Rita M. *Buddhism after Patriarchy: A Feminist History, Analysis, and Reconstruction of Buddhism*. Albany: State University of New York Press, 1993.

Harding, Christoper. *Wingspan: Inside the Men's Movement*. New York: St. Martin's Press, 1992.

Harding, Sandra, and Merrill B. Hintikka. *Discovering Reality: Feminist Perspectives on Epistemology, Metaphysics, Methodology, and the Philosophy of Subject*. Dordrecht: D. Reidel, 1983.

Hegel, Georg W. F. *Phenomenology of the Spirit.* Trans. A. V. Miller. Oxford: Oxford University Press, 1977.

———. *Philosophy of Right.* Trans. T. M. Knox. Oxford: Oxford University Press, 1967.

Heidegger, Martin. *The Question Concerning Technology and Other Essays.* New York: Harper Torch Books, 1977.

Hobbes, Thomas. "Human Nature." In *The Collected Works of Thomas Hobbes,* ed. Sir William Molesworth. London: Routledge/Thoemmes Press, 1992.

Hochschild, Arlie. *The Second Shift: Working Parents and the Revolution at Home.* New York: Viking Press, 1989.

hooks, bell. *Bone Black: Memories of Girlhood.* New York: Henry Holt and Co., 1996.

———. *Outlaw Culture: Resisting Representations.* New York: Routledge, 1994.

———. *Sisters of Yam.* Boston: South End Press, 1993.

———. *Ain't I a Woman? Black Women and Feminism.* Boston: South End Press, 1981.

Ibsen, Henrik. *A Doll's House.* 1910.

ILGO v. Giuliani, WL 91633 (SDNY, March 4, 1996).

In Re Fauziya Kasinga, Int. Dec. 3278 (BIA June 13, 1996).

Irigaray, Luce. *I Love to You: Sketch of a Possible Felicity in History.* Trans. Alison Martin. New York: Routledge, 1996.

———. *Je, Tu, Nous.* Trans. Alison Martin. New York: Routledge, 1995.

Jacobson, Marjorie. "Pregnancy and Employment: Three Approaches to Equal Opportunity." In *Boston Law Review,* no. 68 (November 1988).

Jaimes Guerrero, Marie Anna. "Civil Rights versus Sovereignty: Native American Women in Life and Land Struggles." In *Feminist Genealogies, Colonial Legacies, Democratic Futures,* ed. M. Jacqui Alexander and Chandra Talpade Mohanty. New York: Routledge, 1997.

Jencks, Christopher. "The Hidden Paradox of Welfare Reform." *American Prospect,* no. 32 (May–June 1997).

Kant, Immanuel. "On the Relationship of Theory to Practice in Political Right." In *Kant: Political Writings,* ed. Hand Reiss. Cambridge: Cambridge University Press, 1970.

————. *Groundwork of the Metaphysics of Morals*. New York: Harper and Row, 1956.

Kaplan, Morris. *Sexual Justice*. New York: Routledge, 1997.

Klibanoff, Susan, and Elton Klibanoff. *Let's Talk about Adoption*. Boston: Little, Brown and Co., 1973.

Korsgaard, Christine M. "A Note on the Value of Gender Identification." In *Women, Culture and Development: A Study of Human Capabilities*, ed. Martha Nussbaum and Jonathan Glover. Oxford: Oxford University Press, 1995.

Lacan, Jacques. "The Mirror Stage." In *Ecrits: A Selection*, trans. Alan Sheridan. New York: W. W. Norton and Co., 1977.

Le Guin, Ursula K. *Four Ways to Forgiveness*. New York: Harper-Collins, 1995.

Lubiano, Wahneema. "Black Ladies, Welfare Queens, and State Minstrels: Ideological War by Narrative Means." In *Race-ing Justice, En-gendering Power: Essays on Anita Hill, Clarence Thomas, and the Construction of Social Reality*, ed. Toni Morrison. New York: Pantheon Books, 1992.

Luhmann, Niklas. *Love as Passion: The Codification of Intimacy*. Trans. J. Gaines and D. Jones. Cambridge: Harvard University Press, 1986.

Luther, Martin. "95 Theses or Disputation on the Power and Efficacy of Indulgences (1517)." In *Luther's Works: Career of the Reformer*, ed. Harold J. Grimm and Helmut T. Lehmann. Philadelphia: Muhlenberg Press, 1957.

MacKinnon, Catharine A. *Toward a Feminist Theory of the State*. Cambridge:Harvard University Press, 1989.

————. *Feminism Unmodified: Discourse on Life and Law*. Cambridge: Harvard University Press, 1987.

Mamet, David. *Glengarry Glen Ross*. New York: Grove Press, 1983.

Marcus, Sharon. "Fighting Bodies, Fighting Words: A Theory of Politics and Rape Prevention." In *Feminists Theorize the Political*, ed. Judith Butler and Joan W. Scott. New York: Routledge, 1992.

Matlock, Jana. *Scenes of Seduction: Prostitution, Hysteria, and Reading Difference in Nineteenth-Century France*. New York: Columbia University Press, 1994.

Mayer, Ann Elizabeth. "Cultural Particularism as a Bar to Women's Rights: Reflections on the Middle Eastern Experience." In

Women's Rights, Human Rights: International Feminist Perspectives, ed. Julie Peters and Andrea Wolper. New York: Routledge, 1995.

Miller, Arthur. *Death of a Salesman.* New York: Viking Press, 1949.

Mirhosseini, Akram. "After the Revolution: Violations of Women's Human Rights in Iran." In *Women's Rights, Human Rights: International Feminist Perspectives,* ed. Julie Peters and Andrea Wolper. New York: Routledge, 1995.

Mitchell, Juliet, and Jacqueline Rose, eds. *Feminine Sexuality: Jacques Lacan and the Ecole Freudienne.* Trans. Jacqueline Rose. New York: W. W. Norton and Co., 1985.

Morrison, Toni. *Sula.* New York: Knopf, 1973.

Nagel, Thomas. "Personal Rights and Public Space." In *Philosophy and Public Affairs* 24, no. 2 (Spring 1995).

———. *Equality and Partiality.* New York: Oxford, 1991.

———. "Justice and Nature." *Oxford Journal of Legal Studies* 17 (1997): 303–21.

Nestle, Joan. "My Mother Liked to Fuck." In *Powers of Desire: The Politics of Sexuality,* ed. Ann Snitow, Christine Stansell, and Sharon Thompson. New York: Monthly Review Press, 1983.

Newman, Katharine, and Carol Stack. "Finding Work in the Inner City? How Hard is It Now?" In *Russell Foundation Working Papers* (1995).

Nussbaum, Martha, and Amartya Sen, eds. *The Quality of Life.* Oxford: Oxford University Press, 1993.

Obiora, L. Amede. "Bridges and Barricades: Rethinking Polemics and Intransigence in the Campaign against Female Circumcision." *Case Western Reserve Law Review* 47 (Winter 1997).

Okin, Susan Moller. *Justice, Gender, and the Family.* New York: Basic Books, 1989.

Ortner, Sherry B. *Making Gender: The Politics and Erotics of Culture.* Boston: Beacon Press, 1996.

Patterson, Orlando. *Slavery and Social Death: A Comparative Study.* Cambridge: Harvard University Press, 1982.

Peters, Julie, and Andrea Wolper, eds. *Women's Rights, Human Rights: International Feminist Perspectives.* New York: Routledge, 1995.

Pollack Petchesky, Rosalind. "The Body as Property: A Feminist Re-vision." In *Conceiving the New World Order: The Global Politics of Reproduction,* ed. Faye D. Ginsburg and Rayna Rapp. Berkeley: University of CaliforniaPress, 1995.

Popenoe, David. *Life without Father.* New York: Martin Kessler Books, 1996.

Putnam, Ruth Anna. "Why Not a Feminist Theory of Justice?" In *Women, Culture and Development: A Study of Human Capabilities,* ed. Martha Nussbaum and Jonathan Glover. Oxford: Clarendon Press, 1995.

Raine, Nancy V. "Hers: Returns of the Day." *New York Times* (October 2, 1994), sec. 6.

Rawls, John. "Law of Peoples." Paper presented at the Program for the Study of Law, Philosophy, and Social Theory, November 18, 1993, New York University Law School.

———. *Political Liberalism.* New York: Columbia University Press, 1993.

———. *A Theory of Justice.* Cambridge: Harvard University Press, 1971.

Reeves Sanday, Peggy. *Fraternity Gang Rape: Sex, Brotherhood, and Privilege on Campus.* New York: New York University Press, 1990.

Richenberg v. Perry, 97 F.3d 256 (8th Cir. 1996).

Roberts, Dorothy. "The Genetic Tie." *University of Chicago Law Review* 62, no. 1 (Winter 1995).

Roe v. Wade, 410 U.S. 113 (1973).

Romer v. Evans, 116 U.S. 1620, 1634 (1996).

Rosaldo, Michele. "Women, Culture and Society: A Theoretical Overview." In *Women, Culture and Society,* ed. Michele Rosaldo and Louise Lamphere. Stanford, CA: Stanford University Press, 1974.

Ruddick, Sara. *Maternal Thinking.* Boston: Beacon Press, 1989.

Sacks, Oliver. *The Man Who Mistook His Wife for a Hat and Other Clinical Tales.* New York: Summit Books, 1970.

Salecl, Renata. *The Spoils of Freedom: Psychoanalysis and Feminism after the Fall of Socialism.* New York: Routledge, 1994.

Sanchez-Trujillo v. INS, 801 F.2d 1571 (9th Cir. 1986).

Schemo, Diana Jean. "The Baby Trail: A Special Report; Adoptions in Paraguay: Mothers Cry Theft." *New York Times* (March 19, 1996), sec. A.

Schneider, Elizabeth. "Particularity and Generality: Challenges of Feminist Theory and Practice in Work on Women-Abuse." *New York University Law Review* 67, no. 3 (June 1992).

Schurmann, Reiner. *Heidegger on Being and Acting: From Principles to Anarchy.* Bloomington: Indiana University Press, 1987.

Schwalbe, Michael L. *Unlocking the Iron Cage: The Men's Movement, Gender Politics, and American Culture.* New York: Oxford University Press, 1996.

Scott, Joan Wallach. *Only Paradoxes to Offer: French Feminism and the Rights of Man.* Cambridge: Harvard University Press, 1996.

Sen, Amartya. "Gender Inequality and Theories of Justice." In *Women, Culture and Development,* ed. Martha Nussbaum and Jonathan Glover. Oxford: Oxford University Press, 1995.

———. *Inequality Reexamined.* New York: Russell Sage Foundation; Cambridge: Harvard University Press, 1992.

Showalter, Elaine. *Sexual Anarchy: Gender and Culture at the Fin de Siècle.* New York: Penguin Books, 1990.

Smart, Carol. *Feminism and the Power of Law.* New York: Routledge, 1989.

Stacey, Judith. *In the Name of the Family: Rethinking Family Values in the Postmodern Age.* Boston: Beacon Press, 1996.

Stack, Carol. *All Our Kin: Strategies for Survival in a Black Community.* New York: Harper and Row, 1974.

Sullivan, Andrew. *Virtually Normal: An Argument about Homosexuality.* New York: Alfred A. Knopf, 1995.

Taylor, Charles. "A World Consensus on Human Rights?" *Dissent* (Summer 1996).

———. *Sources of the Self.* Cambridge: Harvard University Press, 1989.

Toubia, Nahid. "Female Genital Mutilation." In *Women's Rights, Human Rights: International Feminist Perspectives,* ed. Julie Peters and Andrea Wolper. New York: Routledge, 1995.

Turkel, Studs. *Working.* New York: Pantheon Books, 1974.

Ulane v. Eastern Airlines, Inc, 742 F.2d 1081 (7th Cir. 1984).

United Nations. *The World's Women, 1995: Trends and Statistics.* New York: United Nations 1995.

Universal Declaration of Human Rights, G.A.Res. 217(II), Dec. 10, 1948.

Vanzi, Mark. "Panel Okays Bill that Would Let Gay Couples Adopt: Legislation Would Undo Rules Backed by Wilson." *Los Angeles Times* (April 3, 1997), sec. A.

Walkowitz, Judith. "Male Vice and Female Virtue: Feminism and the Politics of Prostitution in Nineteenth-Century Britain." In *Powers of Desire: The Politics of Sexuality,* ed. Ann Snitow, Christine Stansell, and Sharon Thompson. New York: Monthly Review Press, 1983.

————. *Prostitution and Victorian Society: Women, Class, and the State.* Cambridge: Cambridge University Press, 1980.

"Wealth in Black and White." Bureau of the Census, 1986.

Weiss, Benjamin L. "Single Mothers' Equal Right to Parent: A Fourteenth Amendment Defense against Forced Labor Welfare 'Reform.'" *Law and Inequality,* no. 15 (Winter 1997).

Wekker, Gloria. "One Finger Does Not Drink Okra Soup: Afro-Surinamese Women and Critical Agency." In *Feminist Genealogies, Colonial Legacies, Democratic Futures,* ed. Jacqui M. Alexander and Chandra Talpade Mohanty. NewYork: Routledge, 1997.

West, Robin. *Narrative, Authority, and Law.* Ann Arbor: University of Michigan Press, 1993.

Williams, Patricia J. *The Alchemy of Race and Rights.* Cambridge: Harvard University Press, 1991.

Williams, Wendy W. "Equality's Riddle: Pregnancy and the Equal Treatment/Special Treatment Debate." In *Feminist Legal Theory,* ed. D. Kelly Weisberg. Philadelphia: Temple University Press, 1993.

Willis, Ellen. "Feminism, Moralism, and Pornography." In *Powers of Desire:The Politics of Sexuality,* ed. Ann Snitow, Christine Stansell, and Sharon Thompson. New York: Monthly Review Press, 1983.

Woolf, Virginia. *A Room of One's Own.* London: Harcourt Brace and Co., 1929.

* Index *

abortion, 82–83, 108, 203–4n.10, 214n.32
abstraction, 38–39, 53
abuse, 54–56, 112, 126, 222n.45
addiction, and pregnancy, 81–85
adoption, 30; in current law, 97–99; demand for open records, 107–8, 110–11, 130; gays and lesbians and, 97, 126–27, 207n.28; informal, 99–100; international, 97, 105–7, 109; single women and, 42
adoption agencies, 108
African Americans, 138–39; and informal adoption, 99–100. *See also* women, African American
alcoholism, 82–83
Alexander, Jacqui, 92–93; quoted, 112, 119, 157–58
All Our Kin (Stack), 217n.5
Anna J. v. Mark C., 286 Cal. Rptr. 369 (Cal. App. 1991), 220–21n.41
anthropologists, feminist, 15
anthropology, 62, 70
antiabortion groups, 83
Argentina, adoption in, 103–4
Asia-Pacific Forum on Women, Law, and Development, 151
asylum status, in U.S. immigration law, 172–73
Austin, Carol, quoted, 105–7
authority, paternal, 133–34, 141, 144
autonomy, 63; erotic, 158

Bahamas, gays and lesbians in, 157–58
banishment to realm of phenomenal, 21, 31, 60; men and, 146

Beauvoir, Simone de, quoted, 199n.61, 199n.65
birth mother: decision to give up baby, 108; decision to reject role of mother, 110; fear of, 110, 127; lesbian as, 126–27; media and, 96; as mother, 107–8; relinquishment of rights to child, 98, 100, 102; rights of, 104–11; trauma of, 99
birth mothers' organizations, 96–97
Blackmun, Justice Harry, 28, 42, 77–78; quoted, 203–4n.10
Blankenhorn, David, *Fatherless America,* 131
bodily integrity, 202–4n.10; need for protection of, 54; right to, 36–37; self-violation of, 53; and sexual imago, 34–37
body, female, 21–22. *See also* female genital mutilation
Boston, St. Patrick's Day Parade controversy, 210n.59
Bowers v. Hardwick, 478 U.S. 186 (1986), 39, 41–42, 205n.17
Brave New World (Huxley), 128
Brennan, Justice William, quoted, 204–5n.17
Bruno, Joseph, 207n.33
Butler, Judith: *Gender Trouble,* 70; quoted, 183, 205–6n.21

capability rights, 117
castration: fear of, 145; symbolic, 142
censorship, 25
Chesler, Phyllis, 220–21n.41
child care: Alexander's views on, 93; Okin's views on, 93–94; publicly funded, 128
child custody. *See* custody

245

ABOUT THE AUTHOR

Drucilla Cornell is Professor of Law, Political Science, and Women's Studies at Rutgers University. She is the author of numerous books, including *The Imaginary Domain: A Discourse on Abortion, Pornography, and Sexual Harassment* and *Transformations: Recollective Imagination and Sexual Difference.* She has also edited and coedited several books, including *Feminism and Pornography* (forthcoming) and *Deconstruction and the Possibility of Justice* (with Michel Rosenfeld and David G. Carlson).